Domestication of Media and Technology

Domestication of Media and Technology

*Thomas Berker, Maren Hartmann,
Yves Punie and Katie Ward*

Open University Press

Open University Press
McGraw-Hill Education
McGraw-Hill House
Shoppenhangers Road
Maidenhead
Berkshire
England
SL6 2QL

email: enquiries@openup.co.uk
world wide web: www.openup.co.uk

and Two Penn Plaza, New York, NY 10121-2289, USA

First published 2006

A catalogue record of this book is available from the British Library

ISBN-10: 0 335 217 680 (pb) 0 335 217 699 (hb)
ISBN-13: 978 0335 217 687 (pb) 978 0335 217 694 (hb)

Library of Congress Cataloguing-in-Publication Data
CIP data applied for

Typeset by BookEns Ltd, Royston, Herts.
Printed in the UK by Bell & Bain Ltd, Glasgow

Contents

Authors' biographies

Maria Bakardjieva is Associate Professor in the Faculty of Communication and Culture at the University of Calgary. She is the author of *Internet Society: The Internet in Everyday Life* (Sage, 2005) and co-editor of *How Canadians Communicate* (University of Calgary Press, 2003). Her research examines the everyday uses of information technology in various social and cultural settings.

Thomas Berker is research fellow at the Norwegian University of Science and Technology in Trondheim. Previously he has done research on internet use in everyday life and on transnational knowledge work. His current research focuses on the interplay between technology, energy efficient architecture and everyday life. His publications include *Internetnutzung in den 90er Jahren*, a book on internet use during the 1990s (Campus, 2001).

Leslie Haddon is a visiting research associate at Chimera, Essex University and a part-time lecturer at the London School of Economics. He has worked on academic, commercial and policy-related projects examining the social shaping and consumption of ICTs. His numerous publications include co-authorship of *The Shape of Things to Consume: Bringing Information Technology into the Home* (together with Cawson and Miles, Avebury, 1995), and his book *Information and Communication Technologies in Everyday Life: A Concise Introduction and Research Guide* (Berg, 2004).

Maren Hartmann teaches and researches at the University of Erfurt. In the past, she has worked at several universities both in the UK and in Belgium, partly on European research projects. Her Westminster-based PhD analysed metaphoric user vocabularies in and around cyberspace and has been published as *Technologies and Utopias* (Reinhard Fischer, 2004). She is also currently co-editing (with Joachim Höflich), *Mobile Communication in Everyday Life: Ethnographic Views, Observations and Reflections* (Frank & Timme, forthcoming 2006).

Deirdre Hynes is a lecturer in Information and Communications at Manchester Metropolitan University. Her PhD, 'Digital Multimedia Use and Consumption in the Irish Household Setting' (2005, unpublished), focused on issues of domestication of the internet. She was also involved with the European project, 'Strategies of Inclusion of Gender in the Information Society'.

Sun Sun Lim is Assistant Professor at the Communications and New Media Programme, National University of Singapore. Her research interests are the social implications of new media and ICTs, specifically, new media and family communication and public perceptions of new technology. Her current research projects focus on the domestication of ICTs by middle-class families in Asia, and public perceptions of new media piracy. Her articles have been published in the *Asian Journal of Communication*, the *Australian Journal of Communication* and *Media Asia*.

David Morley is Professor of Communications at Goldsmiths College, University of London. His specialisms include audience research and studies of cultural consumption in relation to television and the domestic uses of new communications technologies. He also works on communications technologies, media markets and cultural identities from the perspective of cultural geography, in relation to questions of globalization and cultural imperialism. His most recent book is *Home Territories: Media, Mobility and Identity* (Routledge, 2000).

Jo Pierson is currently working as senior researcher for SMIT (Studies on Media, Information and Telecommunication), part of IBBT (Interdisciplinary Institute for BroadBand Technology), Brussels. He also teaches at the Vrije Universiteit Brussel. His core expertise is situated in the field of innovation strategy research on the use of fixed and mobile media technologies. Other research areas include e-inclusion issues and information society policy at European and national level.

Yves Punie is senior Research Fellow at the Institute for Prospective Technological Studies (IPTS), Seville, one of the seven joint research centres of the European Commission DG JRC. He holds a PhD in Social Sciences from the Free University of Brussels where he worked as interim Assistant Professor and as researcher at SMIT (Studies on Media, Information and Telecommunications). Among others, Yves Punie has published on the domestication of ICTs; on the social and technological aspects of Ambient Intelligence in Everyday Life; on the future of the media and the media industries; on social capital in the knowledge society; and on privacy, security and identity in the future information society.

Els Rommes is assistant professor Gender, Pedagogy and ICTs at the Institute for Gender Studies at Nijmegen University and guest-professor at Bremen University. She studies and has published on, amongst others, gender inclusive design practices, strategies of including women in the information society, education and training, (digital) cities and ITCs in every day life contexts. Presently, she studies adolescents' professional choices, gender and heteronormativity.

Anna Maria Russo Lemor is currently a research consultant in a German firm and a lecturer at the University of Saarland, Germany. Her work focuses on the role of new and old media as symbolic sources, resources, and environments, within individuals' perception and display of their social and cultural identities. Her dissertation, based at the University of Colorado at Boulder, consisted of a qualitative study on the role of mass media and ICTs in single parents' everyday life and their meaning-making practices.

Roger Silverstone is Professor of Media and Communications at the London School of Economics and Political Science, and an original contributor to the formulation of domestication as a way of analysing the consumption of information and communication technologies, most notably in Consuming Technologies (jointly edited with Eric Hirsch, Routledge, 1992). He has published several books and articles in this field. He has recently edited *Media, Technology and Everyday Life in Europe* (Ashgate, 2005) on behalf of the European Media and Everyday Life Network (EMTEL) and is currently writing *Morality and Media* for Polity Press (forthcoming, 2006).

Knut H. Sørensen is Professor of Sociology of Technology at the Norwegian University of Science and Technology in Trondheim. His research interests include technology and everyday life, gender and technology, sustainable energy, technology policy, and knowledge studies. He has published several books and articles related to these topics, including *Making Technology Our Own? Domesticating Technology into Everyday Life* (co-edited with Merete Lie, Scandinavian University Press, 1996).

Katie J. Ward is a Research Fellow in the School of Health and Related Research at the University of Sheffield. She has worked previously on research projects in the UK and Ireland concerning media consumption in the domestic environment. She is currently carrying out research relating to e-health. Her other research interests include gender, the consumption of media and qualitative research methods. She has published in these areas.

1 Introduction

*Thomas Berker, Maren Hartmann, Yves Punie,
Katie Ward*

This book is about the 'domestication' of media and technology. Domestication is a concept within media and communications studies, but also within studies of the sociology of technology that has been developed to describe and analyse processes of (media) technology's acceptance, rejection and use. The emergence of the domestication concept represented a shift away from models which assumed the adoption of new innovations to be rational, linear, monocausal and technologically determined. Rather, it presented a theoretical framework and research approach, which considered the complexity of everyday life and technology's place within its dynamics, rituals, rules, routines and patterns. This work was developed in several, mostly European (specifically, British and Scandinavian), countries over the last twenty years. Crucial to the development and application of the concept were several factors. One of them was the funding of European research networks that actively developed and embraced a domestication approach.

We would like to acknowledge that without these networks, particularly EMTEL (European Media, Technology and Everyday Life), in both its phases, this book would not have been written. EMTEL I was funded by the European Commission and ran from 1995 until 1998 under the 4th Framework 'Human Capital and Mobility' programme and later as EMTEL II, from 2000 until 2004, as a research and training network under the 5th Framework programme 'Improving the Knowledge Potential'.[1] This book is the result of our involvement and research in the EMTEL network and it not only looks back at the origins of the concept, but also applies and develops it in the present-day (and future) context. The book is also unique in its critical engagements and reflections on the domestication concept, as well as in its range and depth of engagement with recent empirical material. It is the first of its kind and as such we hope it will not disappoint the reader. Not every author in this book has been directly involved with the EMTEL network, but all of them have critically reflected upon it, and – in one way or another – discussed or applied the domestication concept.

Whether this concept was once, is still, and will be useful in the future to help to understand what happens with media and technology when they are acquired and used, is the focus of discussion for the individual contributions collected here. If doubts can be cast as to whether the concept and approach are still valid, we believe that any study of acceptance, rejection and use of new technologies, in particular information and communication technologies (ICTs), is necessary in a culture where media technology and content are ubiquitous. As modern societies increasingly become technology-mediated, we need to understand our daily interactions with technologies on the streets, in schools, in the town hall, the hospital, at home and in the office. Looking for an understanding of the role of technology in everyday life is ultimately trying to understand what characterizes modern life.

There are many routes into a book that collects applications of and reflections on a concept soon to enter its third decade. The chapters following this introduction tell their own story about the nature of domestication in past and present theoretical and empirical applications. We have avoided forcing them into one encompassing frame of reference, but in addition to the individual empirical and theoretical accounts of domestication, there are common themes, concerns, and storylines that surface repeatedly in this book, relating to users' relationships with, and acceptance and rejection of ICTs.

What is domestication?

Domestication, in the traditional sense, refers to the taming of a wild animal. At a metaphorical level we can observe a domestication process when users, in a variety of environments, are confronted with new technologies. These 'strange' and 'wild' technologies have to be 'house-trained'; they have to be integrated into the structures, daily routines and values of users and their environments. In many cases, these are domestic environments, in particular households. Despite claims about their limitations (see Sørensen, Chapter 3 and Hynes and Rommes, Chapter 7) and critical reflections on their constitution, these households form a major, but not exclusive, focus within this book. Many of the contributions explore the manifold dynamics working between technological artefacts, users and households. Indeed, the technologies, like wild animals, seem to have their own strong will. Households, too, are increasingly recognized as problematic and wilful entities and this theme is explored in some of the contributions in this volume (for example, Russo Lemor's discussion of single-parent families and the way in which the structure of the household plays a significant role in the domestication process).

The process of domestication also implies, at a symbolic level, that in the long run, technologies, like pets, can become part of the family. Some technologies continue to 'disobey', some only from time to time, and many become an integral part of everyday life. When the domestication of technologies has been 'successful', the technologies are not regarded as cold, lifeless, problematic and challenging consumer goods at the root of family arguments and/or work-related stress, but as comfortable, useful tools – functional and/or symbolic – that are reliable and trustworthy. This is often the case with the phone, radio and television. They have all lost their magic and have become part of the routine. However, just as young puppies (and older dogs) can cause damage in the household and arguments between family members, the domestication of technological artefacts is seldom complete. In that incomplete process, the dynamic between 'domesticator' and the 'domesticee' constitutes and recreates the mediated environment. It is not just about adapting technologies to people, but also about people creating an environment that is increasingly mediated by technologies. Re- and de-domestication processes can take place – adapting and morphing to meet the changing needs of users, the constitution of households and workplaces.

The chapters in this book focus not only on these processes and the continuity of routines and patterns of everyday life, but also consider the breaking of routines and the discontinuity of some processes. It is less about the short-term new or spectacular, but rather about the medium and longer-term impact and negotiation of technologies in everyday life. When the technology becomes an ordinary tool like every other tool, it risks escaping attention, not only from researchers and academics but also from policy-makers. The technology will only exist in aggregated statistics relating to, for example, the information society: far from what 'real' users do. Consider, for instance, the challenge for Europe, to 'become the most competitive and dynamic knowledge-based economy in the world capable of sustainable economic growth with increased job opportunities and greater social cohesion', formulated at the Lisbon Council of 2000,[2] where progress towards reaching specific goals is usually measured and described in quantitative terms (for example, R&D investment percentage, productivity per capita, employment numbers).[3] Complementary to such an approach, this book will highlight the technology's challenge and potential as experienced by users in their everyday environments. Although it may be less visible in short-term statistics, a significant part of the ICT potential may only then begin to materialize when users adopt the technologies as tools for being connected, for communication, information, entertainment and transactions – or when users decide to reject technologies.

The metaphor of media and technology as an untamed animal coming into the household and other environments, and undergoing a process of domestication, changing and being changed, was inspired by a set of theoretical assumptions and concepts about households and the process of consumption and incorporation of media and technologies into the fabric of everyday life. Following Giddens (1984), the household was described as the locale where very basic relations of trust and *ontological security* are formed. The household, however, is simultaneously an economic entity, which plays a role in producing and reproducing goods and services. This double quality was captured in the notion of *moral economy*, a term borrowed from E. P. Thompson (1971), where the household is presented as in constant exchange with the economy that surrounds it, thus operating within and constituting a transactional system. Furthermore, domesticated media and technologies are *doubly articulated*: they are part of the household's private as well as the public sphere; they are material artefacts and bearers of meaning in more than one sense (see Hartmann, Chapter 5). Domestication is the process in which the household and its surroundings; the private and the public; and the moral and the formal or objective economy are related to each other, becoming mutually constitutive (Silverstone *et al.* 1992).

This account of a theoretical framework, which was developed mainly by Roger Silverstone, David Morley, Leslie Haddon and Eric Hirsch (for example, Silverstone and Haddon 1996; Silverstone, Hirsch and Morley 1990), gives – if anything – an impression of the ambition and scope of its original conception. Tackling the tricky question of how practices in everyday life are related to grander social processes and structures, the concept proves to be particularly useful for the empirical in-depth analysis of daily media consumption. The dimensions of domestication distinguished by Silverstone *et al.* – appropriation, objectification, incorporation and conversion (Silverstone *et al.* 1990, p. 19) and which were slightly revised later – have served as apt heuristic devices in numerous studies. They still do so today (see Hynes and Rommes, Chapter 7; Pierson, Chapter 11; Ward, Chapter 8) and some of the original formulations have also been scrutinized and developed further (see Bakardjieva, Chapter 4).

Context and application

Domestication emerged as a concept within media, communications and technology studies during a particular academic trajectory. These roots should not be forgotten when explaining and exploring the concept's usefulness. Applicable in empirical research while maintaining theoretical depth, domestication filled a gap both in media and communication studies and science and technology studies. Most notably, it provided ways to refute technological and media determinisms and rationalistic biases.

Domestication represents a step away from the belief in the one-sided transformative power of technology: an area that the domestication approach clearly develops further was the study of innovation and diffusion. Until the mid-1980s, diffusionism was the main perspective in innovation research. The most prominent diffusionist author was Everett M. Rogers with his seminal book *The Diffusion of Innovations*, first published in 1962 and now in its fourth revised edition (Rogers 1995). Diffusionism focuses on the adoption of (technological) innovations by individuals or other decision-making units, at a micro-level, and on the spread of innovations within a social system at a macro-level. Adoption is conceived as a rational 'innovation-decision process'. Rogers has described this process as rather linear and as a set of mechanical curves relating to adoption and diffusion. Most of the terms used by Rogers to describe this spread (such as 'early adopters' and 'late adopters') have now become part of the everyday language to describe adoption and diffusion patterns. Nonetheless, the linearity and overtly rationalistic bias of this model have been challenged.[4]

The domestication perspective provides the means to begin overcoming some of the shortcomings of Rogers's diffusion of innovations. Subsequently, many authors have stressed the importance of the *cultural* appropriation of science and technology instead (for example, Sørensen *et al.* 2000). Domestication also provided an alternative to other determinisms that prevailed within media and communication studies at about the same time (see Hartmann, Chapter 5). While the diffusionism approach points to the technological aspect of the double articulation of technologies, the 'media aspect' is equally important. Here the domestication concept was arguing against a textual determinism that had dominated much of – at least British – media and communications research (see Moores 1993). Instead, domestication offered to research media and technology use in context, defining daily life routines, social embeddedness and similar issues as relevant for the media consumption process. The idea of the active user of technologies (is similar to the idea of the active (television) viewer. Both are turned into an active (media) consumer as an attempt to move away from television audience studies towards a wider view on media use in general; to move from the *text* to the *context*. This shift throws light on the significant emphasis on qualitative research and ethnographic research methods in the study of ICT consumption in everyday life (see Ward, Chapter 8).

While turning away from rationalistic biases, technological and textual determinism, the notion of domestication avoided the replacement of one set of single-sided assumptions with another and instead gave way to a more complex and balanced account. In challenging technological determinism, domestication took technology seriously, which in itself is unusual within the media and communication studies frameworks. Neither did it follow those social constructivist authors who – in a socio-determinist manner – suggested that 'relevant social groups' lead the principal interpretative flexibility of every technology to a closure, thus shaping its resulting function and form (cf. Wajcman and MacKenzie 1985). The temptation to focus exclusively on the spheres of everyday consumption was also resisted. Providing tools to analyse the exchanges between everyday practices and the encompassing cultural and societal structures, studies of domestication – unlike other emerging media ethnographies at the time – did not lose track of the bigger picture while allowing deep explorations into micro-practices of everyday life.

Methodology

Research work documenting and analysing the process of domestication has captured the manifold dynamics associated with the consumption of technology in the home and beyond. The study of the domestication of media technology has relied largely on qualitative research methods, which encapsulate the nuances of consumption and the way that users inscribe artefacts with meaning to give them a place in the network of the home and everyday life. Silverstone and Hirsch (1992), in examining the relationship between media technology, consumption and the domestic sphere, emphasize the dialogue between the psychological, social, economic and political, which highlights significant factors such as the gendered nature of users' relationship with technology and the status of media technology as both objects of desire and 'transmitters of all the images and information that fuel those desires' (1992, p. 3). Media technologies are highly symbolic and have a significant status in the organization and lived experience of everyday life and, as such, have demanded a methodology that explores the nuances of their symbolism, appropriation and interpretation in the context of consumption.

Drawing on anthropological literature as one starting point to examine the significance of ICTs in the home, Silverstone *et al.* (1992) and Silverstone and Haddon (1996), among others, provide a framework for thinking about the role of ICTs in the household as both objects and 'transmitters' of media content. The authors present the household as 'a transactional system of economic and social relations'. This model of the household as a 'moral economy' provides a framework for the exploration of the transformation, negotiation and inscription of meaning on to media technologies. It facilitates an insight and understanding of the 'biography' of an object as it is appropriated and introduced into the domestic environment. The process of consumption and of embedding the object into the household is one of sense making, of transforming the alien object to ascribe it meaning in the symbolic reality of the household.

Exploration of this process of meaning making requires a method that allows space for an explication of the dynamic relationship between users; the technological artefact; wider culture; the technology's positioning within the public and private spheres; and its doubly articulated biography. Research with a focus on the domestic context has involved ethnographic observations, interviews, diary keeping and maps of domestic space. For example, Eric Hirsch (1992) presents an ethnographic case study relating to ICTs. In focusing on one family, Hirsch presents detailed ethnographic observations about a family and the way in which the consumption of ICTs are appropriated and transformed in the context of a family's relationships and moral environment. The approach raises questions about the role of this specific technology in engendering certain tensions and conflicts, and allows an exploration of the way that family members approach the balancing of consumption, against a backdrop of an increasing presence of ICTs with long-term 'moral actions' within the family.

In exploring the use and consumption of ICTs within the home, interviews have also been used to complement the ethnographic approach. Sonia Livingstone (1992), in examining how families account for their use of domestic technology, emphasizes the way in which practices and patterns of behaviour both highlight and constitute human relations and lived experience in the household. Using the 'personal construct approach' (p. 115), which considers the ways individuals construct their 'phenomenological word' (p. 115), Livingstone allows space for the perspectives of individual family members in the context of the ethnographic method, and stresses the way in which 'accounting practices' used by participants to explain the role of technologies in the home reflect gender relations as they are played out in the family.

Leslie Haddon (1992), in his study of the processes surrounding the home computer, employed a qualitative analysis for the interpretation of empirical data. In focusing on the meaning attributed to technological artefacts within the dynamics of the family, Haddon illustrates the domestication process, where technology is resisted and accommodated in the domestic sphere; the way in which the family negotiate the status of the technology before its acquisition; and the process through which individual identities and the collective family identity are formed in relation to the family itself and the outside world. However, he also highlights some of the limitations of family-based studies and suggests that processes outside the home interact with the activity within the home. Hence 'home computing' is not confined to the domestic sphere, but extends and is shaped by wider public and values gendered cultures.

The studies carried out in the 1990s have provided a scholarly context for more recent studies focusing on the role of computers in the domestic context. For example, Maria Bakardjieva (2001, and Chapter 4 in this volume) emphasizes the need to design research, which explicates the intricate everyday practices in which internet use is embedded. Using in-depth interviews to elicit the production of narratives describing the domestication process; 'tours' of participants' home and computer space, which involved looking at the way in which participants organized their electronic artefacts; and interviews with the whole family, she was able to design research that facilitated an exploration of the home and internet as a 'heterogeneous network' integrating technical, social and cultural factors.

Elaine Lally (2002), in her study of domestic computer users, aims to examine how participants respond to a culture which is powerfully entwined with ICTs and defined by home computer use and internet access. She used data from in-depth interviews to explore how computers are transformed from anonymous objects into artefacts that play a central role in home building – becoming deeply embedded in the everyday lives of users. To enhance her approach, Lally also presents case studies of families in order to portray the significance of the relationship between 'technology, home-building and ownership' (p. 11). The case study is illustrated using photographs that emphasize the significance of spatial arrangements relating to the computer in the context of home building and integration into existing patterns of everyday life. Similarly, Deirdre Hynes (see Chapter 7) used 'diary keeping' with her participants as a means to enhance the data collected using in-depth interviews in participants' homes.

The domestic household context and its domestic media was the original and primary focus of domestication studies (hence the name of the concept). This has, in the meantime, changed and is still changing. Originally chosen as a 'clearly identifiable case of a situated reality' (Silverstone and Haddon 1996, p. 71), the household was thoroughly conceptualized as 'the product of a particular set of historical conditions which emerged with industrial societies' (Silverstone and Hirsch 1992, p. 5) – and within a certain group of industrial societies, we might add. Societies (and with them households) have changed within the last twenty years; a significant fraction becoming less and less 'clearly situated'. New uses of media and technologies and related services have entered everyday life. Furthermore, they are often tightly connected with a fundamental restructuring of daily routines. The articles collected here all in their own way apply domestication to the present. They accept the challenge, both theoretically and empirically to examine whether domestication as a concept and analytical tool still holds.

Future domestication research might need to embrace the possibilities offered by new technologies to monitor and log user behaviour. Data from these sources could be instructive as they can provide detailed, personalized and longer-term traces of user behaviour. They can also provide another view on the possible contradictions between what people do and what they say they do with ICTs. Massive and detailed monitoring and logging of what users do with the technologies, however, could raise ethical questions, especially if people are not aware they are being traced.

Introducing the book and its articles

More than fifteen years have passed since the early and most influential contributions to the concept of domestication were published. The contributions to this book collect past, current and, to a lesser extent, future applications of the concept, and critically reflect on its theoretical legacy and offer comments about further development. Domestication can be seen as a whole theoretical approach to media (and/or other technologies) and its role in everyday lives of households, people or other kinds of organizations. Domestication can equally be defined as a research tool, a method on how to research the technologies' entry into everyday lives. We mirror the distinction between these two uses of the concept in the structure of the book. The first part comprises of reflections on the role of the domestication concept in media and technology studies over the last few years. The starting point is thus a theoretical one. In the second part, diverse empirical studies are presented that apply these theoretical reflections. Domestication has here been applied and used as a research tool to examine the manifold dynamics that emerge between users and technologies.

To begin with, **David Morley** (Chapter 2) focuses on how we can understand the contradictory dynamics through which communications technologies have been domesticated at the same time that domesticity itself has been dislocated. These issues are explored in the context of the ways in which the newly mobile ICTs of our era are now claimed to be leading to the 'death of geography'. Drawing on studies of the contextual use of a range of technologies, above all the television, the chapter offers critical perspectives on de-historicized discourses in which the 'new media' of our times are currently inscribed, and on the ways in which even the latest technologies are often domesticated for the most traditional purposes. Morley's call for historical contextualization reminds us that changes usually occur gradually so that much of the extreme excitement about new media does not necessarily stand the test of time. Still, this does not mean that nothing ever changes – rather that change occurs in unanticipated ways. In line with the claims of early domestication studies, Morley argues that the most important historical role of broadcasting media has been their role in the transformation of the relationship between private and public spheres. Here, he observes far-reaching changes as in the case of mobile phones, which are used to create a private space around the speaker, wherever he or she may be.

Similarly, **Maren Hartmann** (Chapter 5) sees the changes in the relationship between public and private spheres, which are connected to new ICTs, as one of the greatest challenges to studies of domestication. She refers back to early accounts, in which the concept of the double articulation clearly stressed that media needed to be taken seriously as technology in context, but also in terms of what the media conveyed as content. She maintains that this claim has never entirely been met by research and, if taken seriously in its equitable appreciation of media text and context, could help to understand the actual complexity of media adoption and use in everyday life. This is discussed in the light of early empirical applications of the domestication framework, Hartmann's own research, and newer empirical studies developing further the notion of domestication. One of her main points is a methodological one. According to Hartmann, the double articulation of media in everyday life can only be captured with extensive empirical research including methods and analyses of the actual media content. It is through a critical return to 'media ethnographies' that Hartmann seeks to arrive at a notion of the *triple articulation* which allows an integrated analysis of individual communication, more general symbolic content (for example, the 'flow' of TV) and the context of consumption.

Knut Sørensen (Chapter 3) also returns to the early days of the domestication concept in a contribution that provides a necessary counterpoint to much of the rest of the book. He offers 'the Norwegian strand' of domestication – or what he calls the 'technology studies version' (see also Lie and Sørensen 1996). This builds on the traditions of the social studies on science and technology rather than on a media and communication studies framework. Its particularity is based on the idea of a combination of actor–network theory (ANT) and the domestication concept. Thus, the concentration is not on households, but it takes inspiration from industrial sociology. Similar to much of the constructivist work, it argues against early sociological strands that framed science and technology as the driving forces behind social change. Instead, social learning is part of the suggested multi-sited, multi-actor process of technology adoption. All this is exemplified through examples from the domestication processes of both the motorcar and mobile phones in Norway. Moralities and use patterns emerge clearly from these analyses. For Sørensen, domestication is about individuals' ways of combining things, meanings and actions as well as their interdependence, offering a changed emphasis on the fundamental ideas relating to domestication.

Maria Bakardjieva (Chapter 4) on the other hand, attempts to free the concept further of some of its original pitfalls. Building on her own research work on home-based internet use and her application of the concept, Bakardjieva shows both how useful it has been to frame media use within everyday-life contexts and where its usefulness stops. She criticizes in particular the moral economy concept in terms of its suggested stability, and she sees the boundaries around the households as much more porous than the original domestication suggests. Finally, she critically reflects on the idea of consumption as a conceptual framework. With her emphasis on phenomenological sociology, she offers an analysis of the two-way dynamic between the household and its social environment. Her chapter clearly offers a way of extending the domestication concept into the future. It builds on current limitations and turns them into future strengths.

Another limitation of the original concept and its initial accounts is that the household of domestication was that of Western industrial societies. **Sun Sun Lim** (Chapter 10) overcomes this limitation by introducing us into the homes of Chinese urban middle-class families. ICTs are embraced and viewed as instruments of upward mobility, symbols of success and crucial conduits for *guanxi* (social network building). Such families are intensively using ICTs to enhance familial interaction and seek societal endorsement. Underlying this trend is China's rising economic wealth and its one-child policy. With only one child to dote on, middle-class Chinese parents actively create a media-rich environment for their children through the purchase of new ICTs, believing that these products have great educational value. Based on interviews with the parents and children of twenty middle-class families in Beijing and Shanghai, this chapter assesses the functions of ICTs in the Chinese family context. Sun Sun Lim uses the notion of domestication and its framework of appropriation, objectification, incorporation and conversion mainly as an empirical tool. Moreover, her exploration of the relationship and connections between ICT, household constellation and grander societal and cultural aspects is exactly what characterizes domestication as a theoretical approach.

Jo Pierson (Chapter 11) also shows how domestication works in an environment that is similar to, and distinct from, earlier applications of domestication in household settings. He investigates small businesses and their appropriation of ICTs. These environments are characterized by the blurring of boundaries between work sphere and private sphere. The article shows how the 'professional domestication' incorporates a paradox of progress and inertia concerning the innovation process. Interestingly, the empirical basis for making these arguments comes not only from qualitative in-depth research but also from a survey of micro-enterprises in Flanders. As such, Pierson makes a case for combining both qualitative and quantitative approaches to domestication.

The contribution from **Deirdre Hynes** and **Els Rommes** (Chapter 7) examines the practical and political usability of the domestication concept. They, too, move the concept beyond its original framework. Hynes and Rommes present two comparative case studies examining the domestication experiences of participants taking introductory internet and computer courses in the Netherlands and Ireland. Like Pierson, they see the domestication concept as applicable beyond the household and extrapolate it to teaching and public environments. In examining the meanings that are attached to the technology as a result of participating on a course, Hynes and Rommes suggest that social and cultural capital are key influences on the domestication process, with historical patterning of social inequalities impacting on the capacity to domes-ticate a technology. In explicating how a course can impact on domestication, the authors focus on the four stages of the process and suggest that a course design, which takes into account the social and cultural capital of users, can play a large role in the level of success users experience in domesticating ICTs.

Similarly, **Katie Ward** (Chapter 8) refers to the four stages of domestication as analytical approaches to home-working. Boundary management, in a home infiltrated by work, poses a challenge to those attempting to successfully segregate 'work' from 'home/family' life. Drawing on the stories of home-workers, it is suggested that the attempts to integrate the internet and work into the domestic environment emphasize the conflictual and dynamic nature of the domestication process, where home-workers can be seen as both actively shaping the technology to meet the needs of the individuals in the household, while also making specific changes to existing domestic routine and ritual to accommodate the intrusion of the technology and distinguish work from leisure and family time.

The contribution from **Anna Maria Russo Lemor** (Chapter 9) also considers the phases of the domestication process and pays close attention to power dynamics within single-parent families. It focuses on the importance of considering family arrangements as an influential factor in individuals' attitudes towards media and their consumption practices within the contexts of everyday life. This chapter analyses how the processes of appropriation and incorporation of media and ICTs as symbolic resources in single parents' everyday life are influenced by social and material constraints, which impact their project of making a 'home'. Furthermore, it is not only material constraints that impact on family practices but also social and emotional ones. The informants' experiences with the ex-partner's media habits influence the attitudes of these parents after divorce or separation, which burden their already difficult process of negotiation between their desires and the social and economic conditions of their lives.

Leslie Haddon adds to this range of empirical applications (Chapter 6), where he reviews a range of British empirical studies conducted in the 1990s. The chapter indicates how the studies helped to elaborate and illustrate themes discussed in early formulations of the domestication framework. A number of diverse user groups (such as single parents and the young elderly) were studied to explore themes relating to ICTs and the relationship between work and home and the boundaries and dynamics of households. He then considers how the forms of analysis emerging in this process were made relevant for both those developing ICTs and related policy issues such as ICTs and social exclusion.

Last, but by far not least, **Roger Silverstone** (Chapter 12) provides a critical reflection of both the domestication concept as such and the book as a whole. He opens the concept up to new challenges, but also picks up some of the ghosts that have haunted domestication over the years (such as the assumed disappearance of the household as a site for something called the moral economy). Before turning to the current challenges, Silverstone explores the origins of the concept, its theoretical predecessors and – to some extent at least – its theoretical legacy. It is interesting to then see that the most prominent challenges for domestication today, in Silverstone's interpretation, lie particularly with the moral aspects of media use. In some sense, there is a continuity of concerns that might be somewhat surprising. But the original challenges have now been broadened, since boundaries are disappearing and mobilities are increasing. In this context Silverstone points out, we need to be aware that domestication is indeed problematic when it is a process of closure. Rather, he proclaims, we should take the disruption seriously – the potential for disruption that technologies and their uses entail. Taking up this challenge could lead us to use media technologies to locate ourselves in the world and to take up the global moral challenges that will continue to haunt us.

Outlook

The domestication concept has reached its third decade. The contributions in this edited collection provide rich, varied and actual accounts of how media and technologies are domesticated by people in their everyday context. They show that the approach has evolved and that the analysis, like the process itself, is dynamic, changing and sometimes incomplete. Domestication as a conceptual and methodological approach has potential for the future and can be adapted to a changing socio-economic and technological context.

At the time when domestication was first developed, new information and communication technologies consisted mainly of stand-alone devices: a personal computer, video recorder, compact disc, satellite television and the telephone. The technological context of today is drastically different. The internet has become a widely used medium and its nature is still changing not only as a result of high-speed access via broadband networks and 'always on' connections, but also of popular applications such as online auctions or weblogs. The internet bubble may have disappeared – but not the internet itself. Users have played a crucial role in this process: peer-to-peer computing has become the largest user of internet bandwidth; mobile phones have become a huge success; both indicating that technologies and applications are not necessarily used as desired or expected by developers and providers.

These processes, the technologies and especially their users, require researchers to re-think our understanding of domestication in the future, again and again. One example for the necessary reorientation is the move towards more 'invisible' technologies, technologies that move into the 'background', a process usually described as 'ubiquitous computing' or 'ambient intelligence'. The latter is currently at the core of European Information Society Technology (IST) research[5] and the idea is that computing becomes so small, cheap and interoperable that it will be embedded in the environment and everyday objects. Technology will operate in the background while computing capabilities will be everywhere and always connected (ISTAG 2001).[6] Although the physical disappearance of the technology is not the same as its psychological disappearance, which is one aspect of the domestication concept, one possible future question is how people will react to the physical disappearance of computing. It could well be that the more invisible technologies are, the more difficult they become to 'tame'. Ironically, the physical disappearance of computing could disrupt rather than facilitate its acceptance (Punie 2005).

Domestication research suggests that only when the novelty of new technologies has worn off; when they are taken for granted by users in their everyday-life context that the real potential for change is visible. Documenting and understanding these changes in modern societies that increasingly become dependent on information and communication technologies constitutes one of the most important challenges for domestication research in the future. The objective of this book is to provide a first important step into that direction.

Notes

1. See www.lse.ac.uk/collections/EMTEL and http://www.emtel2.org/. The EMTEL2 Deliverables are also published in: Silverstone, R. (ed.) (2005) *Media, Technology and Everyday Life in Europe: From Information to Communication*. Ashgate Publishers Ltd: London.
2. See for respective documents: www.europa.eu.int. Closer to users is the eEurope programme of the European Commission because its focus is on supporting the diffusion and use of ICTs in different context, but the impact of daily, continuous ICT usage is also there not a priority (see http://europa.eu.int/information_society/eeurope/2005/index_en.htm).
3. See for instance, Facing the challenge: The Lisbon strategy for growth and employment. Report from the High Level Group chaired by Wim Kok, Luxembourg, European Communities, November 2004.
4. For a discussion of diffusionism, see Punie and Frissen 2000.
5. http://europa.eu.int/information_society/policy/ambienti/index_-en.htm. See for an overview of Ambient Intelligence and for its possible links with an everyday-life (domestication) approach: Punie 2005.
6. In studies such as ISTAG (2001), it is anticipated that people will interact intuitively with this intelligent environment, which is meant to be aware of the specific characteristics of human presence and preferences, is supposed to take care of needs and is capable of responding intelligently to spoken or gestured indications of desire.

References

Bakardjieva, M. (2001) 'Becoming a Domestic Internet User'. Unpublished paper presented at the *E-Usages* Conference, Paris 2001, pp. 28–38.

Giddens, A. (1984) *The Constitution of Society*. Polity Press: Cambridge.

Haddon, L. (1992) 'Explaining ICT consumption: the case of the home computer,' in (eds) R. Silverstone and E. Hirsch, *Consuming*

Technologies: Media and Consumption in Domestic Spaces. Routledge: London, pp. 82–97.

Hirsch, E. (1992) 'The long term and short term of domestic consumption. An ethnographic case study', in (eds) R. Silverstone and E. Hirsch, *Consuming Technologies: Media Consumption in Domestic Spaces.* Routledge: London, pp. 208–26.

ISTAG (2001) 'Scenarios for Ambient Intelligence in 2010' (edited by K. Ducatel, M. Bogdanowicz, F. Scapolo, J. Leijten and J.-C. Burgelman), IPTS-ISTAG, European Commission, Luxembourg, www.cordis.lu/ist/istag

Lally, E. (2002) *At Home with Computers.* Berg: Oxford.

Lie, M. and Sørensen, K. H. (1996) 'Making technology our own? Domesticating technology into everyday life', in (ed.) K. H. Sørensen, *Making Technology Our Own? Domesticating Technology into Everyday Life.* Scandinavian University Press: Oslo, pp. 1–30.

Livingstone, S. (1992) 'The meaning of domestic technologies: a personal construct analysis of familial gender relations,' in (eds) R. Silverstone and E. Hirsch, *Consuming Technologies: Media and Consumption in Domestic Spaces.* Routledge: London, pp. 113–31.

Moores, S. (1993) *Interpreting Audiences. The Ethnography of Media Consumption.* Sage: London.

Punie, Y. (2005) 'The future of Ambient Intelligence in Europe: The need for more everyday life', *Communication & Strategies*, 1st quarter 2005, pp. 141–65.

Punie, Y. and Frissen, V. (2000) 'Present users, future homes. A theoretical perspective on acceptance and use of ICT in the home environment'. Unpublished position paper for the Media@Home project, TNO, Delft, September 2000.

Rogers, E. M. (1995) *Diffusion of innovations*, 4th edition. Free Press: New York.

Silverstone, R. and Haddon, L. (1996) 'Design and the Domestication of Information and Communication Technologies: Technical Change and Everyday Life', in (eds) R. Mansell and R. Silverstone, *Communication by Design. The Politics of Information and Communication Technologies.* Oxford University Press: Oxford, pp. 44–74.

Silverstone, R. and Hirsch, E. (1992) 'Introduction', in (eds) R. Silverstone and E. Hirsch, *Consuming Technologies: Media and Information in Domestic Spaces.* Routledge: London and New York, pp. 1–15.

Silverstone, R., Hirsch, E. and Morley, D. (1992) 'Information and communication technologies and the moral economy of the household', in (eds) R. Silverstone and E. Hirsch, *Consuming Technologies: Media and Information in Domestic Spaces.* Routledge: London, pp. 15–32.

Silverstone, R., Hirsch, E. and Morley, D. (1990) 'Information and communication technologies and the moral economy of the household', in (ed.) A.-J. Berg, *Technology and Everyday Life: Trajectories and Transformations*. University of Trondheim: Trondheim, pp. 13–46.

Sørensen, K., Aune, M. and Hatling, M. (2000) Against linearity: on the cultural appropriation of science and technology,' in (eds) M. Dierkes and C. von Grote, *Between Understanding and Trust. The Public, Science and Technology*. Harwood Academic Publishers: Amsterdam, pp. 237–57.

Thompson, E. P. (1971) 'The moral economy of the English crowd in the eighteenth century', *Past & Present*, vol. 50, pp. 76–136.

Wajcman, J. and MacKenzie, D. (1985) *The Social Shaping of Technology: How the Refrigerator Got its Hum*. Open University Press: Milton Keynes.

PART I
Updating domestication: Theory and its history

2 What's 'home' got to do with it? Contradictory dynamics in the domestication of technology and the dislocation of domesticity[1]

David Morley

This chapter is written in an attempt to update perspectives on the domestication of the media for the contemporary period, characterized as it is by significant changes in household composition, technological changes in the modes of media delivery systems and changes in modes of media regulation. My own involvement in this field of research has now been a long one – beginning with the plans to incorporate research into modes of household consumption in the *Nationwide Audience* research project (Morley 1980) which were then actualized in my research into domestic viewing practices in *Family Television* (Morley 1986) with its specific focus on the gendering of modes of media consumption. My subsequent involvement in the research on 'Household Uses of Information and Communication Technologies' directed by Roger Silverstone at Brunel University from 1987 to 1990 further confirmed, for me, the importance of studying contextualized modes of media consumption in their natural environments, if we are to escape the problems of technological determinism (see Morley and Silverstone 1990; Silverstone and Hirsch (eds) 1992). My involvement in that project also consolidated my conviction of the importance of anthropological perspectives on material consumption (cf. Miller 1988) in analysing the symbolic meanings of communications technologies. In this respect, Bourdieu's (1972) early work on the gendered organization of space in the Berber house had long been an important talisman for me.

This anthropological perspective thus influenced both how I modelled the gendering of modes of media consumption in the Family Television study and later, my approach to the analysis of television – and the TV set itself – as being a meaningful 'visible object' in the symbolic field of the home, as much as a visual medium (Morley 1994; cf. also Leal 1986). Clearly, not only has much changed around us, since

the time of those earlier studies, but this perspective on the domestication of the media has also now become well established – and has been
applied to a range of other technologies beside television – including the
domestication of the computer (cf. for example Lally 2002).

My concern here is how to re-situate this perspective on the
domestication of the media as we are now also facing the converse
process of the technologically mediated dislocation of domesticity itself.
It is now a commonplace that the new networks of electronic
communication, in and through which we live, are transforming our
senses of locality/community and, on a wider geographical scale, our
senses of 'belonging' to either national or transnational communities. In
this context, it has been argued that we need to develop what Larry
Grossberg calls a 'politics of dislocation' which is concerned with 'what it
[now] means to be situated in particular places ... what different ways (or
modalities) of belonging are possible in the contemporary milieu ... and
the various ways people are attached and attach themselves (affectively)
into the world' (Grossberg 1996, pp. 185–6); see also Allon 1999).

This brings me to the question of what 'home' has got to do with any
of this. In this connection, I want to point to one – perhaps specifically
British – articulation of these anxieties, which is represented by the
growing saturation of UK primetime television with 'house and garden'
and 'lifestyle, health and cooking' programmes (Brunsdon *et al.* 2001).
The filmmaker Patrick Keiller (2002) notes that 'until quite recently, it
seemed as if the house, and domesticity in general, had become
unfashionable subjects, in an era characterized by mobility', whereas
nowadays, on British TV, 'images of domesticity flood the screen'. Keiller
is referring to the recent proliferation on British TV of 'makeover'
programmes about how to furnish, decorate, buy or sell your house. In
one of his stand-up routines, the Scottish comedian Billy Connolly
dismissively describes these programmes as showing no more than
'people sitting in their house, watching pictures of other people in their
house – get a fucking life!'. However, following Brunsdon *et al.* (2001), I
want to suggest that these programmes can also be read symptomatically
as reflecting the contemporary obsession, in the UK at least, with the
materiality of 'home' in the form of the privatized lifestyle of the
domestic house(hold).

John Sinclair (2002) argues that the spatial reality of 'home is now
often displaced by its virtual meanings, as mediated by culture and
communications'. It used to be said that one of the most unrealistic
things about TV fiction in the UK was that it never showed people doing
that most common of all leisure activities – watching TV at home.
However, nowadays one of the most popular situation comedies on
British TV is *The Royle Family*. The key formal feature of the programme is

that the camera is placed in the position of the TV set, observing the viewers as they watch it. The narrative premise of the programme is that, for many people, family life and watching TV have become indistinguishable to the extent that, in this fictional household, it is almost entirely conducted from the sitting positions of the viewers clustered around the set. Certainly, one could argue that some part of the programme's popularity is based on its (groundbreakingly) realistic representation of much of UK domestic life, which takes precisely this form.

As I have argued elsewhere (Morley 2001), under the impact of new technologies and global cultural flows, the home nowadays is not so much a local, particular or 'self-enclosed' space, but rather, as Zygmunt Bauman (2001) puts it, more and more a 'phantasmagoric' place, as electronic means of communication allow the radical intrusion of what he calls the 'realm of the far' (traditionally, the realm of the strange and potentially troubling) into the 'realm of the near' (the traditional 'safe space' of ontological security). Electronic media can thus also be argued to produce a psychic effect, which we might describe as that of the 'domestication of elsewhere' – a process whereby Hollywood brings images of the streets of the 'global cities' of the world to people everywhere, without their having ever visited them.

I was very struck recently when a friend, who lives in a small village in Central America, brought his 12-year-old daughter, who had hardly been out of the village in her life, to visit London. Of course, this young girl was thoroughly familiar with much contemporary Hollywood film, which circulates, even in her rural location, on video. She had seen screen images of all the tourist sights of London on film, but her actual experience of the scale and nature of the city was a quite different matter. For her, London was both thoroughly 'familiar' (from film) and yet totally strange, and the contradictory nature of this experience was evidently hard for her to digest.

The contemporary media may well provide us with a secondhand sense of the 'global familiar' and also with what (in the words of the Tina Turner song referred to obliquely in my title) we might describe as a set of 'secondhand emotions' about them. But we should still remember that, whatever range of imagery they may be familiar with, for most viewers, their 'horizons of action' – that sense of the scale on which they can act meaningfully in the world – are still very limited. Moreover, despite all the talk of 'postmodern nomadology', so is most people's actual experience of geographical mobility. Thus, global cultural forms still have to be made sense of within the context of what, for many people, are still very local forms of life.

The (much-advertised) 'death' of geography

Among other things, new communications technologies have been trumpeted as heralding the ultimate 'death' of geography. One striking contemporary example that would seem to point in this direction is the growth of telephone 'call centres' based in India which, because of its combined low-wage economy and high level of indigenous English language skills, now handles a lot of the customer service calls for a variety of British businesses. The workers in these call centres are given crash courses on contemporary British culture and are carefully trained to present to their callers a highly developed form of 'virtual Britishness', entirely disguising their actual geographical location. They are encouraged to use 'English-sounding' first names to identify themselves when answering the phone and to disguise their Indian accents. Their computer screens show Greenwich Mean Time and the current temperature in the UK and they are required to operate on British time for the convenience of their callers. They have to keep up with British daily news and soap operas and consult local British weather reports, the better to engage their callers in sympathetic conversation (Harding 2001).

The point here is that, while these call centres no longer need to be on the geographical territory of the UK in order to deal effectively with British customers, they are not (as the advocates of postmodern nomadology might claim) just anywhere, nor indeed are they in any significant sense 'deterritorialized'. They are located where they are precisely because of the history of British imperialism, which implanted the English language and many aspects of British culture throughout the long history of Britain's imperial presence on Indian soil, leaving behind a low-wage economy when it pulled out of India in 1949. The supposedly 'deterritorialized' geography of our postmodern era is much more legible if one reads it as a set of secondary or 'shadow' geographies created through the complex history of imperialism.

Moreover, despite widespread dissimulations of the kind practised in these call centres, cyberspace still has a very real geography. As research at the Centre for Advanced Spatial Analysis in London has shown, the relative density of internet web connections per square kilometre in different geographical locations varies enormously, and access to these technologies (and to the 'connectivity' that they offer) depends very much on where you are located in both geographical and social space (Dodge and Kitchin 2001). The distribution of these new technologies frequently mirrors established structures of power, and flows of internet traffic tend to follow the routes laid down by previous forms of communication.

Besides, as research in the 'Globalised Society' project, based in Copenhagen, has shown, despite all the claims about how the internet heralds the death of geography, 'where are you?' is (still) one of the most insistent questions in internet chatrooms, and questions like 'where do you live?' (or, more technically, 'where are you mooing from?') are posed frequently (Sunden 2001, p. 15). All this seems to suggest a continuing desire to reterritorialize the uncertainty of location inherent in online worlds. To make a parallel with my comments above about the use of British time and British cultural norms in Indian call centres, the Copenhagen researchers also found many examples of what they call the 'taken-for-grantedness of America as place and culture on the net' (2001, p. 18) so that, in effect, America (and American time) still provide the perceptual horizon of what we might call the 'online real'.

To take an example from another technological realm (to which I will return later), as on the internet, the first question in many mobile phone conversations is 'where are you?' Notwithstanding Meyrowitz's (1985) argument that the advent of broadcast TV means that 'we' (whoever that is) now live in a 'generalised elsewhere', rather than a specifiable place, and despite Wark's (1994) claim that we no longer have roots or origins, only aerials and terminals, it seems that we do still inhabit actual geographical locations that have very real consequences for our possibilities for knowledge and/or action (Hagerstrand 1986).

It is also worth considering what all these utopian visions actually mean in practice. Not so long ago, while I was at home reading Thomas Friedman's (2000) latest book about the 'wired world' and the inexorable triumph of globalization, it took three whole days of engineers coming and going, huffing and puffing in their frustration, before they got a dedicated computer phone line connected to my house. Perhaps that is just a particular experience of British inefficiency, but the journalist Mary Dejevsky has also written of the hair-tearing frustrations she experienced in trying to transfer an email account from the USA to another country (Dejevsky 2001). For all their wonders, these technologies are only as good as the material, social and institutional structures in which they are embedded, from the reliability of the local phone lines, to the electricity supply, to the efficiency of the relevant bureaucracy.

Mediated histories

Surrounded, as we are, by future-orientated debates about the impact of new communications technologies, it may well be that the first thing we need, if we are to avoid the twin dangers of utopianism and nostalgia –

and to avoid the historically egocentric error of treating the dilemmas of our own age as if they were unique – is some way of placing these futurological debates in historical perspective.

This concern, of course, leads us to one of the central issues in historical work: the question of periodization and the issue of how to distinguish between the developing forms of media access and provision as they are transformed by processes of institutional, economic, political, technological and cultural change. We have some guidelines to work with here. John Ellis (2000) rightly points to the necessity to distinguish, in the realm of TV broadcasting, between what he calls the 'age of scarcity' (when there were few channels), the 'age of availability' (as the number of channels on offer to the viewer gradually increased) and the current 'age of plenty and uncertainty' (as we move into a multi-channel broadcast environment, replete with remote controls, time-shift videos and audience fragmentation). The key issue is what exactly is being transformed here and how, in response to these changes, we need to adjust our analytical paradigms. Here, alongside Spigel's (2001b) helpful genealogy of models of domesticity and media consumption, we might usefully also consult Robert Allen's (1999) work on the current transformation of the film industry. Allen's analysis focuses on the way in which, in the USA, not only has domestic video now become the main mode of film consumption, but film-on-video itself now functions, crucially, as a form of marketing for sales of the ancillary products that today constitute the industry's main source of profit. What Allen's and Spigel's analyses offer us is a way of tracing the interconnections between demographic changes in household structure, cultural defini- tions of domesticity, modes of media consumption and their retroactive effects on modes of industrial production.

Technologies, contexts and traditions

Todd Gitlin tells a story about the difficulties faced by a customs officer because a man who the officer is convinced is smuggling something, turns up at his border post week after week, driving a truck. The guard can never find the contraband, which he is convinced is hidden somewhere, until he realizes that what the man is in fact smuggling is the trucks themselves. In this metaphor, we are evidently the customs officers, too often suspicious of the ideological or discursive vagaries of media content, while ignoring the more significant fact of the transformation of the fundamental modes of media presence in our lives (Gitlin 2001, pp. 3–4). Without necessarily falling into a mode of technologically determinist analysis, Gitlin's story usefully points our attention towards what Stanley Cavell (1971) calls the 'fact' of TV; or what Medrich (1979) calls the 'habit of living with television' as a 'constant presence'; or to what Jeffrey Sconce (2000) has more recently called the process of TV's 'colonisation of the home'.

In parallel with Spigel's (1992) work on the history of TV's entry into the North American home, Tim O'Sullivan in the UK (1991) and Shunya Yoshimi in Japan (1999) have investigated the crucial symbolic role played by the acquisition of TV in the development of postwar consumer cultures. Just as Yoshimi points to the significance of the TV, along with the washing machine and the refrigerator, as the 'three sacred things' in the symbolic repertoire of Japanese consumer culture in this period, one of O'Sullivan's respondents, looking back on the 1950s, remembers that 'when a house had got a television aerial and a car – then you could say they'd really "arrived"' (1991, p. 166).

However, the dynamics at play in the introduction of TV and other media to the home are complicated. If, as Barthes (1980, p. 1) once argued, TV 'condemns us to the family, whose household utensil it has become, just as the communal stewing pot was, in times gone by', so too we have to note the ways in which the nature of domestic life itself has effects on how TV is consumed. We have also to consider how TV programming has itself been designed for the specific forms of (distracted) spectator attention routinely available in the home. Moreover, as Spigel (1992) points out, the material structure of the home itself was also gradually redesigned, in architectural terms (for example, the invention of the 'through lounge'), to accommodate the needs of TV viewing. There is a complex symbiosis at play here, as TV and other media have adapted themselves to the circumstances of domestic consumption while the domestic arena itself has been simultaneously redefined to accommodate their requirements.

Given my own previous involvement researching the range of different appropriations and interpretations made of a range of technologies by households of different types, I am unsympathetic to any technologically determinist approach that would conceptualize communications technologies as responsible for transforming our lives in any automatic way. Even the very latest technologies can always be adapted (or 'domesticated') to suit very traditional purposes. The most popular website in the UK is now 'Friends Reunited' (http://www.friends-reunited.com), which, as its name implies, allows people to rediscover old friends from their schooldays – clearly a fundamentally nostalgic project, even if in hi-tech form. According to Manzoor (2003), the site now has 8 million members – rather more than those who belong to trade unions or attend church each week in the UK. The websites now set up by Turkish migrants in Europe for the purpose of facilitating 'arranged marriages' demonstrate the same capacity for 'tradition' to recruit technology to its purposes (see Robins and Aksoy 2001).

Clearly, any conception of a static realm of tradition that is then transformed by new technologies will be unhelpful here; rather, what we need is a conception of how 'mobile' traditions incorporate new technologies as they develop. As the German ethnologist Herman Bausinger rightly argues, far from imagining that we have now passed into some new period, in which tradition is a thing of the past, we must recognize that folk culture is alive and well in the world of modern technology and busily recruiting and adapting new technologies to old purposes (Bausinger 1990).

The domestication of TV

The development of historical work on the communications media has been one of the key developments of the recent period: notably that of Paddy Scannell (1996) in the UK; Spigel (1992) and Sconce (2000) in the USA; and, from a longer-term perspective, that of Siegfried Zielinski (1999) in Germany. However, despite these honourable exceptions, when media history is addressed, it is still too often conceived either in institutional or technological terms.

My own primary concern in this respect is with what Maud Lavin (1990) calls the 'intimate histories' of living with a medium such as broadcast TV. This Lavin describes as involving 'a collection of personal memories of growing up with TV ... [of] how the TV set [has been] gradually incorporated into the home, family and leisure time ... and [the] history of how we design our spaces, habits and even emotions around the TV' (1990, p. 85). This is a question of how our personal memories – especially of childhood – are formulated around media experiences such as emblematic programmes and TV characters. In this respect, we might usefully draw a parallel with Gaston Bachelard's (1994) analysis of how the material structure of the house provides the 'trellis' around which childhood memory is entwined – but perhaps we now need to extend the analogy so as to think also of how that trellis now has a mediated, as much as a material, structure.

From this perspective, we perhaps also need to treat TV not so much as a visual medium, but as a visible object (Morley 1995) because, as Matthew Geller (1990, p. 7) puts it, too often we simply 'look through' the object of TV to the images it provides, while the set itself remains, as it were, 'invisible' to us and we ignore its role as a totemic object of enormous symbolic importance in the household. It is in this context that we must also address the long history of TV's domestication, as we trace its journey from its initial position as a singular 'stranger', allowed only into the most public/formal space of the house (in the living room), through the development of the multi-set household and TV's gradual penetration of the more intimate spaces of our kitchens and bedrooms, to the point where the new individualized/personal media delivery systems, in their latest portable and miniaturized forms, might more properly be conceptualized as 'body parts'.

The domestic history of TV is by no means singular in this respect. Eliseo Veron in France details the similar pathway traced by the 'journey of the phone' in the household, as it gradually multiplied and moved from the public space of the hallway into the other rooms of the house (Veron 1991). To jump forward for a moment, when we come to the era of the mobile phone, not only is it entirely personalized – and very much understood by many of its users as just as much a 'body part' as their wristwatch – but it becomes, in effect, the person's virtual address, while their land line becomes a merely secondary communication facility (and one of seeming irrelevance to many young people).

Simon Frith (1983) rightly pointed to the historical role of broadcasting technologies in enhancing what he called the 'pleasures of the hearth', leading, as a consequence, to what he described as the 'rediscovery of the home' as a site for domestic leisure activities that had previously taken more public forms. The contemporary issue, in this connection, is what the emergence of public forms of TV and of the new personalized communications technologies now do to correspondingly destabilize the centrality of the domestic home.

Clearly, in the present context, we have to move beyond media studies' historically rather exclusive focus on TV so as to address the contemporary significance of a broader range of communications technologies. However, I also want to argue that we need to transcend the unfortunate media-centrism of much work in this area by decentring the media in our analytical framework, so as to better understand the ways in which media processes and everyday life are so closely interwoven with each other. That problem will not be solved by contemporary proposals to modernize media studies by reconceptualizing it as 'web studies' or suchlike, as this would simply put the internet at the centre of the equation, where TV used to stand. Such a move would merely replicate a very old technologically determinist problematic in a new guise. The issue is both to understand how new and old media accommodate each other and coexist in symbiotic forms and also to better grasp the ways in which we live with them.

New times and new formats

Even if we need to avoid the dangers of any overly generalized nomadology of postmodern life, mobilities, of one sort or another, are clearly central to our analysis. In this context, the extended family has now sometimes to be seen as stretched out across the long-distance phone wires, especially for migrants who often spend a high proportion of their wages on phone calls home. This, as Richard Rouse (1991, p. 13) puts it, allows them 'not just to "keep in touch", but to contribute to decisionmaking and participate in familial events from a distance'.

All of this shows how people have adapted to the capacities that these new technologies offer to allow them to literally be in two places at once. What is more, as Kevin Robins and Asu Aksoy (2001) argue in their study of Turkish migrants in London, this ability to oscillate between places is now, for many migrants, no more than a banal fact of their everyday lives, as they routinely move backward and forward, at different points in the same day, between British and Turkish TV channels, local face-to-face conversations and long-distance phone calls to distant relatives or friends. To this extent, twisting Raymond Williams's nostrum, Robins and Aksoy insist that, for many migrants, it is now transnational culture that is 'ordinary'.

However, new technologies are not only relevant to the lives of migrant families. Brockes's (2000) report on research by Jan English-Lueck and James Freeman (of San Jose State University in California) reveals a picture of a situation where the new modes of electronic communication have themselves become the very infrastructure of family life. This, they argue, is especially so among busy, middle-class 'dual career' families, living tightly scheduled lives, where parents have to balance the continually conflicting demands of work and family. In this situation, the issue of which parent is to pick up which child from which place and at what time, is negotiated daily by the participants, on the move, by mobile phone and email. When they get home, the children may reel off their activities for the next day while the parents dutifully enter them into their palm pilots, checking for problems with the scheduling of their other appointments as they go, and promising their children to page them confirmation of their 'pick-up' point/time by mid-afternoon of the next day. This is a world in which virtual parenting now has to carry some part of the burden of child care and where being in electronic contact with a child (welcoming them home with a text message, hoping that they've 'had a good day') is what 'good parenting' is now about.

Clearly, family life is changing around us, as people adapt to new technologies and find ways to deal with new structures of work and mobility, and, for all its continuing ideological centrality, the nuclear family household is declining rapidly in the West. It may not be possible (or even, ultimately, important) to work out which is the chicken and which is the egg in this respect, but we have to develop a mode of analysis that can articulate these changes in household demographics with the rapid growth of individual 'personalized media delivery systems'. Certainly, in the UK, the 'multi-screen' household is now the norm and this affects household life in profound ways. Many commentators have also pointed towards evidence of the internal fragmentation of the home, for example the trend, in many households, towards the serial 'grazing' of microwave meals by individual family members at separate times, replacing the family meal. One might also make an argument that a technology such as the Walkman, routinely used by many young people to create their own autonomous space both within the household and outside, is an intrinsically solipsistic technology – or, in Stephen Bayley's striking phrase, a 'sod-you machine' for switching off unwanted interaction with others (Bayley 1990).

It may be that, in order to place these demographic and technological changes in household structures and technological forms in a broader theoretical framework, we also need to turn to Ulrich Beck's theories of 'individualization' (see Beck and Beck-Gernsheim 2002). Beck's overall claims about the demise of class structures may be overblown (so far as the UK is concerned, at least), but the central idea of the fragmentation – and indeed the 'individualization' – of both audiences and the media technologies that service them, is evidently pertinent here.

Domesticating the future

Questions of the future and of technology are, of course, inextricably intertwined with each other, not least because the future (and increasingly the present) is now defined so much in technological terms. If the future represents, for many people, a troublesome realm of constant change, much of this trouble comes to be symbolized by (and in) technological forms. The question, therefore, is how this problematic technological realm can be naturalized and domesticated so as to make it less threatening and more manageable for its inhabitants.

Many years ago, Bausinger (1984) argued that the everyday was coming to be characterized in the affluent West by what he called the 'inconspicuous omnipresence of the technical'. In the research on the domestic uses of information and communications technologies, in which I have been involved (Silverstone and Hirsch 1992), one of the most striking findings was how, in many households, people went to a great deal of trouble to disguise the presence of communications technologies in their homes, often hiding TV sets, computers and wiring in wooden cabinets or behind soft furnishings. The point is that, if an increasing array of technologies has now become naturalized to the point of literal (or psychological) invisibility in the domestic sphere, we need to understand the process of how that has come about.

The other reason why a historical perspective on new media should be central to our approach is because the dynamic of making technologies consumer-friendly in practice often means inserting them into recognizable forms from previous eras. To this extent, technological innovation often goes along with a continuing drive to make the technofuture safe by incorporating it into familiar formats, icons and symbols.

For example, an advert for one of the latest multifunctional home entertainment systems takes the form of an image of family life which shows the new system installed in just the kind of traditional wooden cabinet that, as Spigel's (1992) research shows, housed early TV sets, when they were first introduced. Moreover, the advert's imagery, in which everyone in the family group is shown smiling under the benign gaze of the father, could almost be derived directly from a Norman Rockwell portrait of suburban family life in the USA in the 1950s. The potentially problematic nature of the new technology is thus neutralized by being shown as happily incorporated into the reassuring symbolism of this most conventional of homes.

With the advent of the electronic 'dreamhouse' – whether in the earlier versions that Spigel (2001b) describes in the 1950s and 1960s, or nowadays in Bill Gates's own 'fully-wired' domestic paradise, as analysed by Allon (2000) – we arrive at a new situation. Here, rather than electronic technologies being domesticated, as in the case of the 'smart house', the domestic realm itself is mediated and made fully electronic. In this vision of the household, the technologies are no longer merely supplementary to, but constitutive of, what the home itself now is.

All this leads us back to a new version of Raymond Williams's (1974) vision of 'mobile privatization' in so far as the technologies that can be used to engage in the new 'virtual' forms of in-home 'travel' are now far more powerful than Williams ever imagined. However, it is necessary to remember that the houses that were built in 'Levittown' in the postwar USA also had, as one of the key defining characteristics of their desirability, TVs built into their sitting-room walls. The electronic home itself has a history, which we would do well to remember, as we puzzle over its future (Hayden 2002). Moreover, to return to the issue of the domestication of 'futuristic' forms of technology, as Allon (2000) points out, even Bill Gates represents the form of family life that he envisages conducting in his fully-wired 'dreamhouse' in the most conventional suburban terms possible – which shows the extent to which futurology is almost always as much 'backward' as it is 'forward looking'.

And now? De-domesticated/ing media?

So far, I have traced the long story of the gradual domestication of a range of media, most particularly TV, and have taken the 'smart house' as the culmination or 'end point' of this story, where the home itself becomes a fully technologized/wired place and comes to be defined by the technologies that constitute it. However, it could be argued that we now face the beginning of a quite different story, where the narrative drive runs in the opposite direction, towards the de-domestication of the media and the radical dislocation of domesticity itself. In many countries, TV began as a public medium, watched collectively in public places, and only gradually moved into the home and then into its further interstices (a story that Yoshimi (1999) traces out, to telling effect, in the history of this medium in Japan). However, it is evident that, having thoroughly colonized the home, TV has now re-escaped from its confines. Nowadays, we find TV everywhere, in the public spaces of bars, restaurants, launderettes, shops and airports, as Anna McCarthy (2001) documents in her study of what she calls 'ambient TV' in the USA.

These developments should also be understood in the broader theoretical context of debates about the ongoing transformation of the relationships between the public and private spheres. In this regard, Mattelart (1995) rightly argues that, for many years now, public space has been gradually transformed by the increasing presence of advertising. Public space is now replete with commercial messages, visually – whether on large-scale billboards in the street or on the back of bus tickets – or aurally – as in the message on the UK telephone service that tells you that time itself is now 'sponsored by Accurist'. Thus, Abercrombie and Longhurst (1999) argue that, given the ubiquity of media of all forms in the contemporary world, the old distinction between those who are part of the media audience and those who are not is now quite outmoded for the simple reason that we are all now, in effect, audiences to some kind of media almost everywhere and all of the time.

But there is yet another dimension to this problem, which was first identified in studies of the cultural significance of the Walkman, as a technology that transformed the relations of the public and private, allowing its users to privatize public space by retreating into their own protective aural bubble of sound, setting their experience of public places to their own privatized soundtrack (Bull 2000; Chambers 1990; du Gay *et al*. 1997). If the Walkman is, in this sense, a privatizing technology, then, to pick up again my earlier comments on 'individualization', the mobile phone is perhaps the privatizing (or individualizing) technology of our age, par excellence.

Evidently, one of the things that the mobile phone does is to dislocate the idea of home, enabling its user, in the words of the Orange advertising campaign in the UK, to 'take your network with you, wherever you go'. Like the Walkman, it also insulates its users from their actual geographical setting. Often the user pays no attention to those who are physically close by, while speaking to others who are far away. To that extent, it might also be argued that the mobile phone often functions not only as a psychic cocoon for its user, but even as a kind of mobile 'gated community' (Luke 2003).

It is usually taken for granted that the mobile phone is principally a device for transcending spatial distance. But just as we know that a large percentage of the world's email is sent between people working in the same building, the mobile phone seems also often to be used in counter-intuitive ways. It is often used not so much to transcend distance as to establish parallel communications networks in the same space (that is, text messaging by pupils in school) and, indeed, it often appears to be used collectively, especially among groups of young people when they are together (Weilenmann and Larsson 2002).

As we know, the mobile phone call also radically disrupts the physical space of the public sphere in a variety of ways, annoying others with its insistent demand for attention or imposing 'private' conversation on those near its user. It is also interesting to see how these developments have also given rise to a whole new set of debates, focused on this technology, about the etiquette of communications. However, there is evidently more than a question of etiquette at stake here, fascinating as it is to see the speed at which new modes to regulate the device have been developing, such as 'quiet carriages' on trains, notices in restaurants and ads in cinemas banning their use (Harris 2003).

The mobile phone is often understood (and promoted) as a device for connecting us to those who are far away, thus overcoming distance – and perhaps geography itself. It has been described as enabling the emergence of an even more mobile descendent of the flaneur: the 'phoneur' (Luke 2003). However, just as I pointed to the continuing pertinence of the question 'where are you?' in internet chatroom conversations, the first question in many mobile phone conversations, as we all know, is often 'where are you?' (answer: 'I'm on the train/stuck in traffic/I'll be a bit late...'). It seems that geography is not, in fact, dead at all and that what the mobile phone allows is endless anxious commentary on our geographical locations and trajectories. Perhaps one might even say that the mobile phone is, among other things, a device for dealing with our anxieties about the problems of distance created by our newly mobile lifestyles and with the emotional 'disconnectedness' that this geographical distance symbolizes for us (Tomlinson 2001).

George Myerson argues that 'the mobile is the object which most closely embodies the spirit of the changing environment. If you want to assure yourself that you belong to the new century, this is the object to have in your hand' (Myerson 2001, p. 1). Linking back to my earlier comments on the symbolic significance of new technologies, Timo Kopomaa pushes the point further, arguing that the mobile phone has now acquired a particularly important symbolic role for many of its users – to the extent that it should be understood, he argues, as 'a portable magic charm', as the 'device that makes everything OK' (Kopomaa 2001, p. 38).

One curious measure of the mobile phone's symbolic significance in contemporary British culture is the fact that it has now replaced the umbrella as the item most frequently left behind on London underground trains (Adams and Sangara 1999). This is a particularly interesting phenomenon, as there is no effective network coverage on most of the underground, meaning that these phones were left behind by people who had felt compelled to have them to hand even when they could not use them for any practical purpose.

To pose matters a little more theoretically, the geographer Yi Fu Tuan (1996) distinguishes between 'conversation' (substantive talk about events and issues: a discourse of the public realm) and 'chatter' (the exchange of gossip principally designed to maintain solidarity between those involved in the exchange: what Tuan calls a 'discourse of the hearth'). Drawing on Tuan's distinction, John Tomlinson (2001) rightly argues that the discourse of most mobile phone use can be characterized as a form of phatic or gestural communication. In these terms, the mobile phone fills the space in the public sphere with the chatter of the hearth, allowing us to take our homes with us, just as a tortoise stays in its shell wherever it travels. To this extent, Tomlinson argues, we would be mistaken to see these new technologies simply as tools for the extension of cultural horizons; rather, he claims, we should see them as 'imperfect instruments, by which people try ... to maintain some sense of security and location' amidst a culture of flow and deterritorialization (2001, p. 17).

If one of the key historical roles of broadcasting technologies has been their transformation of the relations between public and private spheres, then the questions that face us now concern what these new technologies do to those relations and how they, in turn, may be regulated and domesticated. We now find ourselves in a world where we are all audiences to one or another medium, almost all of the time, and where, after its long process of domestication, TV and other media have now escaped the home – to (re)colonize the public sphere. While the domestic home itself might now be said to have become a fully technological artefact, it also seems that domesticity itself has now been dislocated.

As we wander the public realm, protected by the carapaces of our Walkmans and mobile phones, it may be a good moment to repose Heidegger's (1971) question about what it means to live in a culture of 'distancelessness', where things are neither near nor far, but, as it were, 'without distance'. But as soon as we make this connection to these earlier debates, we have to recognize that the questions we face today, while undoubtedly urgent, are not in themselves new. Moreover, we have to recognize, with Spigel (2001a, b), that, if we are ever to get any critical perspective on the discourses of futurology that now surround us, we shall certainly need to put them into a fuller historical perspective than that which they recognize for themselves.

Note

1. This article was previously published in the *European Journal of Cultural Studies*, vol. 6, no. 4. We are grateful to Sage for permission to reprint.

References

Abercrombie, N. and Longhurst, B. (1999) *Audiences: Sociological Theory and Audience Research*. Sage: London.

Adams, R. and Sangara, S. (1999) 'Londoners losing track of phones', *Financial Times*, 27 September.

Allen, R. (1999) 'Home alone together: Hollywood and the family film', in (eds) M. Stokes and R. Maltby, *Identifying Hollywood's Audiences*. British Film Institute: London.

Allon, F. (1999) 'Altitude anxiety: Being-at-home in a globalised world'. PhD thesis, University of Technology, Sydney.

Bachelard, G. (1994) *The Poetics of Space*. Beacon Press: Boston, MA.

Barthes, R. (1980) 'On leaving the movie theatre', in (ed.) T. H. Kyung, *Apparatus*. Tanam Press: New York.

Bauman, Z. (2001) *Community: Seeking Safety in an Insecure World*. Polity Press: Cambridge.

Bausinger, H. (1990) *Folk Culture in a World of Technology*. Indiana University Press: Bloomington.

Bausinger, H. (1984) 'Media, technology and everyday life'. *Media, Culture & Society*, vol. 6, no. 4.

Bayley, S. (1990) *Design Classics: The Sony Walkman*. BBC Video: London.

Beck, U. and Beck-Gernsheim, E. (2002) *Individualisation*. Sage: London.

Bourdieu, P. (1972) 'The Berber house', in (ed.) M. Douglas, *Rules and Meanings*. Penguin: Harmondsworth.

Brockes, E. (2000) 'Doing family in Silicon Valley', *Guardian* (G2), 17 May, pp. 8–9.

Brunsdon, C. (1997) 'Satellite dishes and the landscape of taste', in *Screen Tastes*. Routledge: London, pp. 148–64.

Brunsdon, C., Johnson, C., Moseley, R. and Wheatley, H. (2001) 'Factual entertainment on British Television: The Midlands TV Research Group's "8–9 Project"'. *European Journal of Cultural Studies*, vol. 4, no. 1, pp. 29–62.

Bull, M. (2000) *Sounding Out the City*. Berg: Oxford.

Cavell, S. (1971) *The World Viewed: Reflections on the Ontology of Film*. Harvard University Press: Cambridge.

Chambers, I. (1990) 'A miniature history of the Walkman'. *New Formations*, vol. 11.

Collet, P. and Lamb, R. (1986) *Watching People Watching Television*. Independent Broadcasting Authority: London.

Dejevsky, M. (2001) 'If only globalisation were as common as protestors fear', *Independent*, 6 August.

Dodge, M. and Kitchin, R. (2001) *Mapping Cyberspace*. Routledge: London.

du Gay, P., Hall, S., Janes, L., Mackay, H. and Negus, K. (1997) *Doing Cultural Studies: The Story of the Sony Walkman*. Sage: London.

Ellis, J. (2000) *Seeing Things: Television in an Age of Uncertainty*. I. B. Tauris: London.

Friedman, T. (2000) *The Lexus and the Olive Tree*. HarperCollins: London.

Frith, S. (1983) 'The pleasures of the hearth', in (ed.) J. Donald, *Formations of Pleasure*. Routledge: London.

Geller, M. (ed.) (1990) *From Receiver to Remote Control: The TV Set*. New Museum of Contemporary Art: New York.

Gitlin, T. (2001) *Media Unlimited*. Metropolitan Books: New York.

Grossberg, L. (1996) 'The space of culture, the power of space', in (eds) I. Chambers and L. Curti, *The Post-Colonial Question. Common Skies, Divided Horizons*. Routledge: London and New York, pp. 169–88.

Hagerstrand, T. (1986) 'Decentralisation and radio broadcasting: On the "possibility space" of a communications technology'. *European Journal of Communications Studies*, vol. 1, no. 1.

Harding, L. (2001) 'Delhi calling', *Guardian* (G2), 9 March.

Harris, K. (2003) 'Keep your distance: Remote communications, face-to-face and the nature of community'. *Journal of Community Work and Development*, vol. 4.

Hayden, D. (2002) *Redesigning the American Dream: Gender, Housing and Family Life*. W. W. Norton: New York.

Heidegger, M. (1971) 'The thing', in *Poetry, Language, Thought*. Harper & Row: New York.

Keiller, P. (2002) 'Build, don't repair', *Independent* (Review), 9 May, pp. 16–17.

Kopomaa, T. (2001) *The City in Your Pocket: The Birth of the Mobile Information Society*. Gaudeamus: Helsinki.

Lally, E. (2002) *At Home with Computers*. Berg: Oxford.

Lavin, M. (1990) 'TV Design', in (ed.) M. Geller, *From Receiver to Remote Control: The TV Set*. New Museum of Contemporary Art: New York.

Leal, O. (1986) 'Popular space and erudite repertoire: the place and space of TV in Brazil', *Cultural Studies*, vol. 4, no. 1.

Luke, R. (2003) 'The phoneur: Mobile commerce and the digital pedagogies of the wireless web', in (ed.) P. Trifonas, *Pedagogies of Difference. Rethinking Education for Social Change*. Routledge: London.

Manzoor, S. (2003) 'The friend for life', *Guardian* (G2), 3 January, p. 5.

Mattelart, A. (1995) *Advertising International*. Routledge: London.

McCarthy, A. (2001) *Ambient Television*. Duke University Press: Durham, NC.

Medrich, E. (1979) 'Constant television: The background to everyday life'. *Journal of Communications*, vol. 26, no. 3.

Meyrowitz, J. (1985) *No Sense of Place*. Oxford University Press: Oxford.

Miller, D. (1988) *Material Culture and Mass Consumption*. Oxford: Blackwell.

Morley, D. (2001) 'Belongings: Place, space and identity in a mediated world'. *European Journal of Cultural Studies*, vol. 4, no. 4, pp. 425–48.

Morley, D. (1995) 'Television: Not so much a visual medium, more a visible object', in (ed.) C. Jenks, *Visual Communication*. Routledge: London.

Morley, D. (1994) 'Television – not so much a visual medium, more a visible object', in (ed.) C. Jenks, *Visual Culture*. Routledge: London.

Morley, D. (1986) *Family Television*. Comedia: London.

Morley, D. (1980) *The Nationwide Audience*. British Film Institute: London.

Morley, D. and Silverstone, R. (1990) 'Domestic communications'. *Media, Culture & Society*, vol. 12, no. 1.

Myerson, G. (2001) *Heidegger, Habermas and the Mobile Phone*. Icon Books: London.

O'Sullivan, T. (1991) 'Television Memories and Cultures of Viewing 1950–65', in (ed.) J. Corner, *Popular Television in Britain*, British Film Institute, London.

Robins, K. and Aksoy, A. (2001) 'From spaces of identity to mental spaces: Lessons from Turkish-Cypriot cultural experiences in Britain'. *Journal of Ethnic and Migration Studies*, vol. 27, no. 4.

Rouse, R. (1991) 'Mexican migration and the social space of postmodernism'. *Diaspora*, vol. 1, no. 1.

Scannell, P. (1996) *Radio, Television and Modern Life*. Blackwell: Oxford.

Sconce, J. (2000) *Haunted Media*. Duke University Press: Durham, NC.

Silverstone, R. and Hirsch, H. (eds) (1992) *Consuming Technologies*. Routledge: London.

Sinclair, J. (2002) 'Review of David Morley's home territories'. *International Journal of Cultural Studies*, vol. 5, no. 1, pp. 111–13.

Spigel, L. (2001a) 'Media homes: Then and now'. *International Journal of Cultural Studies*, vol. 4, no. 4.

Spigel, L. (2001b) *Welcome to the Dreamhouse*. Duke University Press: Durham, NC.

Spigel, L. (1992) *Make Room for TV*. University of Chicago Press: Chicago, IL.

Sunden, J. (2001) *The Virtually Global: Or, the Flipside of Being Digital*. University of Copenhagen, Global Media Cultures Working Paper No. 8.

Tomlinson, J. (2001) *Instant Access: Some Cultural Implications of 'Globalising' Technologies*. University of Copenhagen, Global Media Cultures Working Paper No. 13.

Tuan, Y. F. (1996) *Cosmos and Hearth*. University of Minnesota Press: Minneapolis.

Veron, E. (1991) *Analyses pour Centre d'Etudes des Telecommunications*. Causa Rerum: Paris.

Wark, M. (1994) *Virtual Geography*. Indiana University Press: Bloomington.

Weilenmann, A. and Larsson, C. (2002) 'Local use and the sharing of mobile phones', in (eds) B. Brown, N. Green and R. Harper, *Wireless World*. Springer: London.

Williams, R. (1974) *Television: Technology and Cultural Form*. Fontana: London.

Yoshimi, S. (1999) 'Made in Japan: The Cultural Politics of "Home Electrification" in Postwar Japan'. *Media, Culture & Society*, vol. 21, no. 2.

Zielinski, S. (1999) *AudioVisions: Cinema and Television as Entrances in History*. University of Amsterdam Press: Amsterdam.

3 Domestication: the enactment of technology[1]

Knut H. Sørensen

Doing technology – or not

The modern human lives with technology. Everyday life is a continuous engagement with artefacts: physically, mentally, emotionally and morally. At least in the relatively wealthy OECD countries, this situation has become trivial. We expect to live with technologies as matters of fact; we seldom question their place in modern society. And if we do, it is because we expect improvements and new technological options. Thus, we do not just take for granted the experience of having modern technology continuously at our fingertips. We have also come to presume that there will be a continuous supply of new artefacts and systems, and that new versions of the established ones will be offered to us.

Of course, there are controversial technologies. Some are the object of long-standing heated controversies, like nuclear power. Others are questioned occasionally, like television and the car. In fact, there are a number of such technologies that seem to invite moral exchanges about their use. How many hours should children be allowed to watch television, if at all? Should you not use public transport rather than your car to get to work? Under what circumstances should mobile phones be turned off? These debates are important reminders that even if technology's place in modern life is a matter of fact, its use and meaning are not. The practice of technology in everyday life is far more complex and ambiguous.

In this chapter, I inquire into the complexities of human performance or enactment of technologies, related to what is commonly seen as ownership and use. These activities may be conceptualized as the domestication of technology, and this chapter attempts to elaborate this concept and suggest some of its benefits. The argument begins with the assumption that people construct their own technological practices, but in interaction with other people's practices. To start with, the focus is on the way individuals and groups of individuals create assemblages or networks of artefacts, meaning and action in their everyday life. However, most technologies involve the construction of social institutions of infrastructure and regulation as well as collective repertoires and repositories of action and meaning. Thus, we need to approach the analysis of 'doing of technology' as a multi-sited, multi-actor process. The aim of this chapter is to show how the domestication perspective may be helpful in this respect.

This way of framing the issue may be seen to circumvent the set of problems often presented by invoking concepts such as autonomous technology or technological imperative (Winner 1977). They refer to a long-standing anxiety of modern society that technology is out of control, that machines are taking command. Much of the literature that has pursued this perspective seems to take the idea of 'out-of-control' too literally and assumes the technological imperative to be too effective. Most inventions never see the light of day. Most innovations never become household goods. These simple facts should caution against simplistic beliefs that technologies have to be used once they have been conceived.

Nevertheless, the issue of technology as an imposed force on everyday life should not be dismissed too quickly. Even if the idea of a technological imperative is misleading, there may be strong social influences that push us to use certain technologies. This is evident from efforts to analyse what may be conceptualized as non-use of technologies (Wyatt 2003; Sørensen 1994). Clearly, the phenomenon of non-use is a strong indication that people frequently have a choice with regard to what technologies they appropriate, but this choice may not always be exercised at will. In fact, non-use may take a lot of effort as the use of many technologies may be conceived as part of 'normal' behaviour. Of course, non-use may be interpreted as a result of technophobia. Some argue that this is a widespread phenomenon that affects between a quarter and one third of the population worldwide (see Brosnan 1998). However, Wyatt (2003) argues that non-use is a strategic decision, made because the technology does not appear particularly beneficial or interesting, or because of active resistance. Thus, we have to be aware that ownership or use of a particular technology or a set of technologies may be enforced as well as resisted. To study the enactment of technology, we have to use an approach that is sensitive to the fact that this doing is influenced by choice as well as discipline, by enthusiasm as well as resistance. What should such an approach look like? To clarify the advantages of the domestication approach, it is useful to look into some precedent efforts.

Reductionist approaches

In general, technology has been and still is a marginal issue in the social sciences. This is reflected in the striking absence of technology and technological development as topics in standard textbooks. Most social theorists circumvent technology in the same way as nature, climate and physical landscape, probably because this allows them to analyse society as a purely social phenomenon, undisturbed by any considerations related to the material dimensions of human existence. Moreover, the exceptional efforts to analyse how technology interacted with humans were based on varieties of technological determinism or at least technological reductionism. Technology was understood as an autonomous force that had well-defined impacts on people and society, and social change could be explained in terms of technological progress (MacKenzie and Wajcman 1999). To understand the challenges at hand, let us briefly consider two of these efforts: the early sociology of technology and industrial sociology.

The first explicit attempt to develop a sociology of technology came from American sociologist William F. Ogburn and his collaborators. They made thorough, empirical efforts of analysing and assessing technology and technological development (Gilfillan 1970; Allen *et al.* 1957; see also Westrum 1991). While Ogburn's prediction that a personal aeroplane would replace the car with hindsight appears ridiculous, this is not a sufficient reason to neglect the approach. His sociology of technology consisted of two parts: the first was his theory of inventions; the second was concerned with social effects.

Ogburn's first part the theory of inventions – was integrated into a larger theory of social evolution. This theory was based on four key concepts: *inventions, cultural accumulation, diffusion* of inventions, and *adaption* of one part of the culture to another. The rate of inventions, according to Ogburn, grew exponentially with cultural accumulation, implying an acceleration of human progress (Ogburn 1964 [1950], pp. 17–32). The second part of Ogburn's sociology of technology was concerned with social effects. Similar to multivariate statistical analysis, social effects of technology were to be identified through an analysis of variations: 'Since cause and effect are always variables, then, an effect cannot be explained by something that has not varied' (Ogburn 1957, p. 13). The crucial point was the perception of technology as a more or less continuously changing feature of modern society because of the exponential growth of inventions. This was contrasted to humans who were perceived as constants: 'We say that the automobile creates motels, though actually it is the human beings who do the creating, because the variable is the automobile and not the human beings' (*ibid.*, p. 15). Consequently, we may describe this methodological approach as *technovariate*. The concept emphasizes the fact that the main characteristic of the methodology is to compare social systems or social events through their classification, based on the stages in the development of a given technology. To Ogburn, technology was the only independent variable in his analysis of social change.

Nevertheless, the effects of technology are perceived as products of human action and not as a necessary outcome of new technology:

> By granting that we may choose to use a radio receiving set in several different ways, if enough people use a radio to listen to music, then it may be said that a radio has a social effect upon our musical enjoyment. If enough choose to listen to reports of the news, then broadcasting has a social effect upon our civic education.
>
> (Ogburn 1957, p. 18)

In most of the work of the Ogburn group, social effects were deducted from technology in a rather sweeping manner. Put a little crudely, what they did was to make an inventory of new phenomena that could be linked to a specific technology in a given period (like radio, television, the automobile and so on). Linking meant observing that the technology played a role in the phenomenon, like increased physical mobility or different strategies of keeping informed about what happened in society. Since they, as I noted above, tended to perceive technology as the main source of social change, such new phenomena were attributed to technology.

To the very limited extent that standard sociology touches upon issues of technology and technological change, a similar analytical move may be found in the analysis of technology as an external force of variation. Take for instance Talcott Parsons's grandiose contribution to social theory, *The Social System* (1951). While most of his efforts are concerned with social reproduction, his analysis of social change brings him to science and technology as the main force of social transformations: 'Obviously, one fundamental feature of the institutionalisation of science and its application is the introduction of a continual stream of change into the social system' (Parsons 1951, p. 505). Parsons was more abstract in his analysis of technological change, but no less impressed by the scope of impacts than the Ogburn group.

Industrial sociology came to develop quite a different approach to the analysis of how technology could impact human action. Here, one was interested in the interaction of humans and machines related to processes of mechanization and automation. A machine may be seen as an arrangement that requires certain tasks to be performed. In this way, it may be argued to produce instrumental constraints, for example, along the following four dimensions (Kern and Schumann 1970; see also Bright 1958):

- the technical content of the task or its instrumental structure,
- the temporal structure of the task,
- the spatial structure of the task,
- the technical consequences of not executing the task or the technical sanctions.

This allows for a much more detailed analysis of the interaction of humans and machines than Ogburn's techno-variate method, with greater emphasis on characteristics of the machinery under scrutiny. From this perspective, 'effects' are observed in terms of division of labour, skills, bodily and mental strain, and possibilities of social community. However, the analysis presupposes that technology has definite instrumental constraints, unmediated by human interpretation. While industrial sociology can serve as a reminder of the need to analyse the interaction of humans and technology in detail, its methods failed, particularly through its inability to account for diverse socio-economic outcomes of identical technologies.

The intention of these two approaches, the sociology of technology of the Ogburn group on the one hand and industrial sociology on the other, was to provide empirical insights into the role of technology in society and at work, respectively. Both approaches emphasize the need for detailed analyses and the importance of studying technology in a concrete way, which is important to a domestication perspective. They had outlined an important challenge, even if the problems inherent in their reductionist strategies of inquiry pointed to the need to find other ways to conceptualize the interaction of technology, culture and human action.

Consuming technologies – or domesticating them?

In the early 1990s, a small group related to the newly established 'Centre for technology and society' in Trondheim, Norway initiated a few projects to explore aspects of technology and everyday life.[2] We knew we had to search for non-determinist and non-reductionist approaches – but where? Our research interest was embedded in a long-standing, local interest to study technology from the perspective of users or workers and the call from economic historians like Nathan Rosenberg (1982) to get inside the black box of technology. Ruth Schwartz Cowan (1987) also provided an important stimulus to investigate 'the consumption junction' in relation to the development of technology.

Eventually, we came to engage particularly with two sources of inspiration. One was actor-network theory (ANT) and the effort to develop a semiotic approach to the study of technology (Akrich 1992;

Latour 1988, 1992). From this endeavour came above all some new concepts that helped the analysis of technological artefacts as embodiments of designers' ideas about the ways users were supposed to apply their designs. Design was seen to 'define actors with specific tastes, competences, motives, aspirations, political prejudices and the rest', based on the assumption 'that morality, technology, science, and economy will evolve in particular ways'. Designers inscribe their visions of the world in the technical content of the new object (Akrich 1992, p. 208). This inscription Akrich calls a *script*: 'Thus, like a film script, technical objects define a framework of action together with the actors and the space in which they are supposed to act' (*ibid.*). These ideas also resonated well with designer guru Donald A. Norman's suggestion that artefacts could be considered as *affordances* related to human action, a mixture of suggestions and facilitations with regard to how designs should or should not be used (Norman 1988; see also Pfaffenberger 1992).

Another important idea in ANT was that the script could be contested by users, who consciously would try to override inscriptions. Latour (1992) suggested that the actual use of an artefact could be understood as a dynamic conflict between designers' programmes of action, inscribed in artefacts, and users' anti-programmes that countered or circumvented these inscriptions. The outcome could not be predicted; it had to be observed through empirical investigations.

The second source of inspiration came from media studies and the proposal to study information and communication technologies (ICTs) in everyday life through concepts like the moral economy of the household and domestication (Silverstone *et al.* 1992, 1989). Silverstone and his colleagues thereby presented a suggestive and very promising theoretical scheme to study the use of technology, proposing to do this by analysing four dimensions or stages in a household's dynamic uptake of a technology: (1) appropriation, (2) objectification, (3) incorporation, and (4) conversion. This scheme integrated action and meaning. Silverstone *et al.*'s main focus was on the household, where the concept of the moral economy was invoked to emphasize that the economic circulation of ICT commodities was paralleled by a transactional system of meaning:

> To understand the household as a moral economy, therefore, is to understand the household as part of a transactional system, dynamically involved in the public world of the production and exchange of commodities and meanings ... At stake is the capacity of the household or the family to create and sustain its autonomy and identity (and for individual members of the family to do the same) as an economic, social, and cultural unit.
>
> (Silverstone *et al.* 1992, p. 19)

This concept of domestication was attractive in two main regards. First, it presupposed that users played an active and decisive role in the construction of patterns of use and meanings in relation to technologies. Second, it suggested that a main emphasis should be put on the production of meaning and identity from artefacts. This meant a fundamental break with technological determinism, as well as a move away from a long-term tendency to interpret technologies in mainly instrumental terms, as purposive tools.

The growing scholarly interest to study ICTs provided a common ground of investigation for media studies and technology studies.[3] Still, these two fields of inquiry do have their different analytical focusing devices and research questions. Thus, arguably, there is a media studies version of domestication as well as one emerging from technology studies. These two versions are in my opinion compatible, but there are important dissimilarities due to the fact that the two versions have been employed for different purposes. Thus, to some extent, the resulting conceptual and theoretical work has pursued different problems and made use of different intellectual resources. I will try to clarify some such issues by looking into some characteristics of the technology studies version.

A technology studies approach to domestication

The technology studies approach to domestication developed from an emphasis on the analysis of specific artefacts, initially primarily the analysis of the computer and related commodities (Aune 1992, 1996; Berg 1996; Håpnes 1996). In addition, there was an expressed concern to study domestication as a negotiated space of designers' views and users' needs and interests. Thus, in this version, domestication was less about household consumption and more related to the construction of a wider everyday life (Sørensen *et al.* 2000; Lie and Sørensen 1996). As a starting point, domestication was used as a metaphor for the transformation of an object from something unknown, something 'wild' and unstable, to become known, more stable, 'tamed' (Lie and Sørensen 1996; see also Silverstone *et al.* 1989, pp. 24–5). This kind of analysis is not just concerned with the enactment of technology: in the domestication process people and their socio-technical relations may change as well. Domestication therefore has wider implications than a socialization of technology: it is a co-production of the social and the technical.

Hence, the domestication concept could be seen to have a wider potential than its apparent situatedness within the moral economy of the household. First, from a technology studies point of view, domestication invites a focus on three main, generic sets of features (Sørensen *et al.* 2000):

- The construction of a set of practices related to an artefact. This could mean routines in using the artefact, but also the establishment and development of institutions to support and regulate this use.
- The construction of meaning of the artefact, including the role the artefact eventually could play in relation to the production of identities of the actors involved.
- Cognitive processes related to learning of practice as well as meaning.

Pursuing the generic potential, domestication becomes a multi-sited process that transcends the household space, and in which the sites interact. Østby (1995), for example, shows how the historical integration of the car in Norway may be understood as a process in which the set-up of national institutions and collective discourses are involved together with the production of individual practices. Similarly, Brosveet and Sørensen (2000) suggest how the uptake of multimedia technologies and the way these technologies are made available – for example, for households – involve the extensive production of a wide variety of institutions and standards at a national level. Spilker (1998), Levold (2001) and Lagesen (2005) have taken the perspective into yet another direction. Here, the domestication concept is employed to analyse master students, computer scientists and computer science students, respectively. The aim is to sensitize readers to the ambivalent and ambiguous acts of development and positioning that take place when the students and the computer scientists become or evolve as professionals.

Such observations may be taken further by drawing on ANT as a theoretical resource. First, the 'taming' of an artefact may be understood as a process where a script or a programme is translated or re-scripted through the way users read, interpret and act. Second, domestication may be seen as the process through which an artefact becomes associated with practices, meanings, people and other artefacts in the construction of intersecting large and small networks (Sørensen 1994). Only rarely do we domesticate things in isolation.

Using a slightly different vocabulary, the domestication of artefacts may be understood as the complex movement of objects into and within existing socio-technical arrangements. In contrast to the standard assumptions of diffusion theory (Rogers 1995), such objects are not immutable; they are – at least in principle – mutable and may change through their movement. De Laet and Mol (2000) describe this phenomenon as the fluidity of technology. Their example, a kind of water pump, may be particularly open to reconfiguration, due to the lack of sharp and solid boundaries, the potential for collective and shifting 'authorship' with regard to the technology, and the absence of precise criteria for what may be considered successful functioning. However, following Law's (2004) suggestions, we should not just be aware that objects may be mutable; they may even be elusive and/or multi-vocal. This is not so much a quality of the object as a situational issue related to the kind of network within which the object moves or becomes stabilized.

On the other hand, the domestication perspective may add concrete sensibilities to the rather abstract ANT vocabulary. First, it represents a reminder of the temporal aspect of change processes which may be understood as social learning, the important observation that the use of technologies might be transformed over time and that the trajectory of these modifications is important (Sørensen 1996). Domestication may end in the sense that the artefact is forgotten or thrown out, but the process is irreversible in the sense that its traces cannot be completely removed. Second, the domestication perspective adds subjectivity to ANT through its focus on practice, meaning and learning. Domestication implies not only the movement of objects in a network, but also a series of joint enactments between human and non-human elements of the network and in the intersections of network.

Andrew Feenberg (1999) has criticized the use of the domestic metaphor in the domestication perspective: 'The metaphor connotes the narrow confines of the home however it is reformulated, and thus privileges adaptation and habituation in a way that short circuits the appeal to agency' (Feenberg 1999, p. 108). Given the emphasis on social inequalities, like gender or social class, in many domestication studies (see Haddon 2004; Lie and Sørensen 1996), this critique seems misplaced. Social conflict, discipline and power are inherent in most domestic practices, within households, organizations or nations. Arguably, agency starts out from the familiar, even if the aim is to transcend well-known territories. When domestication of artefacts may appear to involve adaptation and habituation, it is through hindsight – the knowledge of what actually happens.

To clarify this point, it is important to investigate domestication processes that extend in time and space. In the following sections, I discuss two examples of such domestication processes, which are presented by drawing on some of the technology studies vocabulary introduced above. The first is a brief outline of the Norwegian appropriation of the car, to demonstrate the multi-sitedness, multi-vocality and emergent character of a long-term enactment of technology. The second is a study of gender and mobile telephony that looks into the tension between diversity and standardization of use. Both examples are also intended to highlight an additional aspect of domestication, namely the co-production of norms and enactment of technologies.

The successful construction of the Norwegian car

There are a few attempts to manufacture cars in Norway. They have all failed, including the latest effort, the electrical car *Th!nk*. Still, from a domestication point of view, the headline 'The Norwegian car' makes sense. It is an allegory that suggests a specificity of cars in Norway that distinguishes them from Swedish or German ones, even when the cars technologically speaking are identical (Sørensen 1991).

To make the argument and to indicate the fruitfulness of studying domestication at a national level, I begin by considering the early historical process through which cars became introduced and embedded in Norwegian society. In the first stage, in the late nineteenth and early twentieth century, the car in the role of a 'rail-free vehicle' was a contested object. Many municipalities met the car with strong regulations; some even prohibited driving. The car was seen as a scary enemy of the perceived natural order, where transport was conducted by foot, horses, or – at best – railways. In addition, cars were believed to have a destructive impact on roads (Østby 1995, pp. 90f.). On the other hand, other actors invoked the car to signify progress. A main supporter, Hans Hagerup Krag, general manager of the Norwegian Highway Directorate from 1874 to 1903, suggested – as early as 1899 – an increase in public grants to improve roads to prepare for the use of cars: '[I]t would be of great harm, if the nation – due to a lack of resources to improve roads – still for some time should have to do without the great advantages of such means of communication' (Skougaard 1914, p. LI). Two years later, Krag drove a car through the Norwegian mountains from Otta to Åndalsnes, a strenuous journey, to make his contemporaries aware of the car and its – in his opinion – great possibilities. Krag also sent his subordinates to other countries to study highways but also cars and driving (Kristiansen 1975).

There are probably many similarities between the Norwegian domestication of the car and what happened in other countries with respect to the building of infrastructure and the regulation of car ownership, driving, and the construction of roads. However, Per Østby (1995) identifies important specific qualities of these processes in Norway. He shows how Norwegian efforts were shaped by the lack of a national car industry, a long-standing concern for the balance of trade with other countries, and high costs of road building in a mountainous and sparsely populated country. This resulted in high duties and strict import controls. Between 1934 and 1962, people needed permission from a public authority to buy a car.

After 1945, new institutions were designed to provide input to the political planning and regulation of cars, traffic and roads. Many engineers were trained in highway planning and management in the USA. They returned to fill posts in public management, in education, and in a new national research institute for transport economics that was established in 1958. These institutions and the highway engineers came to manage national level domestication of the car in Norway, in the absence of a powerful car industry. In particular, city and highway planning shaped the use of cars, while extensive car ownership and driving was a basic premise for the planning. It is not possible to understand the domestication of the car on the national arena or by individuals without analysing the interaction between car traffic and the construction of roads and highways. The practice of driving has been and still is scripted by engineers and politicians, even if the various scripts have been consistently resisted (Østby 1995; Sørensen and Sørgaard 1994). What we see is really a complex interaction between a wide variety of objects, resulting in a strong and powerful but also fluid and malleable network, due to conflicting efforts of domestication.

The Norwegian car was initially a luxury, mainly for the few and wealthy, but gradually it came to be the most important means of transport and thus of great economic significance. Culturally, the continuing increase in car ownership meant that it became a household good which, during the 1960s and 1970s, came to be more or less taken for granted. Still, the meaning of the car never stabilized entirely. While some controversies were closed – like the issue of luxury versus utility and triviality – new ones emerged. Thus, the domestication of the car in Norway has taken place in a continuous engagement with moral aspects of ownership and driving. Inspired by literary theorist and philosopher of language, Mikhail Bakhtin, and his ideas about polyphony (Bakhtin 1986; see also Bell and Gardiner 1998; Lagesen 2005), we could say there exists an abundance of contradictory authoritative voices and expectations regarding car ownership and use which Norwegians are in dialogue and negotiation with. Examples include utterances such as:

- 'Cars are an unnecessary luxury'
- 'Cars are needed to provide important social activities, like transport of goods and people, and to perform services, like doctoring'

- 'Cars are an economic problem'
- 'Cars are needed to support economic growth and development'
- 'Cars are dangerous'
- 'Cars are a part of a modern welfare society and a sign of progress'
- 'Cars need to be taxed severely to pay for costs of infrastructure and accidents'
- 'Cars are a threat to the environment'
- 'To drive a car is a human right'
- 'You should rather use public transport' (see Aune 1998; Østby 1995; Sørensen and Sørgaard 1994).

Clearly, this allows Norwegians to find arguments that support both use and non-use of cars. A wide diversity of ways to domesticate or not emerges. However, it would be misleading to see this as an exercise of free choice. Only a small minority of Norwegians do not have access to a car, and most people in this category are either young or old. In the infrastructure offered to Norwegians with regard to where they live, where they work, and where they find shopping and service institutions, car ownership has been inscribed as a clear expectation. In particular, when people have children, argues Aune (1998), this represents a practical demand to acquire a car, because it is commonly perceived that children need to be driven to kindergarten, sport events and social activities. This makes car ownership a social standard, a normal way of life.

But car driving in Norway is a matter of concern. It is recognized as a normal thing to do, but also as something that one should do less of. In this respect, domestication of the car involves the management of moral ambivalence and ambiguity. As a society, Norway has domesticated the car to the extent that car ownership has become normal. Strong disciplining mechanisms set standards for ownership as well as driving, such as traffic rules, police surveillance, road bumps ('sleeping policemen'), mandatory technical controls and parking rules. While car practices remain diverse, subject to individuals' needs, values and creativity, the car has become what we could call a quasi-stable object. It is stabilized in a complex and extensive network, but it also remains mutable. In a deep sense, to drive a car is a messy business (Law 2004).

Mobile phone morality[4]

The mobile phone offers an interesting opportunity to analyse domestication processes since this artefact has very rapidly become a widely used communication device, which involves considerable cultural changes. In particular, I want to look into the construction of technology-related norms that may shape meaning as well as use of the artefact.

On one level, Norway's domestication of the mobile looks very much like a 'critical mass' story, given the very rapid growth of ownership of mobile phones and the dramatic increase in traffic. In 2003, 86 per cent of Norwegians between 9 and 79 years of age owned a mobile phone.[5] The people interviewed in our study acquired their first mobile at different times and for different reasons. Most of the early users got their mobiles through work.

> I got my first mobile in 1995. I needed it at work, and my employer paid for it. At that time, I drove my car every day from Sandefjord to Oslo. Then I could do a lot of work in the car. There were a great number of people I needed to call, and I could spend the time doing this while I was in the car anyway.
>
> (Anders, 42)

The late users got their mobile one to three years before the interview took place. Several had resisted the mobile, and some had even decided that they never wanted a mobile. Resistance was primarily explained in two ways. The first claim was that they really did not need one. The other claim was that they did not want to be accessible at all times.

> I resist it. I feel that I want to protect myself and not be so accessible. This is something I believe is related to my situation at work; all the time somebody wants something from me. Also, socially and family-wise I am at a stage where everyone sells and buys homes in need of refurbishing and wants some assistance.
>
> (Reidun, 50)

Nevertheless, some of the resistant users had become quite active. To be a latecomer does not mean that one has to remain moderate or cautious; it only implies that domestication may be a drawn-out process. Reidun told us that she felt her attitude towards her mobile was changing, but only very slowly.

A striking finding in our research was a gendered pattern of acquisition of the mobile phone. While the male informants either got the mobile through their employer or bought one themselves, all the women received their first mobile as a present. It was given to them by their husbands, boyfriends, sisters, brothers, fathers or other family members. Often, they got a used mobile, available because the giver had acquired a new one. Arguably, we observe a phenomenon that may be called a 'wife mobile' similar to the 'wife car'.

There is a communication logic, which fuels the motive to give away mobiles. To those who own one, their experience suggests that it is very practical – at least for them – that people they relate to also have access to a mobile. As a communication device, mobile phones seem to carry the seed of their own diffusion – an object-generating object. As an increasing part of the population owns one, access becomes increasingly tempting, even a pressing concern. Reidun told that she felt pressured. She vividly claimed that she did not want a mobile, but her children and her parents had 'forced' her to have one, so they could reach her when she spent time alone at their cabin in the mountains. Domestication may thus be disciplined in a quite upfront manner.

The conjecture that there is considerable variation between our informants in terms of their domestication was definitely confirmed. Some of them spend a lot of time, energy and money on communication through their mobiles. They tend to leave their mobiles on at all times, and they send a lot of messages. Some of them also talk to people a lot through their mobiles, but that tends to be related to work. In a typical manner, Anne (26) admits that:

> I have made myself a bit dependent, really. You get accustomed to be accessible when you want to. Sometimes, it is very convenient to be accessible. You decide yourself. You can ignore people; you can turn it off or choose not to respond ... I mainly use the mobile to send messages. Usually about nothing, such small everyday life things. In a way, this is a toy that you buy for yourself. I really don't phone very much.

Anniken (43) got her first mobile through her employer to make her more accessible. Presently, she is a housewife and she mainly refers to her social life and her interest in chatting, when she explains why she needs a mobile: 'Everyone else had one. I missed out on so much when I didn't have a mobile. There were a lot of at-the-moment appointments. Then it was impossible to get hold of me. I had a telephone at home, but it wasn't used in that way.'

The other informants display a pattern where the rationale behind the use of the mobile resembles the one we observe among the heavy users. After a while, they become much more eager users than they had planned to be. This was particularly true for some of the initially resistant. Suddenly they found themselves bringing the mobile with them wherever they went. Another change was that they now rarely turned off the mobile. Instead, they applied the silent mode. Their reason for leaving the phone on even at times when they are unable to or do not want to answer it, is to remain in control: to see who has called and when a message has come in.

The urge to have the phone turned on seems to be due to a feeling of belonging or being part of a group. When they received a text message, they knew someone was thinking of them. To some degree, there was also the fear of being left out. Many of the informants had noticed that there had been a change in the way people made plans. While in the past, they used to make plans in advance, some of the planning was now left to the last minute.

The mobile was also deemed important in love affairs. Marit (30) told us how essential it had been in her last relationship. Within the first couple of weeks, she sent 258 messages to him, and he answered all of them. As the love affair cooled off, messages became increasingly rare. Anniken told a similar story, but on a more positive note. She and her present partner had exchanged 600 messages the first two days after they had met. She had written them all down on paper, which she kept like a treasure. Every now and then she would read them to be reminded of their first days of getting to know each other.

It was common to talk about 'mobile common sense' or 'proper behaviour'. Here, we observe the emergence of a morality as a part of the domestication of the mobile. The main concern expressed by the informants is to avoid disturbing other people. The most active users say moral sense is about not having telephone conversations at weddings, funerals or very nice restaurants. To some degree, they concur that talking on the phone when you are with just one other person should be avoided. However, conversing on the phone during public transport, in cafes and other places where talking is permitted, they find OK. The more moderate users said they would try to keep their voices down and keep the conversation short if other people were around. As a rule they thought people should avoid talking on the phone in public places when other people were close by.

Many informants also said they should be better at turning off the mobile or even leaving the mobile at home. However, all of them acted in the opposite way. They left the mobile at home or turned it off more and more rarely. In a way, one could perhaps say that they became habituated to having the mobile in an 'accessible mode'. For example, they would say that other people were so used to being able to reach them at all times that they got worried if they did not answer. Also, they admitted to feeling restless when they did not know if someone had sent them a message or tried to call them.

That people talk at length about moral aspects of mobile telephony offers no evidence for a well-defined morality related to mobiles. On the contrary, suggested moral rules vary a lot and many admit to breaking the rules they themselves suggest. Clearly, the situation regarding norms for the domestication of mobiles is more ambiguous than in the case of the car. However, many people feel that technologies like mobile phones should somehow be regulated in a normative way because their use raises important moral issues about appropriate behaviour. These concerns are shared by men and women, and there was no clear-cut distinction between the moral narratives offered by men and women informants in the study.

The domestication of the mobile phone is a moral undertaking in a double sense. We have observed that moral concerns are invoked in the account of the domestication process, but also that the construction of such norms is done as a collective aspect of the domestication. People discover a need for norms and struggle to negotiate what they should be (see also Ling and Yttri 2002). In this way, they retain agency, while the mobile phone remains fluid. The construction of norms is of course an effort to achieve stabilization, but it is not effective in this case.

However, the most striking aspect of the domestication of mobiles is the emergence of a more intensive communication practice. Ling and Yttri (2002) propose that mobile phones facilitate 'hyper-coordination' in terms of the instrumental possibility of exchanging information about time and space coordinates. Both men and women use the mobile phone to exchange information and emotional messages, to allow for tighter socio-spatial navigation. However, in most cases, coordination is not that hyper. It is just improved, compared to previous communication technologies. What is new is the emerging feeling that one should be accessible everywhere and at all times. This moral norm seems to strongly influence the domestication of the mobile to achieve accessibility, but as our study shows, the space for diversity remains considerable.

Representing complexity

The idea that technology has social impacts is widespread. In popular accounts, the car reshaped modern society in a fundamental way and the mobile phone is causing deep changes in late modern living. The techno-variate method of Ogburn and collaborators probably resonates much better with popular thinking about technology than domestication does. The suggestion of industrial sociology that machines direct human action seems close to everyday experience. Is there any reader who has not at least once cursed her car or his computer for its spitefulness and uncomfortable interventions?

The challenge of thinking in terms of 'impacts' is at its most evident when new technologies are about to be introduced. If we look at the arguments provided for heavy investments in broadband technology or so-called 3G mobile telephony, they are surprisingly slim. They focus on speed and capacity, as if these features had an immediate social meaning. It is assumed that increased speed and capacity will be translated into something useful, but it is unclear what that utility will be. Broadband and 3G clearly need to be domesticated; it is only after an eventual domestication that 'impacts' may be identified. Impact is hindsight, something we may believe in after the underlying performances have been rendered invisible or uninteresting.

This argument is no denial that technologies are forceful ingredients of modern society; the argument only protests that the forcefulness should be taken to be inherent in technology itself. Actor-network theory has argued that this force emerges from the way technology and culture become enmeshed through delegation and re-delegation of action between human and non-human actants (Latour 1988, 1992). We experience the force of technology through learning and discipline made invisible.

Thus, the main advantage of the domestication perspective is that it is a conceptual device that sensitizes the analyst to the complexity of integrating artefacts into dynamic socio-technical settings, like the household, the workplace, or society. It is a reminder to be concerned with the practical, symbolic and cognitive aspects of the work needed to do this integration, at multiple sites. The brief efforts to analyse the domestication of cars and mobile phones was meant to demonstrate this point and to show the great number of diverse efforts needed to achieve a productive integration.

In particular, I have emphasized the morality of domestication to show the importance of considering the normative aspects of technologies. On the one hand, domestication is disciplined through expectations and norms. A person may feel that she has to bring a car or a mobile phone into her life, even if she does not want to. On the other hand, over time, a collective domestication produces new norms and expectations that influence the way the artefact is used, the meaning it signifies, and the possibilities of learning new ways of doing and thinking about it. In this respect, technologies are deeply moral enterprises.

This observation is related to, but also distinctly different from, the perspective of a moral economy. As developed by E. P. Thompson (1971), the concept of a moral economy is meant to emphasize the importance of non-economic features to explain action and agency. Thompson was concerned with social norms and obligations as given, as preconditions of proper behaviour. The domestication argument, as presented here, is that norms may be understood as contested, fluid, emergent properties of developing technologies. At some point, norms may influence domestication, but the moral aspects of technologies seem to remain dynamic. Maybe this is typical of norms in late modern societies, which suggests that the concept of a moral economy is too strict and stable in a fluid modernity (Bauman 2000).

This does not mean that technologies should be seen as innocent and completely malleable. Rather, the domestication argument is that technologies should be seen as under-determined and not undetermined. Designers inscribe visions and actions into artefacts, and they are probably successful in shaping users' actions quite often. However, this may only be clarified through empirical analysis of actual use, which is the heart of the matter for domestication approaches. The moralities elicited by a given artefact should be observed in the same vein, as cultural resources of the enactment of technology.

Notes

1. The work reported here has been supported by the EMTEL network project as well as by the Research Council of Norway. I thank Margrethe Aune, Maren Hartmann, Vivian A. Lagesen, Hendrik Spilker and Per Østby for useful comments to a previous version.
2. The group included Håkon With Andersen, Margrethe Aune, Anne-Jorunn Berg, Tove Håpnes, Marit Hubak, Gunnar Lamvik, Per Østby, Jon Sørgaard and myself.
3. This has been fruitfully explored in the EMTEL I and II network projects, from which this paper draws inspiration.
4. This section draws on Nordli and Sørensen (2004), a study based on interviews with 21 Norwegian men and women in two age groups, between 25 and 45, and between 50 and 60 years of age. The informants include both early and late adopters. They have been classified as belonging to one of four categories according to use: Pioneer users (first name begins with a P), advanced users (first name begins with an A), moderate users (first name begins with an M), and resistant users (first name begins with an R).
5. http://www.ssb.no/aarbok/tab/t-070230-271.html

References

Akrich, M. (1992) 'The De-scription of technical objects', in (eds) W. Bijker and J. Law, *Shaping Technology/Building Society. Studies in Sociotechnical Change*. The MIT Press: Cambridge, MA, pp. 205–24.

Allen, F. R., Hart, H., Miller, D. C., Ogburn, W. F. and Nimkoff, M. K. (1957) *Technology and Social Change*. Appleton-Century-Crofts: New York.

Aune, M. (1998) *'Nøktern eller nytende'? Energiforbruk og hverdagsliv i norske husholdninger*, Report no. 34, NTNU, Centre for Technology and Society.

Aune, M. (1996) 'The computer in everyday life', in (eds) M. Lie and K. H. Sørensen, *Making Technology our Own? Domesticating Technology into Everyday Life*. Scandinavian University Press: Oslo, pp. 91–120.

Aune, M. (1992) *Datamaskina i hverdagslivet*, Report no. 15, NTNU, Centre for Technology and Society, Trondheim.

Bakhtin, M. M. (1986) 'The problem of speech genres', in (eds) C. Emerson and M. Holquist, *Speech genres and other late essays*. University of Texas Press: Austin.

Bauman, Z. (2000) *Liquid Modernity*. Polity Press: Cambridge.

Bell, M. M. and Gardiner, M. (eds) (1998) *Bakhtin and the Human Sciences*. Sage: London.

Berg, A.-J. (1996) *Digital Feminism*, PhD dissertation, NTNU, Centre for Technology and Society: Trondheim.

Bijker, W. E. and Law, J. (eds) (1992) *Shaping Technology/building Society. Studies in Sociotechnical Change*. The MIT Press: Cambridge, MA.

Bright, J. R. (1958) *Management and Automation*. Harvard Business School Press: Cambridge, MA.

Brosnan, M. (1998) *Techophobia. The Psychological Impact of Information Technology*. Routledge: London.

Brosveet, J. and Sørensen, K. H. (2000) 'Fishing for fun and profit? Norway domesticates multimedia'. *Information Society*, vol. 16, no. 4, pp. 263–76.

Cowan, R. S. (1987) 'The consumption junction: A proposal for research strategies in the sociology of technology', in (eds) W. Bijker *et al.*, *The social construction of technological systems*. MIT Press: Cambridge, MA.

De Laet, M. and Mol, A. (2000) 'The Zimbabwe bush pump: Mechanics of a fluid technology'. *Social Studies of Science*, vol. 30, no. 2, pp. 225–63.

Feenberg, A. (1999) *Questioning Technology*. Routledge: London.

Gilfillan, S. C. (1970) *The Sociology of Invention*. The MIT Press: Cambridge, MA.

Haddon, L. (2004) *Information and Communication Technologies in Everyday Life*. Berg: Oxford.

Håpnes, T. (1996) 'Not in their machines: How hackers transform computers into subcultural artefacts', in (eds) M. Lie and K. Sørensen, *Making technology our own? Domesticating technology into everyday life*. Scandinavian University Press: Oslo.

Kern, H. and Schumann, M. (1970) *Industriarbeit und Arbeiterbewusstsein.* Europäische Verlagsanstalt, Frankfurt a.M.

Kristiansen, G. (1975) *Bil, vei og meninger.* Norbok: Oslo.

Lagesen, V. A. (2005) *Extreme Make-over? The Making of Women and Computer Science.* PhD dissertation, Trondheim: Department of Interdisciplinary Studies of Culture, NTNU.

Latour, B. (1992) 'Where are the missing masses? The sociology of a few mundane artifacts', in (eds) W. E. Bijker and J. Law, *Shaping Technology/building Society. Studies in Sociotechnical Change.* The MIT Press: Cambridge, MA.

Latour, B. (1988) 'Mixing humans and nonhumans together: The sociology of a door-closer'. *Social Problems,* vol. 35, no. 3, pp. 298–310.

Law, J. (2004) *After Method. Mess in Social Science Research.* Routledge: London.

Levold, N. (2001) ' "Doing gender" in academia: The domestication of an information-technological researcher-position', in (eds) H. Glimell and O. Juhlin, *The Social Production of Technology. On the Everyday Life with Things.* BAS Publishers: Gothenburg.

Lie, M. and Sørensen, K. H. (eds) (1996) *Making Technology our Own? Domesticating Technology into Everyday Life.* Scandinavian University Press: Oslo.

Ling, R. and Yttri, B. (2002) 'Hyper-coordination via mobile phones in Norway', in (eds) J. E. Katz and M. A. Aakhus, *Perpetual Contact. Mobile communication, Private Talk and Public Performance.* Cambridge University Press: Cambridge.

MacKenzie, D. and Wajcman, J. (1999) *The Social Shaping of Technology,* 2nd edn. Open University Press: Buckingham.

Nordli, H. and Sørensen, K. H. (2004) 'Diffusion as inclusion? How adult men and women become users of mobile phones', in (eds) N. Oudshoorn, E. Rommes and I. van Slooten, *Strategies of inclusion: Gender in the information society. Vol III: Surveys of women's user experience.* Report no. 66, NTNU, Department of interdisciplinary studies of culture: Trondheim.

Norman, D. (1988) *The Psychology of Everyday Things.* Basic Books: New York.

Ogburn, W. F. (1964 [1950]) 'Social evolution reconsidered', in (ed.) O. D. Duncan, *William F. Ogburn on Culture and Social Change.* Chicago University Press: Chicago.

Ogburn, W. F. (1957) 'How technology causes social change', in (eds) F. R. Allen *et al.*, *Technology and social change.* Appleton-Century-Crofts: New York, pp. 12–26.

Østby, P. (1995) *Flukten fra Detroit. Bilens integrasjon i det norske samfunnet*, Report no. 24, NTNU, Centre for Technology and Society, Trondheim.

Parsons, T. (1951) *The Social System*. The Free Press: New York.

Pfaffenberger, B. (1992) 'Technological dramas'. *Science, Technology, & Human Values*, vol. 17, no. 3, pp. 282–312.

Rogers, E. M. (1995) *Diffusion of Innovations*, 4th edn. The Free Press: New York.

Rosenberg, N. (1982) *Inside the Black Box*. Cambridge University Press: Cambridge.

Silverstone, R., Hirsch, E. and Morley, D. (1992) 'Information and communication technologies and the moral economy of the household', in (eds) R. Silverstone and E. Hirsch, *Consuming Technologies. Media and information in domestic spaces*. Routledge: London, pp. 15–31.

Silverstone, R., Morley, D., Dahlberg, A. and Livingstone, S. (1989) 'Families, technologies and consumption: the household and information and communication technologies', *CRICT Discussion Paper*, Brunel University: London.

Skougaard, J. (1914) *Det norske veivæsens historie*, Volume II. S. and Jul. Sørensens boktrykkeri: Kristiania (Oslo).

Sørensen, K. H. (1996) 'Learning technology, constructing culture. Sociotechnical change as social learning', STS working paper, no. 18, NTNU, Centre for Technology and Society: Trondheim.

Sørensen, K. H. (1994) 'Technology in use. Two essays on the domestication of artefacts', STS working paper, no. 2/94, NTNU, Centre for technology and society: Trondheim.

Sørensen, K. H. (1991) 'The Norwegian car. The cultural adaptation and integration of an imported artefact', in (eds) K. H. Sørensen and A.-J. Berg, *Technology and everyday life: Trajectories and transformations*. Norwegian Research Council for Science and the Humanities: Oslo, pp. 109–30.

Sørensen, K. H., Aune, M. and Hatling, M. (2000) 'Against linearity – On the cultural appropriation of science and technology', in (eds) M. Dierkes and C v. Groete, *Between Understanding and Trust. The Public, Science and Technology*. Harwood: Amsterdam.

Sørensen, K. H. and Sørgaard, J. (1994) 'Mobility and modernity. Towards a sociology of cars', in (ed.) K. H. Sørensen, *The Car and its Environments. The Past, Present and Future of the Motorcar in Norway*. EC, COST Social Sciences, Brussels.

Spilker, H. S. (1998) *Tilegning av faglige rom: hovedfagsstudiet som fenomen og prosjekt*, STS report no. 38, NTNU, Centre for Technology and Society: Trondheim.

Thompson, E. P. (1971) 'The moral economy of the English crowd in the eighteenth century'. *Past and Present*, no. 50, pp. 76–136.

Westrum, R. (1991) *Technologies and Society. The Shaping of People and Things*. Wadsworth: Belmont, CA.

Winner, L. (1977) *Autonomous Technology*. The MIT Press: Cambridge, MA.

Wyatt, S. (2003) 'Non-users also matter. The construction of users and non-users of the internet', in (eds) N. Oudshoorn and T. Pinch, *How Users Matter. The Co-construction of Users and Technology*. The MIT Press: Cambridge, MA.

4 Domestication running wild. From the moral economy of the household to the mores of a culture

Maria Bakardjieva

A slice of life in my virtual household[1]

'You are the greatest, Peter! No one can be like you, but I will do my best.' Hearing these words coming out of the mouth of my youngest son and addressed to his brother certainly warms my heart and almost draws tears into my eyes. The reaction on the part of the older brother is no less emotional. He smiles and stretches out his arms in an impulse to hug the little boy, but alas, his attempt is doomed. The two brothers are looking at each other via a webcam and are talking over the audio function that we only recently managed to get to work. Following the conversation, the younger one sets out to understand how he can draw cartoon-like pictures in the field of the textual chat just like his older brother had done.

As this episode unfolds, I know for sure that we have domesticated the computer, the ADSL connection to the internet, the webcam and the numerous pieces of software involved in the process. By drawing on these 'virtual' technologies our scattered family manages to retain a sense of closeness and realness of its bond. We make an incredibly complex technical system, created by an anonymous army of designers, engineers and others, to serve the simultaneously trivial and essential intimate purposes of our reunion. (In fact, I call the exchange between my boys trivial only to demonstrate analytical detachment. As a mother, I would fight anyone who dares to characterize it that way.) I know that it may be the case that the sense of closeness given to us by the technical system is false. I agree that it would have been much better if Peter could grab his little brother in his arms for real, but the distance between us is an element of the actual situation in which we have half-willingly chosen to put ourselves, pursuing projects of work and study in a mobile and global public world. The technical system has offered us the best possible place to be and act together under these circumstances. It has become a part of our material geographic home by way of the laptop placed on the kitchen table, the tangled cables running along the floor and the connectivity bills that will arrive at the end of the month. And it creates a virtual home for us to inhabit together when our crazy schedules and conflicting time zones permit. We can remain in what Schutz (Schutz and Luckmann 1973) has called 'attainable reach' to each other as 'fellowmen' and women sharing overlapping segments of each other's existence. This allows us to create a shared lifeworld, even if only for a limited duration and with curtailed sensual engagement.

The short episode described above and the technological activities and relations that constituted it did not occur spontaneously or unexpectedly. When I was packing for my visit to a foreign university, I purchased a webcam and put it in my suitcase. When my son was preparing to go to university in another city, we gave him a laptop and a new mobile phone. The moral economy of our family unit was issuing an imperative for us to try to overcome, as far as possible, the distance that was about to stretch between us. And the technical devices applicable toward this goal were growing in relevance and significance to the point where we picked them from the shelf of the computer store and put them alongside our most intimate belongings. Once taken out and installed in our new locations, these devices constantly reminded us of the project they were supposed to furnish and thus turned into tokens of our family bond. But how exactly was the connection between the sleek silver webcam and the heart-warming exchange between two brothers supposed to obtain? We had to work hard (some of us harder than others) before we could figure out how to make the programs run, how to position the camera and manipulate the multiple windows, how to indicate our status of availability or absence. This was actually the easy part. Much more difficult to settle on were the rules of mutual engagement, respect for privacy, tolerance for slow typing, rhythm of turn-taking as well as the coordination between the interactions on the screen and those behind it. Then, really, what do you do, when your mother, your friend and your grandfather are simultaneously calling for your attention from different windows and different points on the globe? These latter questions remain largely unresolved to this day and the fate of the webcam, even of the very idea of online gatherings and chats, hinges upon finding workable answers to them. You do not want your friend peeping in and engaging you in a frivolous conversation while you are frantically typing your way toward a deadline, as much as you do not want your son to shoo you away every time you catch him online and decide to ask if he has eaten his vegetables.

The concept of domestication, as I encountered it in the early 1990s (see Silverstone *et al.* 1992), has been the swing of the theoretical wand that established the significance of feelings, puzzles, decisions and actions like those recounted above to the dynamic of a technological society. The idea of domestic users having a say, albeit through their mostly silent choices and circumscribed activities, in the shaping of the emergent 'information society' was inspiring to me. The stream of literature discussing the impacts of that society and its dominant technologies on individuals and households was so abundant at the time that a glimpse of faith in the mindful, knowledgeable agent represented a welcome change. I had personal reasons to want to believe in the existence of such an agent, of course. Along with millions of fellow East Europeans, I was coming out of the collapse of an authoritarian communist state hopeful that the dictate of a system, be it political or technological, over individuals was not an inevitable state of affairs. Moreover, I had the inside knowledge of someone who had inhabited an authoritarian society and realized that the power of a system could never be so comprehensive as to permeate all aspects of life, to smash all resistance and to cancel all expressions of alternative human creativity. For my own emotional and biographical reasons, I wanted to search for the 'power of the powerless' that Havel (Havel and Keane 1985) had brought to light, if not necessarily to triumph. I was aware of the role of the home as a place of resistance, as a crucible of an 'alternative rationality' which generated and enacted value systems and projects different from those organizing the public world. I knew intuitively that what we did with objects and ideas in the home mattered with respect to our public affairs. The concept of domestication elevated that intuition to the status of a theoretical tenet.

Seen among a larger family of ideas regarding the relationship between technology and society, the concept of domestication represents a vital extension of social constructivism into the field of technology use. When Pinch and Bijker (1987), along with their colleagues, historians and sociologists, laid out the principles of the SCOT approach and other related perspectives, they were focusing their attention mainly on the practices of those professional groups out of whose efforts new technical artefacts emerge. 'Following the actors' was their leading motto and they lived up to it honourably. But the historical cast of actors they were portraying did not include users in any central roles. Users were confined to the background, to the crowd or choir that would appropriately rejoice at the birth of new inventions.[2] Users' trials and tribulations, their monologues and dialogues as they struggled to make sense of newly emergent technical devices were missing from these accounts.

The concept of domestication was among the first to direct the analytical lens to the dispersed and often dissonant micro-developments occurring behind the stage. More than simply pointing that way, it also offered an elaborate map for the explorer to follow as he or she enters the field of domestic life with technologies. Although I, along with others, would later want to revise the original scheme, the subdivision of the process of domestication into appropriation, objectification, incorporation and conversion was really helpful in structuring one's questions and observation plans. The inscription of technical artefacts into domestic values, space and time is indeed definitive to how these artefacts would be perceived and employed in daily practice. Placing, I discovered in the course of my own studies, is equivalent to appraising, and timing to taming. People choose locations for their artefacts strategically depending on the extent to which they would like to encourage or discourage their use by certain inhabitants of the household and/or for certain purposes. They work out elaborate schedules for access and rules of engagement. After a researcher has come across a sufficient number of examples of these embedding decisions, rules and timetables, or in a more technical lingo, use protocols, it becomes hard to see them as something separate from the technical device itself, from its own buttons, voltage, frequencies, and so on. Domestication, thus, produces an additional set of parameters that literally blends with the technical device and determines its nature, purpose and functionality. With this view of technology in mind, users *are* indisputably actors in the technological world.

Domesticating the internet, unleashing domestication

Another propitious discovery I made in the early 1990s was that of the internet. Heralded as a new communication miracle, the internet at that time was still the domain of engineers, programmers and geeks. Those of us who were not trained in the concepts of computer networking had to go through a hard labour of domestication before we could call the medium our own. It was clear to me from the vantage point my two discoveries gave me that the transformation of the internet into a mass medium beginning in the mid-1990s called for domestication-oriented research. What the medium would become, I believed, would be decided in the unglamorous shuffling around the connected computer at home as much as in the pains of the ingenious brains populating the research and development departments of the burgeoning internet industry.[3]

So, I set out to unveil some of the activities surrounding the internet at home and, following the original domestication appeal, to show how appropriation, objectification, incorporation and conversion occurred in the context of the moral economies of households coming in touch with a new communication technology.

Sure enough, the processes stirred by the arrival of the connected computer into households proved to be exciting. But observing them stirred a no less exciting commotion in the neat domestication model I was trying to work with. First of all, no stable moral order (moral economy) could be found reigning in the households that opened up for me to investigate. In fact, most of them seemed to be in a constant struggle to manage change that propped up from all kinds of corners: my protagonists or their children being diagnosed with disabilities, spouses leaving, jobs being lost or found, careers turning around or ending, or countries of residence being left or embraced. Household values and ways of life had to be reinvented and renegotiated almost on a daily basis and that was exactly where the new medium was best fitting in. It was proving to be an excellent change–management tool as well as an initiator of change itself. Notably, my respondents and their families were more interested in employing the medium in order to propel themselves into new realms of activity, knowledge and values than to preserve a static order of habits, identities and relationships.

Second, and most confusingly, the boundaries between the world beyond the doorstep and the 'private' life of the household were ceaselessly cracking and shifting. People were bringing in work from their offices and schools, friends and relatives were coming and staying, giving remote input and advice, demanding time and attention. The physical household was in actuality only a node in a much larger network of significant others, which, to a large extent, determined the nature and rhythms of its preoccupations (for similar observations see Haddon, Chapter 6). Objects such as computers and modems were flowing across the public–private divide and along the interpersonal networks reaching far beyond the doorstep so that it was difficult to say exactly which object belonged to the particular household.

In terms of ideas, too, the conversations between household members were often overpowered and sometimes almost drowned by voices and discourses coming from outside. In many cases the voices of friends and relatives would be as loud and clear as those of television anchors and other public authorities. A significant degree of ventriloqu-tion would occur between these two types of voices. For example, the technically knowledgeable grown-up son would speak in the voice of the IBM ad, or the ad for that matter would assume the intonation of the miserable child whose father had not yet woken up to the necessity of an internet connection for doing homework. Thus the conversations within the household were fraught with references to discourses unfolding in public and semi-public spaces. All in all, after the active presence of intermediate groups and personalities straddling the postulated provinces of public and private life was given due notice and consideration, the definition of the individual household as a self-regulating moral economy became less convincing and the dichotomy between public and private life significantly blurred.

Third, and importantly to me with a view to my desire to grasp the nature of user agency, it was hard to think about the activities, in which my respondents were drawing the internet as consumption. Silverstone and Haddon's (1996) model presents domestication as an instance of the private consumption of commodities produced by industry and distributed by the market. Some of that was certainly taking place when people bought devices and paid subscription fees, but the activities that followed the purchase in the case of the internet were quite different from those involving earlier communication technologies. Instead of slouching back (see Morley's (Chapter 2) albeit disapproving, discussion of this difference) and consuming entertainment and news, people were indeed leaning forward and engaging in all sorts of projects whose trajectory passed through the connected computer at home. Chatting with family and friends, corresponding with fellow hobbyist, contributing to the discussions of a virtual group, consulting sources for work- or study-related assignments, doing research on all sorts of topics, maintaining personal websites and other such active undertakings formed the backbone of internet use at home. Given the sheer number of words typed and sent away in cyberspace by users, the thought that went into them, the ingenuity with which web searches were performed and their unbreakable link with goals pursued in different spheres of offline activity, it was clear to me that the internet connection was much more a tool in a productive process than a consumer good. Even when users were navigating the Net in relation to a consumer product they wanted to buy, they referred to what they were doing as 'research' as they were finding information and carefully weighing it in preparation for their purchase decision.

Thus, while I understand the underlying logic of dichotomies such as public–private and production–consumption forming the central axes of the domestication model, none of them was easy to sustain in the face of the observation material generated by my studies of internet use at home. In my experience, the process of conversion, which the original domestication model represented only as a thin secondary stream of meanings generated by household members and socialized through interpersonal exchanges outside the home, in the case of the internet was abundant and engulfed internet use as a whole. Conversion of individual users' understanding of the internet was taking place when friends and other 'warm experts' (see Bakardjieva 2005) were coming into the home in order to help set up the internet connection and give novices their first lessons in what this medium could actually do for them. The whole stream of content and activity coming out of the home and adding to the substance of cyberspace could also be seen as conversion. Entities such as virtual communities, for example, are constituted exclusively out of what their individual members post in them while sitting in their homes. Personal and group websites, and at a later stage, blogs, are probably the best expression of conversion of private meanings into public items. And even the jingle announcing one of my buddies' appearance at my virtual door converts the meaning that the medium has for him or her into a loud shareable message.

What is left?

If my field observations managed to undermine to a measurable degree the idea of the household as a bounded unit with a stable moral economy on the one hand, and the idea of consumption as the overarching social process under which domestication is subsumed, on the other, what is left of the original domestication concept and model? I believe the most valuable tenet of domestication, to my mind the user agency, remains intact and in fact is let to 'run wild' after these confines are removed. Of course such a liberating gesture cannot be absolute and I have found it necessary to make two substitutions in order to frame the revised concept of domestication in a responsible manner. In place of the idea of the household, I have introduced the concept of 'home' as a phenomenological experience. Home in this definition is not necessarily a real-estate unit, but a feeling of safety, trust, freedom and control over one's own affairs. It is a home-base, 'a fixed point in space from which we proceed and to which we return in due course' (Heller 1984). Home is the terrain on which I believe I have agency to negotiate and change my conditions of existence. It is, as de Certeau *et al.* put it: a protected space at one's disposal where the pressure of the social body on the individual does not prevail, where the plurality of stimuli is filtered, or, in any case, ought to be (de Certeau *et al.* 1998, p. 146). Home is the container of interpersonal relationships that are supportive of my identity project, nurturing of my personal development and, overall, encouraging to the growth of my human capacities. Home is where I, as an agent, maintain my integrity and devise my strategies for action in places less hospitable, or in the face of oppressive forces.

De Certeau, in his discussion of strategy and tactics, recognizes the capacity of social subjects with will and power – 'a business, an army, a city, a scientific institution' to create 'an interior, a place that can be delimited as its own and serve as a base from which relations with an exteriority ... can be managed' (de Certeau 1984, pp. 35–6). For him, ordinary men and women are deprived of such a capacity. They are forced to operate on the terrain of the Other devising subversive tactics. Following bell hooks's (1990) account of the role of 'homeplace' in the survival and struggle of oppressed black people, however, I contend that home represents the 'interior' created by the powerless.

> Black women resisted by making homes where black people could strive to be subjects, not objects, where we could be affirmed to our minds and hearts despite poverty, hardship and deprivation, where we could restore to ourselves the dignity denied us on the outside in the public world.
>
> (hooks 1990, p. 42)

Seen from the vantage point of this, albeit extreme, historical experience, home is the locus where the agency of even the most marginalized is reaffirmed and regrouped. It is that place, 'which enables and promotes varied and changing perspectives, a place where one discovers new ways of seeing reality, frontiers of difference' (*ibid.*, p. 148).

With respect to communication technology, then, home is interesting in that it allows for varied perspectives on the meaning and practical usefulness of a device, and its pertaining content and functionality, to be discovered and enacted. It is the point where the powers of technologies meet with the meaningful activities and self-affirming projects of ordinary users. In the case of the internet, home can literally become a home-base, from which a whole range of actions can be projected onto the outside world. The materiality of the home, certainly, remains important as much as it provides the resources that user agency can mobilize and draw upon the technologies under consideration here being one prominent example.

This substitution of 'household' by 'home' avoids the shortcomings of a static notion and allows for the dynamic of a constantly changing relationship between exterior and interior to be adequately considered. The activities, in which individuals are involved, do not stop or drastically change at the doorstep of the home. On the contrary, they cut through both interior and exterior. The significant difference between the two realms, then, is not that between production and consumption, or between civic involvement and a self-centred 'private' life, but lies in the sense of agency and control in shaping the conditions and choosing the priorities of one's actions.

The second substitution in the domestication model that I find necessary to perform is that of 'consumption' with 'everyday life'. The notion of consumption keeps the analyst captive to the economic understanding of production, with respect to which consumption appears as the subordinate twin. Domestication is consumption when seen from the standpoint of designers, producers and marketers. From the standpoint of users, it is part of everyday life. Everyday life as an analytical category, on the other hand, is a more comprehensive notion than consumption. Phenomenological sociology construes the everyday lifeworld as 'the region of reality in which man [*sic*] can engage himself and which he can change while he operates in it by means of his animate organism' (Schutz and Luckmann 1973, p. 3). It is also the region, in which man experiences other people (his fellow men), with whom he constructs a shared world. These two qualities, taken together, make the everyday lifeworld 'man's fundamental and paramount reality' (*ibid.*). Importantly, the lifeworld is a reality which we modify through our acts and which, for its part, shapes our actions (*ibid.*, p. 6). In Schutz's classification scheme, the counterparts of the everyday lifeworld are other provinces of meaning such as 'the scientific-theoretical' attitude and the province of dreams and fantasies.

From a markedly different position, critical theorist Lefebvre (1991) concurs that, everyday life is 'profoundly related to all activities, and encompasses them with all their differences and conflicts; it is their meeting place, their bond and common ground. And it is in everyday life that the sum of total relations which make the human – and every human being – a whole takes its shape and form' (*ibid.*, p. 97). Opposed to everyday life in this taxonomy are all the specialized and structured activities characteristic of formal organizations and bureaucracies. Notably, Lefebvre does not place production outside of everyday life by confining it to economic organizations. He proposes an extended notion of production where the term signifies 'on the one hand spiritual production, that is to say creations (including social time and space) and on the other material production or the making of things; it also signifies the self-production of a "human being" in the process of historical self-development which involves the production of social relations' (Lefebvre 1971, pp. 30–1).

Everyday life is the sociological point of interaction and feedback between all different types of production. Therefore, even though users are typically excluded from the economic production of technical artefacts, their dealings with technologies constitute a different type of production relatively open to free and creative engagement. Instances of production in this broader sense, I believe, have been captured in numerous studies of home-based internet use. These are the moments in which the internet has been domesticated in the most imaginative and emancipatory sense. To insist on seeing them as nothing more than 'consumption' of a communication technology is detrimental to the analysis.

Furthermore, the home is an important, but not the only, site of everyday life. Communication technologies are being appropriated as means of pursuing significant individual and group projects in numerous settings outside the home that also deserve attention and consideration. In these other settings – such as clubs, classrooms, offices – users draw technologies into their activities and transform them in the process.

... To the mores of a culture

Finally, does domestication research provide any insights into the nature of the social world in which domestic practices are embedded and to which they give substance? A lot of domestication research, including my own, has been preoccupied with the mechanics of *how* home users appropriate or tame technologies. Not enough reflection has been done on what the results of domestication processes are and what they add up to when similarities and differences in patterns of use across households are examined. It would be unfair to accuse early domestication research of being only descriptive. This research did help us see the domestic environment in its rich dynamic and deep structure. However, the analysis it offered limited itself to the micro level and provided no direction as to how these micro patches of social fabric could be woven into a larger whole. What are the upshots of domestication and how do they matter to the distribution of freedom and control, power and knowledge throughout the culture of which they are a constitutive element? Lefebvre's notion of 'critique of everyday life' gives this lapse its proper name. Can domestication research furnish a *critique*, an examination of domestic practices and their larger social consequences from a normative perspective oriented toward change? Can it cast light on possibilities for technological democratization (see Feenberg 1999)?

My research on internet domestication made me experience that deficiency in an acute way. As I was conducting my interviews and observations in households, a heated public debate was raging around the social role and implications of the internet. The polar positions in that debate were bordering on the utopian, on the one hand, and the dystopian on the other. Would the internet prove to be a force of democratic empowerment in matters of economic well-being, personal control over one's life, collective action and political participation, or a source of further alienation, commercial manipulation and hegemonic oppression? And of course, from my perspective, it was logical to ask how the mundane decisions and routines users were devising around the connected computers in their homes could give us any hints about the resolution of that titanic controversy.

Reflecting on the nature of everyday life in the modern world, Lefebvre pointed out that it represents a diptych of misery and power. On the one hand, there is the monotonous existence under the conditions of alienated labour and pre-programmed leisure, but on the other, everyday life holds a tremendous creative potential as much as human spontaneity, sociability and desire form an inseparable part of it. The objective of the critique of everyday life that Lefebvre advocated was to separate what is living, new, positive – the worthwhile needs and fulfilments – from the negative elements: the alienations (Lefebvre 1991, p. 97). Lefebvre advises that the diverse activities making up everyday life should be examined in their historical concreteness and on that basis concrete distinctions between what is 'life-enhancing' (*ibid.*, p. 82) and what alienated should be made. He saw this distinction as a necessary prerequisite for the emergence of a critical and self-critical consciousness, which could transform everyday life.

So, there are two challenges to the original domestication approach to be discerned here. One is the need for a method through which the results of the domestication process unfolding between the walls of numerous homes across society could be summed up and analysed in their similarities and differences. The second is the search for a critical edge that would allow the description and classification to be extended into a critique and blueprint for change.

To address the first challenge I have borrowed and reworked the linguistic concept of *genre*. Similar to speaking a language, using a communication technology represents a formative strand of activities that have their specific motives, intents and recipients, and unfold in typical situations. Discovering how a new technology could fit appropriately into the typical situations constituting the everyday life of diverse groups of people is the main achievement of users. It is the creative and imaginative aspect of domestication. I still remember the day in the fall of 1992 when it dawned upon me that in my situation of an international student in Canada, I could use the internet to subscribe to a newsletter containing information about the dramatic political events unfolding in my native Bulgaria as well as to stay in touch with my family through a relative connected to Bitnet. Such revelations were present in most 'origin stories' that I heard from the users I interviewed in the late 1990s.[4] A long-term immigrant to Canada was discovering that with the help of the internet he could finally restore his bond with his native country painfully missed in his situation. A battered young wife was finding the virtuality of computer communication to be an antidote to her forced isolation from friends and social support outside her home. A woman with a work-related injury was drawing the internet into her efforts at retraining and redefining herself.

Gradually, it became obvious to me that these different everyday-life situations played a crucial role in how people perceived and employed the internet. To emphasize this intrinsic connection between the immediately experienced situation and specific ways of using a new technology and medium, I introduced in my analysis the concept of 'use genre' (see Bakardjieva 2005). 'Use genre' is not dramatically different from a 'way of using', but it suggests much less of a free choice or random origin. It is contingent upon the inbuilt functionalities present in a technology, but is not designer-configured (see Woolgar 1991), rather it emerges out of a concrete practical situation as experienced and defined by a user. It is not synonymous with 'style of use' as the elements of the situation, rather than a personal or social characteristic feature of the user, determine its nature.

Phenomenological as the concept of situation might sound in this specific application, it can also be given a materialistic read. Subjectively experienced and tackled practical situations are generated by a combination of material and ideological forces characterizing the larger social formation at a particular moment of historical time. Looking back at the examples enlisted above, it will be reasonable to suggest that the immigrant's situation of uprootedness and nostalgia has emerged out of global economic and political dynamics sending millions of people on the move away from their places and countries of birth and original identity formation. Throughout different historical periods, the driving forces, scope and speed of these movements have been quite different, of course, but in each of them, characteristic situations of personal experience have come to pass. The situation of the battered wife is quite typical of a male-dominated culture where putting up with an abusive marriage is enforced by economic dependencies and cultural attitudes. This situation is quite distinct, however, in a society where women's education and involvement in the workforce (where else would the wife learn how to use a computer and connect to the internet?), has introduced new elements and resources. The situation defined by a loss of employability and its associated insecurity has everything to do with a post-Fordist economic order and the dissipation of social welfare. Tellingly, in this situation the network itself has been construed as a life preserver to hang on to.

In the same way that speech genres tend to bring together typical situations, with their pertaining speech motives and goals and characteristic language forms (see Bakhtin 1986), use genres feature typical technical forms such as, in the case of the internet, email or browsers, newsgroups, webcams, or various combinations of these. It is not the technical form, however, that defines the genre, rather the specific fit between situation, action plan and technical functionality. I have tentatively attempted to name some of the use genres I have identified in the course of my empirical studies: sustaining globally spread family and social networks, holding together a fragmented national and cultural identity, participating in online support groups, talking back to institutions and organizations, doing research on everyday activities, and so on.

By virtue of their inseparable connection to typical situations that, for their part, are rooted in social relations of a higher order, use genres can be understood as the meeting point between micro-practices and macro structure. Technologies and media institutions represent components of the macro structure. They shape and at the same time are disturbed, challenged and changed by use genres stemming from the lifeworld. By inventing use genres, meaningful and effective in the context of their local situations, users influence the course of technological and media development. This is not always and necessarily an emancipatory process, however. Templates or scripts of use genres are widely propagated through advertising, political, futuristic and techno-cultural discourses. These are equivalent to authoritative statements that become engraved in the imagination of users and effectively highlight the 'proper', 'respectable', 'cool' uses of the technology in question. Not all genres are created equal and not all user-invented genres are intrinsically empowering. There are escapist genres, hate-mongering genres and terrorist genres, as our most recent collective experience with the internet has demonstrated. The point of notice amidst this breathtaking proliferation and diversification of use genres is their intricate connection with forms of life that constitute the human condition in the contemporary global world.

After the intermediate position of use genres between particular patterns of domestication at the micro-level and the macro relations in a society and culture is duly noticed and accounted for, it is time to consider how to address the second challenge to domestication: What is there to be done to turn the study of its genres into a transformative critique?

A critique of everyday life, Lefebvre insisted, endeavours to separate the 'living', emancipatory elements from the alienations. It is certainly not a straightforward task to apply this approach to internet domestication. How are we supposed to sift the 'life-enhancing' activities spun around the internet in everyday life from the old and new alienations that it introduces into it? The touchstone of this evaluation, I believe, is the capacity of the medium to empower users to produce freely and creatively: social time and space, social relations, material or virtual things, as well as their own self identities. By bringing to light such forms of disalienated production, domestication research could demonstrate the varied possibilities for the medium's progressive development discovered by users. Furthermore, it could suggest technical and political choices that need to be made in order to consolidate these fleeting individual discoveries into a stable democratic trajectory.

Fortunately, the tug-of-war between alienation and empowerment involved in internet use does not need to be mapped out from outside or above by an enlightened researcher who applies her elevated criteria to the daily practice of naive subjects. Domestication is the business of mindful, critically-thinking users who may not be employing terms such as empowerment and alienation when gauging their choices and activities, but certainly consider their options carefully with a view to what feels reasonable, right and rewarding to them. The involvement of women in internet domestication clearly illustrates this point.

Unlike competence and role division around other communication technologies, for example, the video recorder (see Gray 1992), women were taking an active part in the domestic appropriation of the internet. Being more often the household member who needed to masterfully juggle work duties outside the home with those inside it, women were often the champions of the internet connection at home. Somewhat 'naturally' the preoccupation of children with the new technology made it imperative for mothers to come to terms with it as well. Most of the time that meant learning how the technology worked and what was to be expected from the content available online. Thus, the entry of the internet into the household, as opposed to its career in the research lab, was marked by the massive participation of women, those managers and conductors of everyday life at home. Following the steps of these new actors in the internet world, it became clear to me that first of all they made it their mission to mitigate the alienating potential of a powerful technological system designed to accelerate unbridled consumption – from Pokémon stickers, technical gadgets and bandwidth to sexual scenes. Along with that, women were discovering the community-maintaining and -building possibilities and embraced the technology in a spontaneous and non-alienated manner. The internet was being used by them as a tool to enhance relationships with their children inside the home, as well as with numerous relatives, friends and complete strangers outside it.

The ways in which users were taking up electronic commerce represented another example of the daily struggle to resist the alienations while making the most of the empowering potential of the medium. As in a heaven of controlled consumption, the internet marshals an incessant parade of banner ads and pop-up windows across users' screens calling attention to different products and consumption possibilities. If the full 'script' of these techniques was to be realized, users would have clicked their way directly from banner ad to order form, to online purchase. Instead, users were blocking or ignoring the pop-ups with all the inventiveness they had in stock and tried to marshal the internet to help them make informed, reflexive and reasonable purchase decisions. The intrusiveness of the commercial appeal was making many users more vividly aware of the intended manipulation of desire. In response, they were firming up their position of resistance and loud protestation against the disrespect to human will and dignity they saw transpiring in this practice. Interestingly enough, some people saw their participation in the domestication-focused study I was carrying out as a way to take these feelings out of their living rooms into the public domain. Users, I fathomed, were hoping and trying to turn my study into a vehicle of conversion.

I have to admit that this turn of events found me, and my guiding domestication model, unprepared. Faced with such an expectation on the part of users participants, a researcher should stop to consider the political potential of his or her own project. After all, how is a domestication study different from a marketing one? What are its unique insights and how can they be applied to the ongoing enterprise of internet (or any medium, or technology) development? Who do they benefit in the final analysis? 'Universities suck knowledge out of people outside the university, put it through a special filtering procedure provided by social science, and confine it to specialists. ... It serves the organization of ruling people, rather than serving people' charges Smith (1992, p. 130). What kind of defence can domestication research put up against such harsh accusations?

As a domestication researcher I certainly did suck up a lot of my respondents' personal time. I enjoyed their patience and goodwill. I learned a lot from them about internet use and the medium's status in society. I led them to believe that I was taking their stories seriously and knew how to retell them so that they would be heard and noted in those powerful quarters that chart the course of future internet development. After all the data is collected and transcribed, analyses performed and shared within the community of my academic colleagues, papers written and published, a lingering question remains: Has my research brought about any benefit to users? Is domestication research indeed guilty of putting the knowledge extracted from users to the service of users' alienation? Or is it simply another 'ivory tower' exercise deprived of any social consequences?

I argue that in order to avoid these possible scenarios, in order to become part of a transformative programme, the results of the critique domestication research performs have to be returned to users themselves as a form of knowledge that enhances their critical and self-critical consciousness. Domestication research has the potential to transform the process of domestication from a silent achievement, an indistinct 'murmur of everyday practices' into a clearly audible legitimate public discourse. This discourse, then, could inform the choices and organize the activities of numerous individuals whose local sites of internet use may be geographically and temporarily dispersed and institutionally various (see Smith 1999, p. 158).

Thus I come to the conclusion that domestication research should be research *for users*, similar to the 'sociology for women' that Smith (1987) has called for. Starting from the immediately experienced local world users inhabit, perceiving this world from their standpoint and absorbing its situated knowledge, domestication research should go on to perform the critique of this everyday world by separating the alienations from the empowerments and unveiling the social forces at play behind the local scene. Importantly, by bringing the 'life-enhancing' achievements of users into view, domestication research has the capacity to contribute to a more inclusive and hence democratic technological development.

Post-scriptum

What is democratic about me chatting with my son over the internet? Is the triviality of extended family communication, now supported by voice and image over IP functionalities, worth the attention that the version of domestication research I have proposed in this chapter draws to it? The possibility of my well-organized working day at the computer being punctured by virtual visits by childhood friends is certainly of an ambiguous value. Down goes my productivity and up rises my feeling of comfort and security in my here and now. These two simultaneous effects would be judged differently from the perspective of different moral economies. Democratic development steps in when the rationality of a mode of use deviating from the hegemonic moral imperative is given a chance to be considered. This is, I believe, a matter of the unglamorous but consequential everyday politics that domestication research is well positioned to bring into view.

Notes

1. Courtesy of Howard Rheingold (1993): 'A slice of life in my virtual community'.
2. Cowan's (1987) contribution being a notable exception.
3. To the misfortune of million investors world-wide, venture capitalists had not heard about domestication and hence the disaster of the year 2000.
4. Curiously, they did not come through so distinctly in the narratives of the users interviewed only a couple of years later. This raises interesting questions about the different stages of domestication throughout the career of a new technology as in the course of time it blends into the background of taken-for-granted assumptions and recipes.

References

Bakardjieva, M. (2005) *Internet Society: The Internet in Everyday Life*. Sage: London and Thousand Oaks: New Delhi.

Bakhtin, M. (1986) *Speech Genres and Other Late Essays* (translated by V.W. McGee; edited by C. Emerson and M. Holquist). University of Texas Press: Austin.

Cowan, R. S. (1987) 'The consumption junction: A proposal for research strategies in the sociology of technology', in (eds) W. E. Bijker, T. P. Hughes and T. J. Pinch, *The Social Construction of Technological Systems: New Directions in the Sociology and History of Technology*. The MIT Press: Cambridge, Mass. and London, pp. 261–80.

de Certeau, M. (1984) *The Practice of Everyday Life*. University of California Press: Berkeley and Los Angeles.

de Certeau, M., Giard, L. and Mayol, P. (1998) *The Practice of Everyday Life*, vol. 2. University of Minnesota Press: Minneapolis, MN.

Feenberg, A. (1999) *Questioning Technology*. Routledge: London and New York.

Gray, A. (1992) *Video Playtime: The Gendering of a Leisure Technology*. Routledge: London and New York.

Havel, V. and Keane, J. (eds) (1985) *The Power of the Powerless: Citizens against the State in Central-eastern Europe*. M. E. Sharpe: Armonk, NY.

Heller, A. (1984) *Everyday Life*. Routledge & Kegan Paul: London and Boston.

hooks, b. (1990) *Yearning*. South End Press: Boston, MA.

Lefebvre, H. (1991) *Critique of Everyday Life. Vol. 1*: Introduction. Verso: London and New York.

Lefebvre, H. (1971) *Everyday Life in the Modern World*. Harper & Row: New York, San Francisco and London.

Pinch, T. and Bijker, W. E. (1987) 'The social construction of facts and artifacts', in (eds) W. Bijker, T. P. Huges and T. J. Pinch, *The Social Construction of Technological Systems*. The MIT Press: Cambridge, Mass., pp. 17–50.

Rheingold, H. (1993) 'A slice of life in my virtual community', in (ed.) L. Harasim, *Global Networks: Computers and International Communication*. The MIT Press: Cambridge, MA, pp. 57–80.

Schutz, A. and Luckmann, T. (1973) *The Structures of the Life-world*. North-Western University Press: Evanston.

Silverstone, R. and Haddon, L. (1996) 'Design and the domestication of information and communication technologies: Technical change and everyday life', in (eds) R. Mansell and R. Silverstone, *Communication by Design: The Politics of Information and Communication Technologies*. Oxford University Press: Oxford and New York, pp. 44–74.

Silverstone, R., Hirsch, E. and Morley, D. (1992) 'Information and communication technologies and the moral economy of the household', in (eds) R. Silverstone and E. Hirsch, *Consuming Technologies: Media and Information in Domestic Spaces*. Routledge: London, pp. 15–31.

Smith, D. (1999) *Writing the Social*. University of Toronto Press: Toronto, Buffalo and London.

Smith, D. (1992) 'Remaking a life, remaking sociology: reflections of a feminist', in (eds) W. K. Carroll, L. Christiansen-Ruffman, R. Currie and D. Harrison, *Fragile Truths: Twenty-five years of Sociology and Anthropology in Canada*. Carleton University Press: Ottawa, pp. 125–34.

Smith, D. (1987) *The Everyday World as Problematic: A Feminist Sociology*. University of Toronto Press: Toronto.

Woolgar, S. (1991) 'Configuring the user: The case of usability trials', in (ed.) J. Law, *The Sociology of Monsters: Essays on Power, Technology and Domination*. Routledge: London and New York, pp. 57–102.

5 The triple articulation of ICTs. Media as technological objects, symbolic environments and individual texts[1]

Maren Hartmann

> ... the increased interaction between genres and media forms strengthens the necessity for media research to emphasize textual aspects of investigation ... this interaction lends a strong argument in favour of textual analysis as part of ... reception theory and media ethnography.
>
> (Drotner 2000, p. 161)

> ... television's meanings, that is the meanings of both texts and technologies, have to be understood as emergent properties of contextualised audience practices.
>
> (Morley and Silverstone 1990, p. 32)

Ten years lie between David Morley and Roger Silverstone's call for research about contextualized audience practices, and Kirsten Drotner's proclamation that textual analyses should be more clearly incorporated into audience research. This tension between the *textual* and the *contextual* analysis is the core concern of this contribution. It is in many ways a return to something that had apparently been left behind: the text. The return will take place through a closer look at the concept of the so-called *double articulation* of media and information and communication technologies (ICTs). The double articulation was a core concept within the early formation of the domestication approach.[2] It stands for 'the ways in which information and communication technologies, uniquely, are the means (the media) whereby public and private meanings are mutually negotiated; as well as being the products themselves, through consumption, of such negotiations of meaning' (Silverstone *et al.* 1992, p. 28).

This particular aspect of (or emphasis within) the overall domestication approach is important for several reasons. First and foremost, the double articulation idea clearly assigns the domestication concept overall a role within media and communication studies. Second, the double articulation touches upon core concerns within long-standing debates about the 'most appropriate' analysis of media consumption. Third, the double articulation idea (especially through its existing limitations) emphasizes the fact that the original formulation of the domestication concept needs to be re-thought in the light of the more recent emergence of diverse forms of digital and mobile media.

The argument in this chapter is for a return to, and reapplication of, the original double articulation concept and a possible extension to a triple articulation. The claim is that this notion was relatively well developed on the theoretical level within the early domestication texts, but was then lost in the 'application' of the domestication concept in actual research.[3] At the point of application the double articulation becomes a methodological question, which then again has implications for the wider theoretical framework of qualitative audience and user research.

I begin with this wider framework to embed the double articulation therein. The following step revisits the early domestication concept before turning – albeit briefly – to its application within empirical research on the one hand and the methodological implications on the other. The final part of this chapter is a deliberation about the double – and a possible triple – articulation concept and its relevance for audience and user research today.

Text–context relationship

> [It] is necessary that we somehow move away from the binary opposition which still haunts cultural studies, that is, the distinction between text and lived experience, between media and reality, between culture and society. What is now required is ... an ethnographic approach ... which brings a renewed rigor to this kind of work by integrating into it a keen sense of history and contingency.
>
> (McRobbie 1992, p. 730)

The binary opposition that haunts this text is not dissimilar: it is the assumed opposition between text and context and the attempt to combine the two. This is an opposition that has haunted especially television research for some time and that has – as yet – not been resolved satisfactorily. For a long time the distinction between reception research's responsibility for the texts (the messages) and audience research's responsibility for the context (cf. Morley 1992, p. 46) was all too easily made. Eventually, however, efforts were initiated to overcome this division. The domestication concept can be clearly located within these efforts. Its theoretical answer to the challenge was the double articulation, wherewith it touches on core concerns within the epistemology of media and communication research.

One – more recent – example of the debate can be found in Pertti Alasuutari's introduction to *Rethinking the Media Audience* (1999), in which he proclaimed that existing research should be rethought. Alasuutari divided media audience research (or rather: 'reception studies and audience ethnography') into three 'generations'. His division begins with Stuart Hall's 'Encoding/Decoding' article (and thus underlines a clear cultural studies paradigm). In contrast to other approaches until that point, Alasuutari claims, Hall favoured the semiotic approach to messages over the technical approach, whereby a particular concentration on the text was initiated. Alasuutari's second generation label is given to audience ethnography, which is signified by an interest in the social uses of television. The shift here is from text to context. Alasuutari labels the third generation – a still emerging one – a constructionist view (Alasuutari 1999, p. 6). In this third generation, media culture as a whole is the focus, increasing reflection is asked for and the sociology of the audience is more important than the psychology. The approach taken is a discursive one, but – and this is the main difference to my interpretation of the double articulation – 'a "reception" study devised along these lines does not necessarily analyse the programme or genre "itself" at all' (*ibid.*, p. 16). While the third generation is broader than the second, it does not necessarily include the first. This shift from one extreme (individual media text) to the other (overall media culture discourse) is the core problem in many attempts at rethinking audiences and uses.

In the same book, David Morley responds to Alasuutari with a reference to his own earlier work (among other things). There Morley argued for 'a model of media consumption capable of dealing simultaneously with the transmission of programmes/contents/ideologies (the vertical dimension of power) and with their inscription in the everyday practices through which media content is incorporated into daily life (the horizontal dimension of ritual and participation)' (Morley 1999, p. 197). He suggests that this combination should not be lost nowadays and even proclaims that content analyses of programmes might need to be reconsidered as appropriate parts of reception studies and audience ethnographies (*ibid.*, pp. 198–9). This is not, it should clearly be noted, a return to an analysis of individual, private readings of media texts. Instead, social meanings are the core foci. Morley remains somewhat ambivalent concerning the individual programme, but he points in the same direction as the double articulation (since he is one of the original authors of this notion, this does not necessarily come as a surprise). We now turn to the domestication and double articulation concepts themselves.

The domestication concept[4]

The early domestication version was formulated as a critique of existing studies on television audiences, which were seen to be problematic in several ways. They were supposedly not accounting for the complexity of culture and the social (cf. Silverstone *et al.* 1991, pp. 205–6). Most audience studies had limited themselves to television rather than taking several information and communication technologies into consideration. If one wanted to understand the importance of media within the conduct of everyday lives of people, however, a broadening was crucial (and still is).[5] The importance of this expansion was only beginning to dawn at the moment of the early formulation of the domestication concept, but it has increasingly been referred to since then. On top of that, the domestication authors promoted an engagement with the household as the site of study. Their ethnographic approach promised an in-depth engagement with this environment that so much represented everyday life. And most of the existing television studies rarely provided enough information about the *dynamics surrounding* media use (with some notable exceptions). Domestication (and related approaches) argued against so-called *Screen*-theory, which had been very important in UK media studies in the preceding years, and refuted the 'abstract text-subject relationship' (Neale in Morley 1992, p. 60), which had led to a limited focus on media content, that is, on cultural texts which inscribed 'subject positions' (cf. Moores 1993, p. 6).

The aim in the domestication concept was not to let go of the focus on media content (albeit not in the psychoanalytical focus of *Screen*-theory) or on the text–subject relationship (analysed, however, in more concrete ways, potentially based on the concept of reading), but to create a different framework, which would add new aspects. These new foci provide reasons for calling domestication a *reception and consumption theory* of the appropriation of technology within the household. Consumption and technology studies as well as a concentration on constructivist approaches were emerging academic interests at the time (cf. Moores 1993; Morley 1992). Similarly, feminist studies had also begun to study media use and the home environment (e.g. Gray 1992; Ang and Hermes 1991; Radway 1984).[6] All this provided the framework for the domestication concept and the double articulation idea therein, in which both the material and the symbolic values present in media use are researched. The most general framework was thus the contextualized processes of the integration of technologies into everyday life. This context is both complex and contingent – and this context was also still meant to include content. All this was theoretically brought together in the concept of the moral economy, another framework for the double articulation idea.

Moral economy

Every household is part of the economic system and as such it produces, consumes and exchanges. It is a transactional system and represents an economic, social and cultural unit. Although this unit is in many ways a process, it also needs to be upheld and temporarily (and repeatedly) fixed. Thus another economy emerges next to the well-known material one: a moral kind, closely linked to processes of consumption and production. This is the so-called moral economy, a core concept within domestication. Here, the household's cognition, evaluations and aesthetics – based on the history, biographies and overall politics of the household – come into play, providing the backdrop for the processes of consumption and production. The moral economy is partly conveyed through the stories that are told and invented within households. Its most prominent form of expression is the household's everyday practices. This economy helps in the creation and sustenance of what Anthony Giddens defined as 'ontological security', the impossible and necessary stability in everyday life, the practical consciousness that keeps out the chaos (Giddens 1991, p. 36). This gives the household a position in time and space and a belief in the world 'as it appears to be' (Silverstone *et al.* 1992, p. 19).[7]

The introduction of any technology into the household challenges the ontological security. The challenge can also be a reinforcement of existing values and/or it can go more or less unnoticed. In principle, however, the (media) technology is a threat to the existing. That is not to say that the technology alone has the power to change and challenge, rather, its adoption into the household is a reciprocal, dialectic process of potential change. In this process, the second articulation (that is, the symbolic environment) moves to the forefront of concerns. The technology itself – as well as, one could claim, its content – comes with certain affordances. These are pre-given limitations or directions – the technology suggests certain ways of how it should be used, what it is for, and so on. The media texts, on the other hand, come with a structurally limited polysemy, as discussed below. These affordances can always be ignored, but mostly they are at least partly recognized, partly taken on. They are part of the overall construction and management of symbolic boundaries of the household which signify the moral economy. The double articulation of technologies is a double challenge for this economy.

Double articulation

The double articulation concept

The concept of the double articulation is a core concept within semiotics.[8] Silverstone *et al.* (1991) state that the origin of the double articulation notion lay in the analysis of natural language use and in the work of André Martinet, a linguistic functionalist (cf. Silverstone and Haddon 1996). Martinet showed that both the morphological (semantic) and phonetic (distinctive) aspects of language (and especially their interconnection) are important for meaning creation (cf. Nöth 2000, pp. 333–4; Silverstone 1994, pp. 122–3). Without these two interdependent structural levels, we could not convey complex meanings with the pre-given resources (the two levels help to structure the principally unlimited possibilities). When Martinet speaks of articulation, he thus actually refers to structure. The first level of this structure (the first articulation) refers to linguistic signs that convey meaning (Martinet's 'moneme'), while the second level are the 'phoneme' (the sounds) that help to distinguish the different monemes. Together, they form the specificity of different words, that is, they make up our language. The most important aspect to consider here is the interdependence of the two levels.

Silverstone and his colleagues actually apply Martinet's double articulation in unexpected (some claim, impossible) ways.[9] They state that meaning creation in relation to media technologies similarly takes place on (at least) two interdependent levels. The technical dimensions are communicating the 'meaning of the commodity as object' (Silverstone and Haddon 1996, p. 62), while 'the texts and communications of the technologies' (*ibid.*) generate the messages. The double articulation hence emphasizes that media are articulated as specific technologies: they are both objects and conveyer of messages. This makes these media the particular and unusual objects of consumption, the particular technologies that they are, which therefore need to be analysed accordingly. Their description as 'media technologies' already hints at the combination of these two aspects. Silverstone and Haddon stress that the technologies need to be articulated first before the messages can be articulated (*ibid.*). The medium *is* not, but it *does become* the message (Silverstone 1994, pp. 82–3) – or, as I would claim, it becomes part of a set of different messages. Put together, the practices and discourses of the production, marketing and use of these technologies constitute the first meanings (Silverstone and Haddon 1996, p. 62).

> ... these technologies are not just objects: they are media. ... information and communication technologies are also objects ... [and] technologies. But [they] ... have a functional significance, as media; they provide, actively, interactively or passively, links between households, and individual members of households, with the world beyond their front door ... in complex and often contradictory ways. Information and communication technologies are ... doubly articulated into public and private cultures.
>
> (Silverstone *et al.* 1992, p. 15)

The latter is a reference to a second important interpretation of the double articulation in the domestication context: media are also doubly articulated as private and public (and as the interrelationship between these two). This argument builds on the previous in the sense that both the technological object and the media messages are imbued with public meanings that are then embedded within the private realm of the household. These two are caught in a process of mutual influence and neither has a fixed boundary.

The history of the concept

Similar to the domestication concept as a whole, the double articulation is set against particular traditions within the above-mentioned study of (television) audiences.[10] The double articulation argues against what David Morley has called the 'textualization' of cultural (and also media) studies (Morley 1992, p. 5; see also Hall 1992, p. 286). Instead Morley promotes an analysis of 'processes of culture and communication within their social and material settings' (1992, p. 5). Despite using a semiotic concept to do so, the double articulation provides an *inclusive* move from the *semiology* to the *sociology* of media use: 'The research questions ... were driven ... by a compulsive fascination with the 'actual practices' of media and information technology use, by a conceptual imperative to provide a framework for understanding reception ... and consumption' (Silverstone *et al.* 1991, p. 219).

This interrelationship between object and messages underlines the complexity of the processes of meaning-making involved in media consumption. Again, one can detect the threefold move from (a) a primary concern with ideology, to (b) positions that regarded audiences as active and content as polysemic, to (c) the actual context of media use. The attempt within the double articulation concept is indeed to research reception and consumption of media in terms of their complexity and multidimensionality. The content and potential ideology – or limited polysemy – form one part of this process:

> ... our understanding of the double articulation of information and communication technologies in public and domestic culture are those that media scholars will recognize. They concern the ideological significance of mass communications, the power of texts, and their articulation and negotiation of the boundaries between public and private worlds: through individual programmes, genres and the schedules of broadcasting.
> (Silverstone *et al.* 1991, p. 219)

The second articulation

While the first articulation of media technologies is easy to pin down – the television set, the radio, the computer as material objects and in their role as consumer objects – the second articulation is less easily named. It includes, as shown above, individual programmes, genres, broadcasting schedules. Mentioned elsewhere are narratives, rhetorics and software. Another form can be to ask 'how the seating pattern is arranged, who watches what with whom, who chooses programmes, and what kinds of talk are defined as appropriate during viewing' (Morley and Silverstone 1991, p. 152), in other words, the use of media in everyday life. The social structures and patterns around viewing are core concerns.

All these aspects underline that media are content-based technologies. From the specific (for example, individual programme) to the more general (for example, the genre) to the most general (for example, the programme flow and surrounding talk): all these aspects matter. The emphasis of the analyses within the domestication framework, however, lay primarily on the most general level. We shall return to this point in the context of the discussion on the double articulation of digital media.

Let us first reconsider the specificity of the second articulation not through the media-specific aspects, but through its consequences. Media technologies connect the private worlds of the users with the public worlds beyond their front door. They enable the participation in the national community. They draw people into a world of public and shared meanings, while they also provide options for the meaning-formation in private worlds. Building on this meaning-formation, the second articulation of media 'provides the basis for an "education", a competence, in all aspects of contemporary culture' (Silverstone 1994, p. 123). Thus media technologies are crucial to our 'being-in-the-world', both as consumers and citizens, as individuals, family-members and more: 'Their difference [of media to other technologies] centres on what we would like to call their articulations and their differential capacity within those articulations, to change culture and society; to engage the user as audience or consumer' (Morley and Silverstone 1990, p. 36).

The possibility for change, however, is limited. It has already become clear that the use of the media is dialectical and problematic. The interpretive power concerning the first articulation is limited through the affordance of technologies, in the second articulation through textual 'affordances of interpretation'. The emphasis in the double articulation concept is on an interpretive power of the media user over the agenda, not over the text (Morley and Silverstone 1990, p. 34). The text itself, however, brings its own limitations – this is exactly why its analysis remains crucial.

> The analysis of the text or message remains, of course, a fundamental necessity, for the polysemy of the message is not without its own structure. ... While the message is not an object with one real meaning, there are within it signifying mechanisms which promote certain meanings ... these are the directive closures encoded in the message.
>
> (Morley 1992, p. 21)

The relationship between text and 'reader' is reworked by Morley and Silverstone (1990, pp. 46–7) to state that: (a) the television-meanings are generated in daily-life activities (beyond the viewing), (b) there is a need to recognize differences between the different media, (c) there are different modalities of engagement, and (d) the construction of meanings is a dialectical process of changing variables (including all of the above). Deconstructing the directive enclosures and engaging with both the modalities and the meaning-construction is a complex process. Only if this is pursued, can the double articulation be made visible. In the research that built on these theorizations, this is not always the case.

Double articulation, empirical research and methods

'What do you include in context and where does it stop?' asked John Corner in 1991 (Corner 1991, p. 23). Let us then ask today, paraphrasing Corner, 'What do you include in "content" and where does it stop?'

There is no easy answer to either of these questions. The question that keeps reappearing and that has not yet been solved is how to adequately research the complexity of the combination of media content and media context to paint a picture of the overall whole.

The application of double articulation

In the 1990s, Roger Silverstone and Leslie Haddon conducted a range of studies that can be described as 'applications' of the domestication concept. Much of this was a follow-up study of the original HICT (The Household Uses of Information and Communication Technologies) study, which had been based at Brunel University and where the original concept had been developed (see Silverstone 1994). The HICT study was based on empirical research, but Silverstone and Haddon's follow-up was more extensive. This follow-up study was designed to last three years. It focused on a different social group each year. These included teleworking households, lone parents and the young elderly (60 to 75 years of age). Each was reported on separately, but the overall theoretical and methodological framework remained more or less the same (Haddon and Silverstone 1996, 1995, 1992; Haddon 1994, and Chapter 6 in this volume). The studies provided very interesting and fruitful accounts of the complexities (and patterns) of media technology adoption into the everyday lives of a set of diverse social groups. The authors offered this account thoughtfully, thoroughly and theoretically embedded.

Nonetheless, the implementation of the domestication concept showed the following problem: the combination of the study of media as both technologies and media and the high stakes involved in this were not necessarily fulfilled. Part of the critique then is not the assumption *that*, but the question *whether* it can actually be done differently.

In Silverstone and Haddon's work on teleworking households, for example, references to the particularities of the media that are being engaged with, are primarily embedded in general descriptions of the everyday use of media technologies within the chosen households and certain characteristics of their patterns of use (Haddon 1994; Haddon and Silverstone 1992). Conflicts about time, place and access are shown and the general difficulty of how to arrange media into routines of work and home are contextualized. Content-wise, broadcasting schedules, shared media times (with family members primarily) and the role of the media to fill in the lack of the social, are mentioned. In this particular case, Haddon explicitly refers to the comparatively small focus on traditional media within the teleworking case study, since the concentration here was on work and the relationship between home and work (Haddon 1994, p. 9). The particular 'old media' meaning-making could, therefore, only partly be explored and it does not become clear how the researched general media characteristics relate to the intricate relationship between public and private worlds of meaning.

The second study, about lone parents, again concentrated on the routines and patterns of media use within a social framework (Haddon and Silverstone 1995). Here too, similar issues about costs, about the use of media technologies to structure (and fill) time, the issue of the phone as a connection to the outside world and such patterns and problems are mentioned. Media content, such as television programmes, is only marginally part of the story (such as in the case of discussions with the children that emerge from the display of family lives on TV that differ substantially from their own reality). How then are we supposed to understand the changes that take place on the content level as well as on the technological and wider social level? How are we supposed to understand the preference of certain media over others if we do only superficially differentiate between the two?

Part of the answer lies in the third case study of the same cycle, which analysed the case of the young elderly (Haddon and Silverstone 1996). This is embedded in the complete final report on the overall study and is thus more complete than the other two (which were primarily referred to in conference presentations). First of all, in the young elderly study a distinction is made between the telephone and the computer on the one hand and radio and television on the other. They are reported on in different sections and have seemingly provoked different kinds of responses from the interviewees. The discussion about the first two technologies (phone and computer) remains primarily on the level of rituals, of personal histories (and thus relates some stories), of issues such as cost, distribution of use, expertise. 'Content' is not discussed in relation to the computer apart from a brief mention of computer games (early versions had been used by some of the interviewees), but this can be explained through both the age of the cohort and the time of the interview (mid-1990s). Content in terms of the phone is discussed in slightly more detail (questions such as 'who do you phone', 'how often', 'how long', 'what do you talk about', etc. form an important part). Most of this, however, is done retrospectively, as overall biographical statements about media behaviours over time.[11]

Radio and television use by the young elderly is again described in terms of its history, its main characteristics, the routines and preferences. The latter, however, clearly include a content dimension. The interview quotes refer to the programmes that have been (or are) listened to or watched, the genres, the changes in content over the years. Generally, both radio and television seem to provide a framework that is difficult to think about without these references. The analysis of engagements with the current day-to-day dealings with certain content, questions about the relationship to the world beyond the front door and similar in-depth analyses of the second articulation are lacking to some degree. Overall, however, the engagement with both articulations is provided (sometimes so much that the interview quotes dominate the text).

Here then is an example of a kind of 'implementation' of the original double articulation concept. It is striking that the second articulation is primarily present in the analysis of the broadcast media, while the interpersonal medium and the multiple medium (the computer) are primarily analysed on the level of the object and the routines. This is partly explained, as outlined, through the age of the cohort in question, but it underlines, yet again, that the transfer of the double articulation idea is not straightforward when it comes to interpersonal and networked media. Most other limitations of the analysis, I want to claim, are due to the (pragmatic) choices of research methods.

Methods

The research methods within the domestication approach are potentially both part of the problem and the solution. In most of the domestication research projects, so-called ethnographic approaches have been used. They consisted of an intense engagement with the subjects in question. In the HICT study, this was initially done through participant observation within the households in question, followed by interviews. The one-week observation was introduced by a one-week time-use diary that household members were asked to fill in throughout the week before the observation. This was completed through talks about photos, drawings of the household, social network plans, lists of the technologies within the household, and so on (Silverstone *et al.* 1991, p. 210).

In the second part of the HICT project, the participant observation was abandoned for more traditional interviews. These comprised several interviews spread out over a number of months (and often several hours long, sometimes followed by invitations to stay on for a little while after the interview – this could then be used for further observations). Similar additional material as in the first part of the study was used to initiate and feed into the interviews. The shift away from a more traditional ethnographic approach was justified both pragmatically (the engagement of a new – male – researcher seemed to suggest the need to remove the participant observation and the first research outcomes had been unsatisfactory), and also content-wise. The latter was expressed through the claim that justifications for, explanations of and fantasies about media use would not be satisfactorily researched in participant observation (*ibid.*, p. 210). The follow-up studies, conducted primarily by Leslie

Haddon (Haddon 1994; Haddon and Silverstone 1996, 1995), followed, more or less, the same path as the second part of the original project (Silverstone *et al.* 1992, 1991). The number of interviews with each participant, however, was drastically reduced (to two, in the case of the young elderly study). The claim for an ethnographic engagement – based primarily on a continuous or at least repeated engagement with the subjects – is thus difficult to uphold.[12]

The second articulation is in many instances a more spontaneous and immediate engagement than the overall incorporation of the media technologies into the household and thus gets a different rapport by the subjects interviewed. Self-reporting alone is, however, problematic. And it filters out engagements with content that have not been turned from the immediate to the systematic (and conscious). The content itself gets marginalized, too, analysed only as flow or pattern and through some memorable exceptions or some generalizable uses (for example, genres). Silverstone and his colleagues suggest that the regulation within households about who uses what (watches what, and who listens to and plays with what) and when and sometimes even how, is the most important part of the engagement with the second articulation. But it does not suffice to cover the range of possible second articulations.

Overall, the move from more traditional ethnographic methods, albeit based on clear reasons, has potentially pushed the possibility of researching the double articulation into the background. To find the double articulation one would need an immersion into content use. One such example, albeit for newer media, has been provided by Maria Bakardjieva and Richard Smith (2001), who were able to reconstruct the interviewees' 'computer space' through an analysis of the folders on their computer, the history and bookmarks of their internet connection, their email boxes, etc. The subjects would take the researcher through these contents and explain their significance and use. This, at least, is one step towards the inclusion of 'content'. Actual observations of internet use, coupled with 'thinking aloud' procedures can also show certain engagements with content (this is, obviously, particularly interesting with new users – cf. Rommes 2002). Overall, several methods (and potentially existing material) can be combined. This ranges from an analysis of SMS messages to content analyses of specific programmes (discussed with the interviewees) to observations of actual media uses (at home and elsewhere). Researching all these aspects for a single group of subjects is definitely a challenge, maybe outright impossible. But the challenge remains. The original focus of it all – the contextual use of media technologies – should not be pushed aside. Since the process is all about the appropriation and re-embedding of technologies (and content) in the local context (see Lie and Sørensen 1996), the content itself cannot be researched separately. It always needs to be analysed in relation to its use and appropriation.

This is thus also a question of research politics, of current funding tendencies and other such 'trivial' matters. It is not surprising that the original domestication research project was conducted by a team, over a longer period of time and with considerable funding behind it.[13] To single-handedly attempt to include all these aspects (and all these technologies in all these situations by all these people) is problematic at least.

This problem was also the origin of this chapter. The reasons lie in my own past research, particularly a project on young Belgian adults and their use and perception of new media (Hartmann 2005, 2004). Domestication did not go far enough to cover at least one apparent problem: especially due to the mobile nature of the interviewees' lives and their individualized uses of diverse bits of content, actual tracing of their diverse engagements with the media were difficult. Patterns were reported, but individual engagements with content were left aside. It was not possible to see the sites they accessed, for example, to clearly understand what particular communicative or other need was fulfilled at that stage, to contrast this with other media uses, etc. Here, participant observations, together with interviews, observations and explanations of use in practice, social network analyses and more, would provide a more detailed picture. This much detail, I claim, is necessary for the engagement with the second articulation. The domestication concept remains crucial despite these flaws, exactly because it offers a starting point which takes media technologies in their different articulations seriously.

Double articulation today

The VCR, the computer and the telephone, each in their different ways provide (or fails to provide) a route for the consumption and articulation of publicly generated messages and exchanges that feed back into the household, and, of course, for privately generated messages and exchanges to be circulated in return. (Silverstone *et al.* 1992, p. 21):

> ... what of cases, such as online communication, where users do not bring technology in from the outside but act through it on the public world? (Feenberg 1999, p. 107)

The difficulty in researching the complexity and contingency of media use research in everyday life is clearly related to the very different characteristics, and growing diversity, of ICTs. Television is more easily identifiable and thus analysable in terms of the 'messages' it offers. How, however, should we interpret the 'messages' of mobile phone conversations? They exist (and are to some degree analysable), but they are mostly interpersonal forms of communication, their 'content' is not meant to be public in the same sense as that of television.[14] This difference does not, however, relieve us from recognizing the importance of the content in relation to the context in relation to the object. Similar questions and difficulties arise in terms of the internet, which offers an array of diverse applications, services, communication and information channels, and so on. What gets lost here (among other things) is the felt simultaneity of social experience that broadcasting – and to some extent also print media – still offered. This question of shared common time (Morley and Silverstone 1990, pp. 40–4) is not pre-given any more to the same extent. Thus the notion of publicness changes. So-called virtual communities might offer alternative spaces of communal identification – potentially with stronger social ties than the still abstract social simultaneity of broadcasting – but this needs an active commitment on the user side: a conscious effort to take part. All this is part of the research process.

One interesting approach to the complexity has come from Leslie Haddon (2001). In a paper on domestication and mobile telephony he suggests that a lot of what could be labelled 'domestication theory' can actually be found in diverse existing research projects – only it is not always called domestication. Haddon starts from the premise that indeed mobile technologies and social networks beyond the home pose a challenge to the domestication concept as it has been thought thus far. But the research he then finds on these issues seems to suggest to him that the continuation of this research tradition is already in place. Similarly, I would like to suggest that a first answer to the plea for a return to the double articulation – as well as an attempt to understand an increasing array of media technologies – could best be covered by bringing together existing research on the diverse aspects of use – both in terms of technologies and texts. As a matter of illustration, I refer briefly to two examples (both of which actually use the domestication concept).

The first comes from Rich Ling and Kristin Thrane (2001). In their research on electronic media in Norwegian homes, they begin from the premise that a more dynamic approach than the existing domestication concept is needed to analyse media research in the home today (Ling and Thrane 2001, p. 6). They thus extend what they perceive as too linear a model and add 'physical zones' (for the display of technology), 'personal spheres' (in which individual use management, often in temporal matters, comes into play) and 'rules' (which guide the overall use and express family 'ideologies' around ICTs) to the existing model. In the analysis of their interview material, Ling and Thrane do not go much beyond the kind of descriptions and analyses that other domestication approaches have also provided, that is, there is no detailed analysis of the second articulation. However, through defining the zones, spheres and rules, they add new dimensions on how to organize research material. Different degrees or versions of the second articulation might, for example, become relevant in the personal spheres in contrast to the shared physical zones (and exactly where they do not overlap). Ling and Thrane also point to the combination of individualization and mobility (*ibid.*, p. 35) that makes a more differentiated analysis scheme necessary.

A greater challenge to the existing concept – although still in reference to it – can be found in a study of internet use in cybercafes by Sarah Lee (1999). She claims that there is no double articulation, since technologies in cybercafes are not seen as a possession, as 'my' objects (*ibid.*, p. 341). What she found instead was the consumption of a communicative experience and of standardized, non-tangible goods (timed access to the net). She thus finds only the second articulation. This picture might change if the customers are regular customers. Here, certain adoption processes could possibly take place (someone might choose the same computer every time, for diverse reasons). Things get more complicated also when we think of, for example, email folders that can be accessed from any computer (depending on the programme one uses). Their arrangement – although it disappears when one leaves the computer – can still suggest a certain 'material' ownership of the technology, as non-tangible as it might appear. Lee does not provide an analysis of what this possible lack of a strong first articulation of the technology could mean for the engagement of the second level. Does it make a difference? Probably so. But that difference in an increasingly media-saturated world, might need to be explored more fully. The question that remains is whether the processes that are analysed here are then still 'domestication' processes.

The above two examples are simply meant to indicate that the expansion to other, existing studies can indeed be fruitful for the reinvigoration of the domestication concept. If nothing else, it seems to underline the problems in researching digital media and their adoption into everyday lives. I want to close, however, with a suggestion that builds on the idea that the domestication concept actually provides a useful concept for analysis today – especially if we take the double articulation seriously.

Triple articulation?

I would like to argue not only for a return to the double articulation, but for an extension to a *triple articulation*. This has already been suggested (and dismissed) in a footnote to one of the crucial domestication texts:

> As Rohan Samarajiva has helpfully pointed out it is possible to distinguish between three, rather than two, dimensions of message and articulation: that grounded in the object, that in the symbolic environment to which the technology gives access, and that of specific 'programme' messages. This is correct. Our argument in the body of the chapter, however, is based on the privileging of the first two. The last – the single text/message – is clearly present and, on occasion, of importance but, as many analysts have noted, it is itself dependent on the generic symbolic environment and insignificant in terms of influence when compared with the overall flow of media messages.
>
> (Silverstone and Haddon 1996, p. 74)

The flow of the television message has indeed been seen as crucial (see for example, Williams 1974; Jensen 1996) and might be the predominant mode of engagement with the medium. In a similar vein, the ritualistic nature of media use has been analysed (for example, Couldry 2003). This goes hand in hand with the use of broadcast media as background media and the general idea that media use as such provides us with ontological security. Similar arguments have been made for mobile telephony and its importance for phatic communication to reassure us (and those around us) of our existence (Tomlinson reference, Chapter 2). My point is not to argue against the importance of these instances of communication. Even less do I want to argue against 'the transformation of the fundamental modes of media presence in our lives' (Gitlin, in Chapter 2). Media are everywhere and it is partly this mediatization phenomenon as such rather than individual media messages that provides the crucial transformations of current social life (as gradual and contingent as they might be) (cf. Krotz 2001).

Notwithstanding my support for these kinds of arguments, I claim that a research approach based on the double articulation concept is equally fruitful and necessary and that all three dimensions need to be taken into consideration: not only the ritual, the overall idea of participation, but also the individual communicative instance, the individual programme, the individual website, the text message, etc. This need stems from the shifts that have taken place in the media landscape since the formulation of the original concept. Especially in relation to changing practices and content, it is interesting to note continuities in habits of engagement (or not), it is important not to lose the impact of 'the media' on our everyday lives beyond and within the shaping processes of meaning-making. To keep sight of that is both to celebrate potential new possibilities as well as to warn about remaining and powerful structures. It is definitely *not* a return to the idea of an independent media message.

Instead, it is a plea to return to the high aims of the original domestication approach and to take these authors by their word. It is exactly the intricate connection between these different aspects of media consumption, reception and use that has thus far only partly been researched. The originators of the concept have provided some good examples. It is now up to us to provide more and especially new ones. It is in many ways a methodological challenge (and partly a research political one). In terms of the methodology, a clear return to ethnography seems necessary.[15] Or at least the repeated engagement with the subjects in question is necessary – simple interviews do not suffice. Underlying all this is still the question of how we are to understand media use in context. In order to do so, we need to become a part of the context – and we need to return to the content.

Notes

1. Different parts and versions of this chapter were presented at the final EMTEL 2 conference in London in May 2003, the IAMCR conference in Porto Alegre in July 2004 and the domestication workshop at the VR Media Lab in Aalborg in November 2004 (as well as at some smaller events in between). I am very grateful for the valuable feedback provided at all these events. In particular, I would like to thank Thomas Berker, Lars Holmgaard Christensen and Jo Helle-Valle for their inspiring comments.
2. It is also still the most clear-cut division between this and other approaches to domestication (compare Sørensen *et al.* 2000; Sørensen 1994, and Chapter 3 in this volume).
3. Others (such as Helle-Valle and Slettemeås 2004) actually suggest that one of the problems with the domestication concept is its lack of theoretical rigour. Their main problem, however, is with the actual domestication concept.
4. This chapter deals primarily with the British – and especially the late 1980s, early 1990s – version of domestication. Other versions and implementations do not provide any sufficient answer to the double articulation problem. Important for the formulation of the early

concept was the funding that the HICT project at Brunel University received (as part of the British ESRC's PICT programme). Later on, European-funded research networks (such as COST248 – which led to COST269 – COST A4, EMTEL, etc.) were also crucial for the spread of these ideas.

5. Although the original assumptions that formed the basis for the concept programmatically included diverse ICTs, much of its conceptual (and methodological) focus is most easily applied to television in the home. Thus the authors constantly found themselves referring to 'television (together with the other media)' (Silverstone 1994, p. 83). By 'the other media' they refer primarily to the phone and the computer. Television, however, is by far not the only media technology that research today – if it wanted to adequately describe and analyse the increasingly complex patterns of everyday life – needs to concentrate on.

6. Another milestone in the development of the theoretical framework was Herman Bausinger's 1984 text in *Media, Culture & Society*, which pre-formulated many of the concerns of the concept, as can be seen in the following summary quote: '(1) To make a meaningful study of the use of the media, it is necessary to take different media into consideration . . . (2) As a rule the media are not used completely, nor with full concentration . . . (3) The media are an integral part of the way the everyday is conducted . . . (4) It is not a question of an isolated, individual process, but of a collective process . . . (5) Media communication cannot be separated from direct personal communication . . . (6) . . .With regard to media offerings the story of the synthetic average viewer surely does not work . . .' (Bausinger 1984, pp. 349–50).

7. As the introduction to this book also points out, the moral economy term was borrowed from E. P. Thompson (1971).

8. Articulation as such is also a core concept within cultural studies, but within the domestication writings, references are made explicitly only to the semiotic origin and not to the cultural studies interpretation thereof. Stuart Hall's concept of articulation, for example, is an attempt at rethinking the question of *determination* and an acknowledgment that discourses, practices and structures are not easily joined, but need to be thought of in relation to each other and as a whole (cf. Hall 1986). Similar divisions can be found in the question of text and context here.

9. I am grateful to Lars Holmgaard Christensen for the criticism he provided on the double articulation in a private email communication (with which, however, I do not agree). He claims, that if we take the structural linguistic origin and Martinet seriously, we cannot

actually speak of two levels that justify the double articulation reference, rather we can speak of different articulations on the *same level* or a set of first articulations. In my own reading, I agree with Silverstone and Haddon (1996), who state that the first articulation is a necessary precondition for the second articulation to emerge and that, therefore, we can speak of a double articulation, since this also points to a structural differentiation (first – second) that contradicts the idea of the 'same level'. More problematic I find that in Martinet, as I interpret him, the second articulation is used to aid the differentiation of the first articulations. This I cannot see in the application of the concept to media technologies (rather to media texts). Here it is important to note that the double articulation in the context presented refers to the media as technology and as content, not as simply different levels within the content, that is, it does not read television messages, for example, as the two levels. The usefulness of the concept to illustrate this particular interdependence of technology and text outweighs in my eyes its potential 'misunderstanding' of the origin.

10. Other approaches in the study of audiences that domestication argued against were 'uses and gratifications' and cultural studies (see Morley and Silverstone 1990, p. 44).

11. Many of the stories told underline the fact that certain patterns of family relationships, life cycles, etc., remain more or less the same and that, therefore, certain patterns of use keep returning and are thus to some degree generalizable (for example, young people talking on the phone for extended periods of time to friends they have just seen).

12. The question what constitutes an ethnographic study within media and communication studies is an ongoing debate that unfortunately cannot adequately be dealt with in this chapter.

13. The ethnographic research, however, was conducted by one researcher alone (or rather: two subsequent researchers).

14. This is not to say that using a mobile phone is not in many ways a very public undertaking (cf. Sussex Technology Group 2001).

15. For a good combination of offline and online research see Miller and Slater 2000.

References

Alasuutari, P. (1999) 'Introduction: Three phases of reception studies', in (ed.) P. Alasuutari, *Rethinking the Media Audience*. Sage: London, pp. 1–21.

Ang, I. and Hermes, J. (1991) 'Gender and/in media consumption', in (eds) J. Curran and M. Gurevitch, *Mass Media and Society*. Edward Arnold: London, pp. 307–28.

Bakardjieva, M. and Smith, R. (2001) 'The internet in everyday life: computer networking from the standpoint of the domestic user'. *New Media & Society*, vol. 3, no. 1, pp. 67–83.

Bausinger, H. (1984) 'Media, technology and daily life'. *Media, Culture & Society*, vol. 6, pp. 343–51.

Corner, J. (1991) 'Meaning, genre and context: the problematics of "public knowledge" in new audience studies', in (eds) J. Curran and M. Gurevitch, *Mass Media and Society*. Edward Arnold: London, pp. 267–85.

Couldry, N. (2003) *Media Rituals – A Criticial Approach*. Routledge: London.

Drotner, K. (2000) 'Trends in young Danes' media uses'. *Media, Culture & Society*, vol. 22, no. 2, pp. 149–66.

Feenberg, A. (1999) *Questioning Technology*. Routledge: London and New York.

Giddens, A. (1991) *Modernity and Self-Identity*. Polity Press: Cambridge.

Gray, A. (1992) *Video Playtime: The Gendering of a Leisure Technology*. Routledge: London.

Haddon, L. (2001) *Domestication and Mobile Telephony*, Paper presented at the conference 'Machines that become us'. Rutgers University, 18–19 April 2001.

Haddon, L. (1994) 'Studying information and communication technologies in teleworking households', in (eds) A.-J. Berg and M. Aune, *Domestic Technology and Everyday Life – Mutual Shaping Processes*. Proceedings of COST A4 Workshop in Trondheim, Norway, 28–30 November 1993. See http://members.aol.com/leshaddon/IC-TRefs.html (accessed 20/11/2004).

Haddon, L. and Silverstone, R. (1996) *Information and Commuication Technologies and the Young Elderly*, SPRU/CICT Report Series, no. 13, University of Sussex, Brighton.

Haddon, L. and Silverstone, R. (1995) *Lone Parents and their Information and Communication Technologies*, SPRU/CICT Report Series, no. 12, University of Sussex, Brighton.

Haddon, L. and Silverstone, R. (1992) *Information and Communication Technologies in the Home: The Case of Teleworking*, SPRU/CICT Working Paper 17, University of Sussex, Brighton.

Hall, S. (1992) 'Cultural studies and its theoretical legacies', in (eds) L. Grossberg, C. Nelson and P. Treichler. *Cultural Studies*. Routledge: New York, pp. 277–94.

Hall, S. (1986) 'The problem of ideology – Marxism without guarantees.

On postmodernism and articulation: An interview with Stuart Hall (edited by Lawrence Grossberg)'. *Journal of Communication Inquiry*, vol. 10, no. 2, pp. 45–60.

Hartmann, M. (2005) 'The discourse of the perfect future – young people and new technologies', in (ed.) R. Silverstone, *Media, Technology and Everyday Life in Europe*. Ashgate: Aldershot, pp. 141–158.

Hartmann, M. (2004) 'Young People = "Young" Uses? Questioning the "Key Generation"', in (eds) N. Carpentier, C. Pauwels and O. Van Oost, *Het On(be)grijpbare Publiek: een communicatiewetenschappelijke exploratie van publiekonderzoek*. VUB Press: Brussels, pp. 355–75.

Helle-Valle, J. and Slettemeås, D. (forthcoming) 'ICT, domestication and context: Perspectives on subjects, objects and sociality'. Unpublished paper presented at the Domestication workshop in Aalborg's Media Lab, November 2004.

Jensen, K. B. (1996) 'Superthemen der Rezeption: Von Fernsehnachrichten zum Fernsehflow', in U. Hasebrink and F. Krotz, *Die Zuschauer als Fernsehregisseure?* Nomos Verlagsgesellschaft: Baden-Baden and Hamburg, pp. 178–96.

Krotz, F. (2001) *Die Mediatisierung kommunikativen Handelns. Der Wandel von Alltag und sozialen Beziehungen, Kultur und Gesellschaft durch die Medien*. Westdeutscher Verlag: Wiesbaden.

Lee, S. (1999) 'Private uses in public spaces'. *New Media & Society*, vol. 1, no. 3, pp. 331–50.

Lie, M. and Sørensen, K. H. (1996) 'Making technology our own?: Domesticating technology into everyday life', in (eds) M. Lie and K. H. Sørensen, *Making Technology Our Own? Domesticating Technology into Everyday Life*. Scandinavian University Press: Oslo, pp. 1–30.

Ling, R. and Thrane, K. (2001) *'It Actually Separates us a Little Bit, but I Think that is an Advantage': The Management of Electronic Media in Norwegian Households*, Telenor FoU Rapport 8/2001.

McRobbie, A. (1992) 'Post-Marxism and cultural studies: a post-script', in (eds) L. Grossberg, C. Nelson and P. Treichler, *Cultural Studies*. Routledge: New York, pp. 719–30.

Miller, D. and Slater, D. (2000) *The Internet: An Ethnographic Approach*. Berg: Oxford.

Moores, S. (1993) *Interpreting Audiences. The Ethnography of Media Consumption*. Sage: London.

Morley, D. (1999) '"Too boldly go . . .": The third generation of reception studies', in (ed.) P. Alasuutari, *Rethinking the Media Audience*. Sage: London, pp. 195–205.

Morley, D. (1992) *Television, Audiences and Cultural Studies*. Routledge: London.

Morley, D. and Silverstone, R. (1991) 'Communication and context:

ethnographic perspectives on the media audience', in K. B. Jensen and N. Jankowski, *A Handbook of Qualitative Methodologies*. Routledge: London, pp. 149–62.

Morley, D. and Silverstone, R. (1990) 'Domestic communication – technologies and meanings'. *Media, Culture and Society*, vol. 12, pp. 31–55.

Nöth, W. (2000) *Handbuch der Semiotik. 2. Aufl.* J. B. Metzler: Stuttgart and Weimar.

Radway, J. (1984) *Reading the Romance*. University of North Carolina Press: Chapel Hill.

Rommes, E. (2002) *Gender Scripts and the Internet: The Design and Use of Amsterdam's Digital City*. Twente University Press: Enschede.

Silverstone, R. (1994) *Television and Everyday Life*. Routledge: London.

Silverstone, R. and Haddon, L. (1996) 'Design and the Domestication of Information and Communication Technologies: Technical Change and Everyday Life', in (eds) R. Mansell and R. Silverstone, *Communication by Design. The Politics of Information and Communication Technologies*. Oxford University Press: Oxford, pp. 44–74.

Silverstone, R., Hirsch, E. and Morley, D. (1992) 'Information and communication technologies and the moral economy of the household', in (eds) R. Silverstone and E. Hirsch, *Consuming Technologies. Media and Information in Domestic Spaces*. Routledge: London and New York, pp. 15–31.

Silverstone, R., Hirsch, E. and Morley, D. (1991) 'Listening to a long conversation: an ethnographic approach to the study of information and communication technologies in the home'. *Cultural Studies: Theorizing Politics, Politicising Theory*, vol. 5, no. 2, pp. 204–27.

Sørensen, K. H. (1994) *Technology in Use. Two essays on the domestication of artifacts*. Senter for Teknologi og Samfunn: Trondheim.

Sørensen, K. H., Aune, M. and Hatling, M. (2000) 'Against linearity: on the cultural appropriation of science and technology', in (eds) M. Dierkes and C. von Grote, *Between Understanding and Trust: The Public, Science and Technology*. OPA: Amsterdam, pp. 237–57.

Sussex Technology Group (2001) 'In the company of strangers: mobile phones and the conception of space', in (ed.) S. Munt, *Technospaces – Inside the New Media*. Continuum: London and New York, pp. 205–23.

Thompson, E. P. (1971) 'The moral economy of the English crowd in the eighteenth century'. *Past & Present*, vol. 50, pp. 76–136.

Williams, R. (1974) *Television: Technology and Cultural Form*. Fontana: Glasgow.

6   Empirical studies using the domestication framework

Leslie Haddon

While the broad theoretical outline of the concept of domestication has been widely cited (especially Silverstone *et al*. 1992) the subsequent British empirical studies are perhaps less well known. The first part of this chapter introduces the history of British domestication projects conducted during the 1990s, with some indications of how all these studies contributed to thinking in the area of ICT policies, as well as observations about how the domestication framework might be extended to social networks. The second part describes how the domestication framework was itself developed by examining some key themes arising principally from the ESRC's Programme on Information and Communication Technologies (PICT). First, it reconsiders both the boundaries of households and the influence of different household compositions on ICT use. Second, it looks in more depth into forces at work beyond the home. Third, it considers how the domestication approach can be combined with complementary forms of analysis, here exemplified by cohort analysis. Finally, it examines factors shaping the longer-term careers of ICTs in the home.

The 1990s domestication studies

The PICT studies, each of which lasted a year, examined how ICTs were experienced by teleworkers, by lone parents and by the young elderly. These target groups were chosen for strategic purposes in order to develop the original domestication framework further, as outlined below. In each of the studies we conducted in-depth interviews in 20 households. Where there were two partners we attempted to see them both separately and together, on the first occasion to appreciate what they had to say independently, and on the second to see their interaction. In addition, each adult interviewee wrote out a week's time-use diary and observations about the home were noted. This included photographing various ICTs and the context in which they were located as well as taking pictures to capture the appearance of these homes and their locale. However, the more detailed ethnographic element of the earliest domestication studies was not repeated. While the first three-year study at Brunel had explored various methodologies, the Sussex research was more focused in this respect, especially due to time considerations. Hence, the central research tool was in-depth qualitative interviews around a set of themes.

The first PICT study, conducted in 1992–93, was of teleworkers (Haddon and Silverstone 1993, 1995a). This group were chosen in order to explore the relationship between home and paid work under conditions when the boundaries between the two were being challenged in a particularly dramatic form by homeworking using ICTs. Some of the insights from this study apply to certain non-teleworkers as well: for example, those who bring some work home after leaving offices, those who allow themselves to be contactable at home and those who work non-standard shifts so that their free time is out of synchronization with other household members and social networks.

The second year of the programme, 1993–94, dealt with lone parents (Haddon and Silverstone 1995). These were chosen in order to explore a household structure that was different from the nuclear families of the earlier Brunel work. But this study also had a number of other dimensions. In practice, the lone-parent households were mostly female-headed, and so they provided an opportunity to look at the dynamics involved around ICTs when no adult males were present. A large number of our interviewees were living on state support, or earned a limited amount. Hence, this was also in part a study of the consequences of poverty and of the strategies to overcome problems and hardship. In those cases involving the break-up of relationships, the research also acted as a study of trauma, of upheaval and the dramatic dissolution and reformation of households and household life.

The final year, 1994–95, was spent examining the young elderly (aged 60–75) (Haddon and Silverstone 1996). This group was chosen in order to reflect upon differences in the experience of ICTs arising at a stage in the life course when the children had left home and paid employment had ended. But the young elderly were also useful for considering cohort effects: the fact that people are born, grow up and live their earlier adult lives at particular historical moments, with particular social and economic conditions and technologies available.

In addition to the PICT studies, there was one EC-funded study of a particular and newly released technology, CD-*i*, (Silverstone and Haddon 1993). Some of this material fed into a book chapter aimed at combining an understanding of how users were conceived in the production process with the domestication approach to analysing ICT consumption (Silverstone and Haddon 1996a).

The first commercially sponsored study (Silverstone and Haddon

1996b) was for the cable company Telewest. Its staff had shown an interest in how the domestication approach might help them to understand the low take-up of their cable service by what is in the UK social class AB: managers and professionals. This 1995–96 study was able to cast some light on the values of this group, specifically how they evaluated TV and associated cable with more TV (which was understandable given cable's marketing strategy at the time). In addition, the study drew upon the interest of domestication analysis in people's time schedules and showed that, after prioritizing the news, the remaining time slots that many of these managers and professionals had for TV watching in the weekdays mitigated against their ability to watch films, one of the key selling points of cable.[1]

The second commercial project arose when the firm NCR was interested in the future of electronic commerce. While this topic provided one important focus, the company was also interested in the internet more generally, as this was the early period of its growth as a mass-market phenomenon. The study focused on a middle-class sample, since this group provided the main adopters at the time of the study in 1998. It explored differences in early experiences of the Net that related to an emerging literature of internet 'apprenticeships' (Jouet 2000; Lelong and Thomas 2001; Horrigan and Rainie 2002; Haddon 2004). But as in the case of the cable study, it examined people's time structures, their time commitments and hence 'free' time slots. It became clear how these provided important constraints on usage that challenged contemporary speculations within the industry about the prospects for increasing online time substantially.

The other novel dimension of this particular NCR study was that it entailed a five-country comparison involving Germany, Italy, the Netherlands, Norway and the UK. This study provided a heightened appreciation of the particular challenges of cross-cultural comparisons of qualitative studies (see especially, Livingstone 2003 on this point). For example, the participants agreed to operate within the domestication framework, covering the same areas in interviews and addressing an agreed set of questions when producing a country report. Even then, there was often some uncertainty as to whether different observations from the various national teams reflected actual national differences or whether they reflected the particular insights and background sensitivities that the researchers brought to the analysis.

A third commercially sponsored study was conducted for Telecom Italia. This involved a five-country survey conducted in France, Germany, Italy, Spain and the UK (Fortunati 1998). The earlier PICT studies had examined the ways that people sometimes developed strategies to control communications. They usually did this either because of the costs of outgoing calls or the disruptiveness of incoming ones, especially if the latter occurred at certain inconvenient times (Haddon 1994). Together with an analysis of the strategies people used to keep their communications private, this focus on control strategies formed one of the strands explored in the survey. A critical perspective as regards what can be and is being measured in surveys was reflected in the questions asked and the statistical tests that were chosen. On the one hand, the survey material contrasted with the bulk of domestication studies that have been associated with qualitative methodologies. On the other, the research explored avenues that, while not being unique, were also not so common in more traditional surveys of ICTs – touching, for example, upon issues of domestic politics.

This 1996 survey provided an opportunity to examine the generalizability of these experiences of communication, to see to what extent controlling communication was an issue for people and the degree to which any strategies aimed at dealing with perceived problems were used.[2] For example, it was striking how much the cost of telecoms was an issue within the European countries studied, across the social spectrum, and how much this affected interactions within households, for example, in terms of complaints about other household members' use of the phone and attempts to limit this use.

In addition to the commercial studies, the domestication framework was also used to explore policy issues.[3] In particular, several publications addressed the issue of social exclusion, looking at how access to, and use of, ICTs related to debates about new 'haves' and 'have-nots' (Silverstone 1994; Haddon 2000). Through considering some of the studies outlined above, especially the PICT ones, it was possible to explore what the presence and absence of ICTs meant to people in everyday life, the possibilities they opened up or closed down. Although the earliest British domestication analysis looked in detail at the processes by which ICTs were fitted into our lives, it never insisted that they had to be. These PICT studies revealed some of the ambiguities felt about ICTs, even well-established ones like the TV and phone, and showed why people might not always choose to embrace new technologies.

Finally, more recent work has explored in principle how the domestication framework could provide insight into the experience of technologies such as the mobile phone. It had always been clear that while the British domestication framework provided insights it also had its limitations through an emphasis on interactions within the household. For example, some of the processes shaping the popularity of technologies occurred outside the home (Haddon 1992). Indeed, some Norwegian work using the domestication approach has looked to other sites outside the home, for example, places where computer hackers meet and develop their individual and collective domestication strategies (Håpnes 1996). The case of portable ICTs, such as the mobile phone, also require us to think how the domestication framework could be expanded to consider how interactions with wider social networks can have a bearing upon the experience of these technologies (Haddon 2003, 2004).

Household structure and dynamics

The PICT studies in particular enabled more reflection upon the effects of household composition on ICT use. Across the studies, we considered ways in which household boundaries could be more porous than had been depicted in the early Brunel studies. For example, this occurred when children from first marriages 'flowed' in and out of a household depending on which parents they were staying with at any one time. Another example would be when adults, and sometimes their children, moved back to their own parents' home when their partnerships split up.

Because the households were asked about their earlier experiences, including earlier experiences of ICTs, it was also possible to appreciate the consequences of the diverse living arrangements they had lived through in the past. This included the degree of communal living experienced by students, by other young adults, as well as by some of our lone parents. Then there were the households shared by just two adults whose relationship could consist of various degrees of closeness: where they might be partners, gay or heterosexual, friends or just otherwise sharing for cost reasons or to provide company. Finally, there were the arrangements whereby families or couples of whatever age define a household primarily as their family, but then have extra people staying with them, be they friends, other relatives, au pairs, longer-term lodgers or bed and breakfast guests.

To the extent that technological resources are shared between a number of people, there can be more complex, collective decisions and negotiations about access and use. Sometimes this can extend to the acquisition of ICTs since these adults can pool group resources to buy new ICTs that might be neither affordable nor justifiable for any individual. For instance, when we applied the domestication perspective to the study of CD-*i*, the earning power and limited demands on the income of one gay male couple was such that they could afford an extremely rich and up-market technological environment. To the extent that individuals in shared households lead separate lives, they sometimes duplicate ICTs like computers or audio equipment. Alternatively, such households can provide the chance for some members to experience the technologies of others prior to acquiring their own set-ups. Finally, particular issues can arise around those ICTs financed on a pay-per-use basis. For instance, some of those lone parents and teleworkers who had lived in shared households recalled the extra interest they had had at that time in monitoring phone usage, as well as devising systems for financing it. Indeed, some had implemented various systems for blocking outgoing calls. Clearly there can be some concern in such shared households with the surveillance and control of technologies.

If we turn now to lone-parent households, although not all of these had a low income, many, usually female, lived on social security payments and/or part-time work. The absence of a second adult could create particular constraints, demands and household dynamics. For example, many lone parents felt trapped in home in the evenings because there was no one else to mind the child. Organizing the logistics of child management, such as getting someone to pick up a child from school, could be more complicated for just one parent. And older children could sometimes achieve a stronger negotiating role as regards household rules when only one parent was present in the home.

Moving on to the consequences for their experience of technologies, limited income often meant that anything beyond very basic ICTs such as the phone or TV was beyond the horizons of many lone parents. The poorer ones also tended to be more conscious of costs such as phone bills, sometimes even rationing their calls and those of their children. Such constraints, and the lack of options to even investigate whether new ICTs and services could play a part in everyday life, can be considered to be one more dimension of deprivation. It shows a lack of ability to have access to the same resources as peers and hence participate fully in the social world. The dynamics of how ICTs were acquired often reflected limited economic resources: for instance, phone handsets, old TVs and VCRs were more likely to be gifts and/or second hand. Apart from the effects of low income, the phone was often more of a social lifeline for those trapped in the home, and certainly it could take on substantial significance as a tool for organizing and coping with daily life. In effect, stronger voting rights for children meant that they sometimes had a larger say in how ICTs were consumed.

We saw at the start of this section that household composition could also be somewhat fluid. This could have implications for ICTs. Travelling between homes meant that equipment was sometimes duplicated in different households, for example, having a video console in both. Or else portable ICTs such as Walkmans were carried from one household to another. Meanwhile, children, or indeed adults, spending time in two different households could experience different rules and regulations, different regimes, relating to ICTs. For example:

> It's the violence that I don't like. Mark loves *Terminator 2* and all those sort of films, which is what he watches. His dad bought him that video and he sees films at his dad's that I would never allow him to watch. We have discussed it but that's just one of those things ... (my ex-husband) makes decisions about what they watch when he's there and he lets them watch horror films and *Terminator* and other things I don't know about.
>
> (Joy)

From her perspective, Joy had lost some influence over this part of her children's lives through not having control when they were at their father's place. Of course, from the children's perspectives, the ability to operate in two different households might have actually given them more freedom. The same applied in Paul's case:

> Their mother has never allowed them to have it because ... I mean my youngest boy, his favourite author is Stephen King. He's into horror and the most horrific video that he could possibly get his little hands on, that's what he'll go for. Mind you they go round their friends' houses and they've all got (these) bleeding videos. You name it, they've seen it.
>
> (Paul)

Lastly, part-time household members can have access to different equipment in different households:

> I believe my husband's got satellite. They've been watching *The Simpsons* round there and they're quite pipped that they can't watch *The Simpsons* here.
>
> (Linda)

Linda's children had clearly expressed some dissatisfaction that she did not have satellite when their father did – she was seen as technologically deprived given their other reference point.

In sum, household composition can be complex, and indeed it sometimes forces us to think about what counts as the boundary of a household and how flexible this is. Moreover, people often have a far wider experience of different household forms and the very transition between household forms can require some readjustment in life, which can itself give rise to new demands on ICTs.

The relationship between home and the outside world

People's experience of ICTs can be influenced by their commitments to, and roles in, social networks outside the home. In principle that had always been acknowledged in the formulation of the concept of domestication. But in the earlier British work much more attention was given to the interaction between household members relating to ICTs and how people presented themselves to the outside world, as shown in the notion of 'conversion' (Silverstone *et al.* 1992). The PICT studies provided a chance to explore the relationship with the outside world in more depth, as later researchers using the domestication were also to do (for example, Lally 2002, looking at social networks and computer use in Australia). Below, the three examples discussed are paid work, unpaid work and links to the extended family.

Commitment to paid employment outside the home influenced the amount of time that was available to spend in the home and hence the time available to use PCs, to watch TV or otherwise participate in other ICT-based leisure. In an era before the mass market for mobile phones, it also influenced the time when people were contactable by phone or free to contact others. Moves towards more flexible working hours and to shift work in organizations operating 24 hours a day had led to more varied times to consume ICTs, although time-shifting technologies such as the VCR and answering machines had enabled people to cope better with being out of synchronization with more mainstream leisure times.

Apart from structuring time, work reached into the home in various ways, certainly as telework but also as overspill work (or in terms of second jobs) where people brought home some work or else initiated or received work-related communications at home. This often led to ICTs coming into the home to support work, either through bringing the laptop home or else re-duplicating in the home work facilities such as the PC. In these studies from the early 1990s, some mobile workers had their next day's work faxed to them at home or else it was relayed to them as a phone message. Nowadays we might anticipate that email would take on this role. Even in the early 1990s, work-related commuting had also led some people to utilize portable ICTs in order to make more productive use of travelling time.

Portable or home-based ICTs acquired for work were subsequently often used for non-work purposes. Teleworkers who would never have acquired a variety of equipment for purely domestic or personal reasons, including PCs, could now justify this because of work and then discover non-work applications (for example, printing out shopping lists, using the home fax for trade union matters). Indeed, the equipment was sometimes free in that it was funded or loaned by an employer or client.

Once in the home, not only teleworkers but also other family members could gain familiarity with the technology, experiment and develop their competences and awareness of its possibilities. The home-based work fax machine was sometimes used to contact relatives, the work photocopier was used for school projects.

But paid work entering the home could also change the experience of existing ICTs. The best example from our research concerned the phone. Where a second work line was not justifiable, the domestic phone took on an additional role as a work tool. As a result, rules concerning its use often had to be renegotiated. Household members, including children, had to learn how to answer appropriately, or when not to answer. Issues arose over other household members blocking the phone line at certain times with their social calls if this might prevent work calls from arriving. And the whole sound regime of the home had to be reviewed. Hence we have examples of teleworkers deciding where the phone was to be relocated and controlling domestic background noise in an attempt to create a good impression of their working environment when dealing with calls from prospective clients and employers. Related issues emerged over access to PCs where telework now competed with computer games, school homework or other applications.

Unpaid work can, of course, include domestic labour, but the focus here is specifically on voluntary commitments outside of home. This can include 'voluntary work' helping others, taking part in committees, running sports clubs, and participating in interest groups, be they hobby-orientated or concerned with wider social issues. Across the PICT studies we found a considerable involvement in the wider community, with greater and lesser degrees of formality. A teleworker might head the school board of governors, a lone parent might organize activities for Gingerbread (the organization of and for lone parents) or a retired person might captain the local bowls team or run a church group. In fact, many of the young elderly were especially active as they sought to replace paid work with constructive and social involvement that could structure day-to-day life, keep them mentally alert and add purpose to life.

These involvements often generated organizing work, administration and other forms of production. For example, teleworker Simon described how he used his equipment:

Simon: I did some tickets for a hockey club. I've organised the last two or three karoake/disco-ey-type things, and I just knock the tickets up upstairs and print them off. When Eliza was born, I scanned a picture of her face in and blew it up and that was the, you know, 'she's arrived', you know.

LH: But do you find because you've got this equipment here, other people come up to you and say, 'well, could you do this or could you do that on your ...'?

Simon: No, nobody's actually asked me. Actually, at church on Sunday, I suggested or offered to do the weekly news-sheets which has gone by the board because the guy who used to do it is no longer doing it. They tend to be sort of hymns and songs which I could put into the computer quite easily. And then just, I want number 1, number 47, number 36, just pop them all together and shove them on the page and print them off.

We have other examples of computers being used to word process school reports, update records of hobby groups (for example, what records have been listened to in music appreciation societies) and handle official correspondence on behalf of clubs or maintain a treasurer's accounts. Equipment such as photocopiers has been used for reproducing the music scores for bands. Meanwhile, the telephone was the medium for organizing outings and other events, arranging speakers and players or calling meetings. Other telecoms equipment such as answering machines and even mobile phones could find similar roles. Less formally, others within social networks made use of our participants' ICTs as a resource, asking if it was possible to use the fax or other facility. Here we see the modern-day technological equivalent of asking to borrow a cup of sugar from a neighbour.

Lastly we have the case of support for and from extended family. This was most acutely illustrated in the study of the young elderly, many of whom had commitments in terms of either caring for their own infirm elderly parents or minding young grandchildren. In managing these tasks, the basic telephone in particular became an important organizing tool for arranging visits and travel, as well as for monitoring developments in their relatives' households or providing security in the case of emergencies. The other technology of significance for the extended family was the camcorder, as either the young elderly or their children took on the role of preserving family memories. However, this was not always embraced by other family members. Retired Chris described why he and his wife Hilda had first acquired a camcorder:

Chris: Because it was a year when there were three big events in the family. Well, big events ... I think the grand-daughter was being born ... my son was getting married, and Hilda and I were going on a Nile cruise.

LH: So how often would you use it now?

Chris: Spasmodically. Mainly holidays, birthdays, Christmas. ... special

> events ... like I'm putting together some films to ... Well, I say films, some of the family for my son out in Oman, for example, just to give Christmas messages and show him what the weather's like, you know; 'This is rain if you'd forgotten.'
>
> *LH*:   So do your various children actually ask you 'Can you come and video this?'
>
> *Chris*:   No, they don't. I poke the camera at them and they say 'Oh no, not again!'
>
> *Hilda*:   We videoed my son's wedding and he still hasn't seen it. They don't want to see it.

Through these various examples we can see the many ways in which what happens outside the home has a bearing upon the organization of domestic time and space and involves commitments which shape the place and use of ICTs in the home, as well as their acquisition and regulation.

Cohort analysis: the influence of earlier life experiences

Applying the domestication framework to the analysis of a particular topic or group does not preclude combining it with other forms or levels of analyses. For example, each of the PICT studies contextualized their subjects by borrowing from the literature analysing the social construction of childhood (for example, James and Prout 1997). The studies reflected upon such things as recent historical developments in work practices, in legislation, in media representations and in financial circumstances. Based on this they could ask what it meant to be a teleworker, a lone parent or young elderly person in 1990s Britain in terms of options, perceptions, expectations, constraints, and so on. Another form of contextualization involved considering the biographies of our subjects, in particular as cohorts of people born at a certain time and sharing some experiences over the course of their lives. This was clearest in the study of the young elderly group, although the form of analysis has a wider applicability.

Many of this young elderly cohort were originally from working-class backgrounds and had undergone upward social mobility in their own lifetime as middle-class occupations expanded. Hence, it was common for them to have lived as a child in somewhat austere conditions from the pre-war era into the early postwar years. Although they had enjoyed more affluence from the 1950s, in certain respects non-consumerist values were retained. Our interviewees would often talk about knowing the value of money. They were careful spenders, interested in getting value for money. They often resisted rushing to buy the latest version of a commodity and had always been more inclined to replace items when they were sufficiently worn out. On the other hand, many had enjoyed a lifestyle that had been somewhat different from the previous cohort: with holidays abroad, a car-oriented culture and shopping patterns long geared to supermarkets. Some had experienced the break-up of traditional working-class communities and many had seen their children and friends move away with the prevalence of generally greater geographical mobility.

The second set of considerations relevant here is at what point in their biographies various technologies became more widely available and how they evolved over the course of this cohort's lives. Radio had become a mass-market product when these interviewees were in their youth. Familiarity with the phone had often come first through work as it became an increasingly common tool in many jobs, especially the expanding white collar ones. Television had made its in-roads into the home in their early adult life in the 1950s and early 1960s. But on the whole this was still not the computer generation. Many of those now nearer to being 75 years old in the 1990s had not lived through office automation during their working lives. Others had actively tried to avoid computers – being very near retirement age they had not wanted to have to take on new ways of working and learn computing skills at this stage. At the same time, their own children had usually been too old to be swept up by the computer and games boom of the 1980s. For most, the computer was beyond their horizons not only because it would be difficult to master but because they could not envisage how they would fit into their lives and routines.

While basic phones, televisions, multiple TVs, TVs with teletext, VCRs and various audio equipment could usually be found in the homes of this cohort, there was a conservatism as regards acquiring newer ICTs, or additional facilities. We saw that they were not impulse buyers and hence acquisitions had to be justified. The young elderly argued in terms of not 'needing' any more equipment, facilities or services rather than not desiring them. They would often point out that they had been without various facilities for all their life so far and had managed. While some were more adventurous, most clearly did not want to try too much experimenting at this stage and so they were not interested in some innovations.

In contrast with some of their own parents, most of this cohort of young elderly were at ease with the phone, having gained competence in using it so early in their lives. Most had had their own phone for many years. It had been and was still important for maintaining social contact with dispersed friends and children. And many knew through years of practice how it might potentially be used – for instance, phoning to pay by credit card or phoning ahead to check whether something was in stock at a distant store to which they had to drive. Phone-related equipment was usually a fairly straightforward extension of the familiar: with modern or additional handsets and some cordless phones. But in the early 1990s, answering machines were still rare among this group and mobile phones virtually non-existent.

Radio listening in the evening had already been largely displaced by TV-watching habits developed over a few decades, but this generation still resisted TV in the morning and during the day. For many musical tastes, if not classical, were predominantly from the pre-1960s popular music era. Although most of our interviewees had been willing to take on a VCR, often at the instigation of their own adult children, at the time of the research satellite and cable were too new, and not justifiable. Apart from some interest in war programmes by those who had taken part in action, the films from their cinema-going days often appealed as did travel programmes relating to their own visits abroad. Some soap operas were attractive because they portrayed a sense of community that they had lost. The fairly universal critical standpoint on forms of realism and particularly sex and violence on TV reflected in part their earlier exposure to broadcasting based on very different values in the 1950s.

Overall, we see the various ways in which past shared experiences have helped to shape habits and routines, values and tastes and the very perception of what that technology can offer. In principle, this form of analysis could be applied to any cohort, as in media commentaries on postwar 'baby-boomers' or more recently in discussions of the specific ICT experiences of children growing up in the 1990s (Haddon 2004). The purpose of discussing it here has been to show how approaches such as cohort analysis can complement domestication framework, adding extra insights.

The longer-term careers of ICTs

Earlier British formulations of the domestication framework paid particular attention to the initial career of ICTs, through the period when they first entered the home and to some extent shortly afterwards. Turning now to the longer-term processes changing the experience of ICTs, one set of factors covered in some depth were the changes in people's circumstances[4] that altered their interest in and use of ICTs. This might include the arrival and growth of children or changes in factors external to the household, such as work (Haddon 2004). In the

PICT studies we focused not only on transitions into telework, lone parenthood and the stage of being young elderly, often involving retirement, but we also observed subsequent and the ongoing changes. For example, the new demands on space and evolving timetables of growing children could lead to changes in where telework equipment was located and when it was used. As the financial position of some lone parents improved, this could lead to them using ICTs that they had previously not considered. And the communication patterns of the young elderly could alter as grandchildren arrived or their social commitments changed.

In addition to these dynamic processes, people's use of ICTs was itself influenced by the new technologies and services on offer. Others have subsequently referred to this in terms of the 'shifting environment' of ICTs (Cummings and Kraut 2002). Of particular interest here is how the entry of new ICTs into the home affected people's relationships to the existing ones (Haddon and Silverstone 1994).

While products such as computer peripherals, videos and satellite, and answering machines can be regarded as separate ICTs, their entry into the home also affected the existing computer, TV and telephone respectively – that is, the generic technologies. Obviously, such additions enhanced the functionality of existing ICTs, adding new options. Less obviously, these additions could create new problems or at least give rise to issues that had to be handled in the household. Some of the parents remembered new conflicts with their children over access to the TV when video games consoles first entered the home. By requiring the TV screen for display, games had competed with broadcast programmes. Other interviewees had been wary of how the additional programme choice offered by the introduction of satellite or cable might make the familiar TV too tempting – they might find themselves watching more TV than thought was appropriate. So both by offering new possibilities and requiring new decisions, what we might call the new TV-video-satellite-game display technology system had gone beyond the boundaries of and was a different entity from the old TV.

The multiplication of technologies and the acquisition of second and third phone lines, TVs, computers, and so on can have implications for the experience of ICTs. For example, in some of the teleworking households we examined, upgrading a computer meant that partners of teleworkers and their children could now have easier access to the old PC. While this meant a change in the 'career' of those particular old computers, it also had implications in terms of the computer's general place in the home. It could reduce conflicts and anxieties arising from the fact that different people wanted to use the machine at the same time. There was a parallel in the case of second TVs. The arrival of a new

TV not only meant a potentially new role for the old set. It could also change the experience of viewing, reducing communal TV watching – and hence 'family time together' – as on occasion some household members retired to another room to watch the programmes they wanted to see on their own TV.

We should not forget how even more minor or mundane innovations can have significant consequences. In the 1980s, the introduction of phone extensions going into private spaces such as bedrooms enabled more privacy for individuals within the home. But that in itself could also lead to conflicts of interest as it allowed some teenage children to evade more easily the surveillance of their parents. Yet, some parents not only wanted to know who was being phoned, but, being conscious of phone bills, preferred such phoning to take place in a space where it could be monitored. As a result, in some households, there had been attempts to deny children the use of the extension phone (and cordless phone, which raised similar issues).

Another instance of change in media is that of the services deliverable via ICTs, most particularly via the telephone, including ordering by credit card, access to technical helplines, to social support lines (for example, the Samaritans), and to chatlines. For some lone parents undergoing the trauma of separation and social isolation, the availability of these support and chatlines had been a social lifeline. In other households, the fear of teenagers running up huge bills on chatlines, or accessing sexlines, had led to some anxiety and conflicts.

ICT-related innovations such as the radio phone-in, initiated by the broadcasting industry, have created whole new forms of messaging. TV competitions, where the audience was invited to phone in with answers – at premium phone call prices – had also required new forms of negotiation within households, with some parents limiting how much their children could take part in these competitions because of the implications for the phone bill. Clearly, the increasing availability of all of these options, making the role of the phone more and more complex, had the potential to cause new types of interaction and regulation within households.

The earliest British formulations of the domestication framework drew attention to the biography of objects over the longer term. But the focus on the first moment of consumption and shortly afterwards and the very metaphor of 'taming the wild' could lead to the misleading view that domestication was a one-off set of process leading to an end-state in which the ICT is finally domesticated. This was not an intended implication, as was even clearer in Sørensen's contemporary observation that artefacts become redomesticated or even dis-domesticated as we give them up (Sørensen 1994). The changes outlined in this section as well as the dynamics of households themselves, serve to underline this principle that domestication is actually an ongoing process where we have constantly to reassess our relation to ICTs over time.

Summary

The history of the 1990s British projects shows how the domestication framework has been 'applied'. For commercial purposes, it helped cast light on the use, as well as non-use, of ICTs. Its appeal to industry lay largely in the fact that much traditional market research is very focused on individuals, and indeed often draws upon theoretical frameworks orientated to individuals such as 'uses and gratifications' model of media use, or Maslow's hierarchy of needs. In the British domestication studies the unit of analysis was the household,[5] or when commenting on individuals at least it placed them in a context where one could appreciate the role of interactions with others as well as the structures, such as time commitments, within which they acted.

The domestication framework has also been 'applied' in the sense of informing policy, the main example being in relation to digital divides or social exclusion. But empirical material has also been policy relevant in terms of being used to comment upon the claims and aspirations associated with the 'information society', be that in terms of questioning broader visions of revolutionary change (Silverstone 1995) or in reflecting upon the practical experience of one icon of that vision: telework.

The second half of this chapter showed how the follow-up PICT studies were designed to fill out the areas that had received less attention in the earliest formulations of domestication. First, the PICT studies highlighted how the composition and dynamics of households were relevant for ICTs. Indeed, they drew attention to ways in which the very boundaries of what counts as a household or a family can be somewhat fluid. Second, the studies looked in far more depth at the implications of relationships with outside world, providing more insight into the context in which households and their members operate.

Third, we saw how in actual studies the domestication framework could usefully be complemented by other forms of analysis. Domestication analysis had always argued how households or families had previous histories or biographies that had a bearing upon current interactions around ICTs. We could now broaden this appreciation of histories to consider the role of generational experiences.[6] Finally, the PICT studies underlined how it was possible to understand the experience of ICTs as an ongoing and dynamic process in the longer term.

Notes

1. The results are described in more depth in Haddon 2004.
2. The original Italian chapter on this topic is Haddon 1998. The full English version of the Italian chapter can be downloaded from http://members.aol.com/leshaddon/Date.html
3. Indeed, when the EC's Bangemann report on the future of ICTs came out in the late 1990s, some of the material described here informed the report to a high level group of experts brought together to respond to this report and develop policy initiative. That contribution was later published as Haddon and Silverstone 2000.
4. Such dynamics have also been considered in a variety of French studies, such as Claisse 2000, looking at evidence on changing gender communications patterns over the life, and Manceron *et al.* 2001, exploring the impact on communication of the arrival of the first child. Both are discussed in more depth in Haddon 2004.
5. Norwegian studies have discussed and illustrated ways in which the framework could be used to understand domestication at a household level and an individual one (Aune 1996; Berg, A.-J. 1997). This individual level of analysis reflects processes described in some of the consumption literature (for example, McCracken 1990), one of the very roots of the domestication framework.
6. The cohort analysis was inspired in large part by the work of Sibylle Meyer and Eva Schulze from BIS in Berlin, with whom we had contact at an earlier stage and who later part participated in the EC sponsored EMTEL network of researchers looking at ICTs in everyday life.

References

Aune, M. (1996) 'The computer in everyday life: patterns of domestication of a new technology', in (eds) M. Lie and K. Sørensen, *Making Technologies Our Own? Domesticating Technology into Everyday Life.* Scandinavian University Press: Oslo, pp. 91–120.

Berg, A.-J. (1997) 'Karoline and the cyborgs: the naturalisation of a technical object', in (ed.) V. Frissen, *Gender, ITCS and Everyday Life: Mutual Shaping Process.* COST A4, 6: Brussels, EC, pp. 7–35.

Claisse, G. (2000) 'Identités masculines et féminines au telephone. Des rôles, des pratiques des perception contrastés'. *Réseaux*, vol. 18, pp. 51–90.

Cummings, J. and Kraut, R. (2002) 'Domesticating computers and the internet'. *Information Society*, vol. 1, no. 83, pp. 221–32.

Fortunati, L. (ed.) (1998) *Telecomunicando in Europa*. Franco Angeli: Milan.

Haddon, L. (1992) 'Explaining ICT consumption: the case of the home computer', in (eds) R. Silverstone and E. Hirsch, *Consuming Technologies: Media and Information in Domestic Spaces*. Routledge: London, pp. 82–96.

Haddon, L. (1994) 'The phone in the home: ambiguity, conflict and change', paper presented at the COST 248 Workshop The European Telecom User, Lund, Sweden, 13–14 April.

Haddon, L. (1998) 'Il controllo della comunicazione. Imposizione di limiti all'uso del telefono', in (ed.) L. Fortunati, *Telecomunicando in Europa*. Franco Angeli: Milan, pp. 195–247.

Haddon, L. (2004) *Information and Communication Technologies in Everyday Life: A Concise Introduction and Research Guide*. Berg: Oxford.

Haddon, L. (2003) 'Domestication and mobile telephony', in (ed.) J. Katz, *Machines that Become Us: The Social Context of Personal Communication Technology*. Transaction Publishers: New Brunswick, pp. 43–56.

Haddon, L. (2000) 'Social exclusion and information and communication technologies: Lessons from studies of single parents and the young elderly'. *New Media & Society*, vol. 2, no. 4, pp. 387–406.

Haddon, L. (1999) 'European perceptions and use of the internet', paper presented at the conference Usages and Services in Telecommunications, Arcachon, 7–9 June.

Haddon, L. and Silverstone, R. (1996) *Information and Communication Technologies and the Young Elderly*, SPRU/CICT report series no. 13, University of Sussex: Sussex.

Haddon, L. and Silverstone, R. (1995a) 'Telework and the changing relationship of home and work', in (eds) N. Heap, R. Thomas, G. Einon, R. Mason and H. Mackay, *Information Technology and Society: A Reader*. Sage: London, pp. 400–12.

Haddon, L. and Silverstone, R. (1995b) *Lone Parents and their Information and Communication Technologies*, SPRU/CICT report series no. 12, University of Sussex: Sussex.

Haddon, L. and Silverstone, R. (1994) *The Careers of Information and Communication Technologies in the Home*. Paper presented at the International Working Conference on Home Orientated Informatics, Telematics and Automation, Copenhagen, 27 June–1 July.

Haddon, L. and Silverstone, R. (1993) *Teleworking in the 1990s: A view from the home*, SPRU/CICT report series no. 10, University of Sussex: Sussex.

Haddon, L. and Silverstone, R. (2000) 'Home information and communication technologies and the information society', in (eds) K.

Ducatel, J. Webster, W. Herrmann and W. Lanham, *The Information Society in Europe: Work and Life in an Age of Globalization*. Rowman and Littlefield Inc.: Maryland, pp. 233–58.

Håpnes, T. (1996) 'Not in their machines. How hackers transform computers into subcultural artefacts', in (eds) M. Lie and K. Sørensen, *Making Technologies Our Own? Domesticating Technology into Everyday Life*. Scandinavian University Press: Oslo, pp. 121–50.

Horrigan, J. and Rainie, L. (2002) *Getting Serious Online*, Pew Internet and American Life Project, [online] available from: http://www.pewinternet.org/ (6 Oct. 2002).

James, A. and Prout, A. (eds) (1997) *Constructing and Reconstructing Childhood: Contemporary Issues in the Sociological Study of Children*. Falmer Press: London.

Jouet, J. (2000) 'Retour critique sur la sociologie des usages'. *Réseaux*, vol. 100, pp. 486–521.

Lally, E. (2002) *At Home with Computers*. Berg: Oxford.

Lelong, B. and Thomas, F. (2001) '*L'Apprentissage de l'internaute: socialisation et autonomisation*', paper for the conference *e-Usages*, Paris, 12–14 June.

Livingstone, S. (2003) 'On the challenges of cross-national comparative media research'. *European Journal of Communication*, vol. 18, no. 4, pp. 477–500.

McCracken, G. (1990) *Culture and Consumption: New Approaches to the Symbolic Character of Consumer Goods and Activities*. Indiana University Press: Bloomington.

Manceron, V., Leclerc, C., Houdart, S., Lelong, B. and Smoreda, Z. (2001) '*Processus de hiérarchisation au sein des relations sociales et diversification des modes de communication au moment de la naissance d'un premier enfant*'. Paper for the conference *e-Usages*, Paris, 12–14 June.

Silverstone, R. (1995) 'Media, communication, information and the "revolution" of everyday life', in (ed.) S. Emmott, *Information Superhighways: Multimedia Users and Futures*. Academic Press: London, pp. 61–78.

Silverstone, R. (1994) 'Future imperfect – media, information and the millenium', *PICT Policy Research Paper* No. 27. Brunel University, Brunel.

Silverstone, R. and Haddon, L. (1996a) 'Design and the domestication of information and communication technologies: technical change and everyday life', in (eds) R. Mansell and R. Silverstone, *Communication by Design. The Politics of Information and Communication Technologies*. Oxford University Press: Oxford, pp. 44–74.

Silverstone, R. and Haddon, L. (1996b) 'Television, cable and AB households', *A Report for Telewest*. University of Sussex: Sussex.

Silverstone, R. and Haddon, L. (1993) *Future Compatible? Information and Communications Technologies in the Home: A Methodology and Case Study.* A report prepared for the Commission of the European Communities Socio-Economic and Technical Impact Assessments and Forecasts, RACE Project 2086, SPRU/CICT, University of Sussex: Sussex.

Silverstone, R., Hirsch, E. and Morley, D. (1992) 'Information and communication technologies and the moral economy of the household', in (eds) R. Silverstone and E. Hirsch, *Consuming Technologies: Media and Information in Domestic Spaces.* Routledge: London, pp. 15–31.

Sørensen, K. (1994) 'Technology in use: two essays in the domestication of artefacts,' *STS Working Papers 2/94.* Senter for teknologi og Samfunn: Trondheim, Norway.

PART II
Applying domestication: empirical work

7 'Fitting the internet into our lives': IT courses for disadvantaged users[1]

Deirdre Hynes and Els Rommes

Introduction

This chapter presents two case studies documenting the domestication experiences of participants taking introductory courses in computers and the internet in the Netherlands and Ireland. Both courses specifically aimed to reach disadvantaged users, for example elderly people, people from ethnic minorities, unemployed, and single parents. All of them live in a disadvantaged area of Amsterdam: 'Westerpark', or in the 'Ballymun' area of Dublin. While neither course was specifically aimed at reaching women, both attracted more women than men. Both courses were offered as part of a community-wide attempt to promote IT skills through free 'introductory' courses conducted in public spaces.

Our aim is twofold. First, we aim to explore the practical and political usability of the domestication concept. Domestication is a notion that calls attention to the relevance of the symbolic meaning of artefacts and to the various phases a user goes through when facing a new technology. We explore the contribution our analysis could make to policy-makers and course developers when designing courses. We argue that, in addition to material resources and tuition, course designers should also address the symbolic resources people bring with them; that is the reasons and motivations to learn and attend the course, and the importance and meaning the artefact holds to the individual. Second, we extend the current conceptualization of domestication to address how introductory computer courses can influence and intervene in the domestication process, especially in more problematic cases.

Little attention has been paid to domestication processes that are problematic, reversed, stopped altogether, or influenced by factors such as the availability of resources or the presence of a course.[2] In other words, the concept ignores the diversity of users. In this chapter, we show that the concept can be used to analyse these kinds of cases and we demonstrate the way in which the organization of the Dublin-based course considered the social and cultural capital of the participants, in the sense that it supported participant interest, motivation and the processes involved in ascribing meanings to ICTs. The Dublin-based course, with its sensitivity to user need, facilitated a greater level of success in the domestication process than the Dutch course.

We start by introducing the concept of domestication: the ways in which it can incorporate more diverse users, and the place a course may have in the domestication process. Following this, we introduce our research methodology and compare the courses we have studied. We discuss the ways these courses influenced the phases of domestication for the course participants. Finally, we conclude with some suggestions on how courses can be improved; ways in which the domestication concept can be adapted to include more diverse users; and we consider the influence of a course on the domestication process.

The concept of domestication

In our understanding, domestication is, first of all, an analytical tool, which helps to illuminate the process where the user makes the technology 'his/her own'; a process through which both the technology and its user are changed. This process takes place through various phases or dimensions and the artefact is fitted into the routines and practices of the everyday life of its user (Silverstone *et al.* 1992; Berg 1996; Lie and Sørensen 1996; Mansell and Silverstone 1996; Frissen 1997; Mackay 1997). Although the term 'domestic' suggests a household environment, the concept is also applicable to other areas of everyday life, such as to study the introduction of computers at work (Sørensen *et al.* 2000; Pierson, in this volume), or in our cases, in a teaching environment and in public settings.

Perhaps the main advantage of the domestication concept is the explicit attention it brings to the symbolical meanings of technologies. By domesticating technology, users may ascribe new and changed meanings to the artefacts (Gay *et al.* 1997, p. 95). According to Silverstone:

> Both [domestication and design] constrain and enable the capacity of consumers to define their own relationship to the technologies that are offered to, or confront, them. These constraints … are embodied in design and marketing and in the public definitions of 'what these technologies can and should be used for'.
>
> (Silverstone and Haddon 1996, p. 46)

In terms of the domestication approach the design of an artefact is seen as enabling and constraining its users, both in its materiality (through design) and by, for example, 'marketing' and 'public definitions'. In this chapter, we suggest that meanings are ascribed to ICTs as a result of participation on a course.

In addition, Silverstone flags that constraints can also be found at the level of the user. In this chapter, we show that users' different access to resources or forms of capital (Bourdieu 1986) is decisive in their ability to domesticate computers and the internet. Of these, social capital points at participation in social networks and the resources that can be mobilized through this network. Cultural capital can be defined as a configuration of achievements, dispositions and value orientations of various forms, whereas economic capital points to the financial resources at our disposal.

Forms of capital are not randomly distributed in society. As Cockburn remarked 'hidden within the innocent concept of resources ... is ... the historical patterning of the social by class, race and gender' (Cockburn 1992, p. 45). Hence, it is important to diversify users, on the basis of age, gender, ethnicity and educational background (Aune 1996; Berg 1999; Sørensen *et al.* 2000), as it is the gendered configuration of resources that influence our capacity to domesticate a new technology. This is especially relevant when studying late adopters or 'laggards': people that are late in adopting new technologies. In general when compared to early adopters: they have less formal education; are less likely to be literate; have lower social status; a smaller degree of upward social mobility; and they have every (financial) reason to be slow in the adoption of new technologies (Rogers 1995, pp. 280, 279). Indeed, we show in our empirical section, that the course participants had very rational motives relating to their lack of resources, for not domesticating the computer sooner.

Dimensions of domestication

How can a course change the domestication process of a technology? The answer to this question may be different for each step of the domestication process. This process is divided into dimensions or phases: 'appropriation' (sometimes called 'commodification'), 'objectification', 'incorporation' and 'conversion' (Silverstone *et al.* 1992; Berg 1996; Lie and Sørensen 1996; Silverstone and Haddon 1996). In the appropriation and conversion phase, emphasis seems to be on the symbolical meaning an artefact has, whereas during the objectification and incorporation dimension, the material expression of the symbolic meaning of the artefact is more relevant.

Appropriation is an activity within which both actual and potential consumers engage. It consists of imaginative work: commodities are constructed as objects of desire (or as something they do not want) and not only to fulfil specific functions but also as a construction of the desire for difference and social meaning (Silverstone *et al.* 1992, pp. 62–3). For some participants, the course influenced their decision to buy and use a computer. And this phase was relevant for those who already had access to computers and the internet, as it influenced their willingness to invest time and energy in attending the courses, complete homework and use more functions of their computers and internet connections. Some users (divided by class, age, gender and ethnicity) never pass the appropriation phase as they never make a 'technology-representation' of computers that fits their self-image; they simply never transform the public meaning of the artefact towards a personal meaning of something that is 'desirable'.

Several authors have noted that in non-domestic situations studying the appropriation phase by users becomes redundant because it is not the users who decide to buy the technology (Sørensen *et al.* 2000; Silverstone 2001). We would like to add to this observation that this is often also the case in household situations, where one member of the household decides for all members whether a computer should be purchased. Haddon, for instance, showed how girls were dependent on the appropriation decisions taken by their brother on what games they would play on the computer: the 'girls "just played" the games which were available' (Haddon 1992, p. 91). Hence, as other feminist researchers of technology (Bakardjieva 2001; Berg 1999), we want to call attention to the importance of who decides which technology is being appropriated, rather than studying the family as a unit and ignoring the different positions of various family members. In both cases we studied all appropriation decisions on what to use during the course, were taken by the course developers, leaving no agency on the part of the user.

During the phase of 'conversion', the personal meaning that the user has attached to the artefact is *conversed*, made part of the public meaning again. During this phase, the user displays his or her ownership and competence both materially and symbolically in a public culture, 'to whose construction it actively contributes' (Silverstone and Haddon 1996, p. 65). Thus, conversion is of importance in explaining how potential new users gain their representations of computers, once again starting the domestication process for new users. In a sense, a course can be regarded as a form of conversion instigated by course designers and teachers, consciously starting or intervening in the domestication process of the course attendees. Hence, depending on how course teachers conversed the meaning of the internet to participants, some of them decided to appropriate a computer at home, whereas others decided not to.

During the incorporation dimension,[3] in order to become functional a technology has to find a place into the routines of daily life. Hence, the main focus in this dimension is a temporal one (when it is used and for how long), whereas during the process of objectification, the object is given a space in the home. The analytical focus is on 'how values, taste or style are expressed in the display of the artefact' (Berg 1999, p. 5). We found that some disadvantaged users never pass these phases, as they never buy their own computer and continue to use computers at public places, with relatives, or during the course hours. Some stopped using computers altogether after finishing the course. In the following sections, we will discuss how the courses we studied contributed to, affected or even hindered the domestication process of computers by disadvantaged (potential users), showing how 'messy' the process can be (Lie and Sørensen 1996).

Methodology

For the Amsterdam introduction courses, four male and six female participants were selected on the basis of age and ethnic background. Their ages ranged between 44 and 70 and three informants originated from a country other than the Netherlands, namely Indonesia, Surinam and the United Kingdom. The informants were also diverse in their family situations and educational and professional backgrounds. Only two of them had a job.[4] On the whole, they seemed to be representative of the course participants in general. A longitudinal approach was adopted.

Semi-structured interviews were held during the time that they were following the course and a year after the course; five of them were interviewed in person and two by telephone. The first round of interviews were either held in the community centre, 'Westerpark', where the course was provided, or in their homes. The second round was held in their homes, to see what place the computer had obtained in the household. The informants were observed during the courses and documents of the course were studied. Interviews were held with the dominant actors who had set up the course, for example the leader of the community centre, the trainer and the course-material developers.

The Ballymun case was part of a wider doctoral project focused on domestic users of new multimedia technologies. Six informants were chosen for this case study from a number of school-run courses. Each informant had access to a computer and the internet in their homes. No informant had any prior training with computers other than tentative use at home. This case study employed both in-depth interviewing and participant observation (at home and at school) to achieve insights into how the computer is regarded in an educational sense (during the course) and also as a domestic technology (as another machine for the home). In addition, time-use diaries were used to get a sense of how the computer/internet fitted into the network of domestic media technologies available. Due to the fact that the informants were also compliant in a comprehensive study of domestic use of ICTs, it was possible to construct an understanding of how attending an IT course was influential in the way the technological artefact was further domesticated.

Description of the courses

Both courses were financed largely by the local municipality.[5] Partly as a result of this, both were aimed at a similar audience of those previously 'excluded' from the information society and participants from disadvantaged areas.[6] Courses were provided in a local community centre in the Dutch case and a local school in the Irish, where the practice of teaching courses of various kinds already existed. Moreover, in this way advantage was taken of the computer equipment and child care facilities available in both places.

Ballymun qualifies as a disadvantaged area of Dublin as the social and economic problems facing the area are complex, including unemployment, educational attainment and progression levels, welfare dependency, drug and substance abuse. The inhabitants of Westerpark, an area of Amsterdam, are very similar to those of Ballymun, and they also have a relatively low income, relatively high unemployment rates and high levels of ethnic minorities, and 80 per cent live in rental houses.

The backgrounds of the informants of both courses were varied but most were from working-class backgrounds and unemployed. The informants in the Irish case study were either parents of young children or had a connection with the school in some capacity, as the courses were school based and aimed at parents of young children attending the local school. The Westerpark case had a wider catchment area due to the decision to locate the course in a community centre. According to an evaluation of the introductory course, a total number of 264 people have participated in 32 course groups (Rommes 2003). Almost half of these people had a non-Dutch ethnicity.

While not overtly aimed at women, they were in both cases in the majority among the course participants. This can partly be explained by the fact that both courses were held one day a week during school hours to facilitate ease of access of minority groups (parents and women) who would otherwise be excluded from attending privately arranged courses. As a further incentive, free child care was provided by the schools to enable parents to avail themselves of the course.

Both courses were initially offered free, taking into account the low level of economic capital available to these groups. However, if students wished to pursue additional tutorials in advanced features of both computers and the internet, they were required to pay a fee. To aid the delivery of the course, public terminals were installed with free access throughout the Westerpark area. In the Ballymun area, public access to the internet was available only in the local library, yet as in the Westerpark study no informant testified to actually using the internet in a public space.

Although both courses were presented as an 'introduction to computers/internet', there were several differences between the courses in terms of course content and course organization. The Ballymun weekly course lasted one and a half hours and was delivered over a 10/12 week term, while, the Westerpark course consisted of four lessons of two and a half hours each.

The first two lessons of the Westerpark were aimed at familiarization with the technology, starting with basic skills, such as turning on the computer, learning to use the mouse, the keyboard and file management. In addition, an introduction to word processing was given, and students were instructed in internet uses and functions. The participants were provided with a course book to compliment the tutorials. The course book was primarily based on technical skills, with only one page dedicated to practical, everyday functions such as useful website URLs. The teachers delivering the course were previously employed by the community centre to teach other computer courses. They were drawn on by virtue of their patience and ability to stand back and allow the students to 'learn by doing'.

Similarly, the Ballymun course also set out to familiarize the course participants with the non-technical uses and functions of computers and the internet. This was achieved through the course content which demonstrated 'everyday' uses of the technology, such as designing household budgets using spreadsheet applications or using the internet to conduct research on summer holiday destinations.

Analysis of the domestication process

This section explores the role that IT courses play in the translation of the computer/internet from foreign object to an object of value and significance. In this process, it is important to address the types of resources participants bring with them. We argue that IT courses should not only provide the material resources for users, such as the hardware, the instruction, or access privileges, but that they should also support the symbolic resources, such as interest, motivation and the importance and meaning of the artefact to the user.

The following sections assess how influential the courses were in the process of domestication. We identify a problem with the 'ideal' four-stage model of domestication proposed by Silverstone. We regard the phases of appropriation and conversion to be intrinsically linked through their association with meaning generation, symbolic importance and value of the technology, while the objectification and incorporation phases are deemed to be concerned with use and material features of the courses. Moreover, a 'stages' model seems to suggest that one stage directly follows the next. We do not perceive such a linearity, especially in the objectification and incorporation dimensions. We show that the domestication process is not necessarily a linear process; users may stop halfway, or skip a stage.

Appropriation and conversion

The motivations and reasons associated with attending the course and getting to know computers are firmly located in the appropriation phase of the domestication process. As explained in above sections, appropriation is concerned with ownership or the first phases of 'getting to know' the technology. This phase is also bound with the symbolic interpretations of the technology.

Respondents from both case studies gave very similar reasons and motivations for attending the course. It seems that the increased visibility of ICTs in all aspects of daily life – from work environments to domestic spheres, has generated a perceived pressure for people to gain technological competencies and computer literacy in order to maintain a grip on modern society.

As a course participant in Ireland remarked:

> I think kids need to know it, for them, because in a couple of years time that's all it's going to be, and that's all it's going to be in the workforce. The computer's for the kids. Whether they're going into the mechanics of it, like fixing things, or whether

they are going into office work, they are going to need computer skills.

(Jenny, Dublin)

Similarly, a Dutch mother and a grandmother stated:

It was more for the children ... it is for the boys' homework. Well, they do grow up in a computer-world. I did not really think of myself when I bought it.

(Judith, divorced mother of two children, Amsterdam)

You have to experience and learn, you have to participate with everything. Especially now I have grandchildren, I want to help them with the computer. And I want to keep in touch with my children in Surinam.

(Eva, 71-year-old grandmother originating from Surinam,
Amsterdam)

From these quotes, it becomes clear that a major source of motivation for (grand)mothers to want to use computers is to be able to support their children (see also Smith and Bakardjieva 2001) and, for some older Dutch women, to keep in touch with their (grand)children. In addition, we get a sense of societal pressures, such as the changing nature of work to include a computer, which has a shaping influence on the ways computers are perceived. Computers are no longer seen as a luxury item or as an entertainment commodity but are now regarded as key instruments associated with education and employment, either for increasing their own chances on the job market, or, more often, for increasing the chances of future employment for their (grand)children.

Some of the Dutch participants seem to have been more motivated by other reasons, as mentioned by John:

I have always said: what do I need such a thing for? Because I do not need it, right? But, well, most of my friends use computers and they talk about the Internet and I think, my God, what are they talking about? ... I really feel like I should join, 'cause otherwise I will be looked at like I am backward. The only one who cannot use a computer.

(John, Amsterdam)

As John makes clear in this quotation, he identified use and knowledge of computers and the internet as means of maintaining a grip on technological advances and for not feeling excluded, which may be very significant for those that have been left out in one way or another, either by being unemployed, disabled or retired. They wanted to keep up with societal change, to avoid falling behind (technologically). The computer for them clearly was associated with a quest for social meaning and the desire for difference (Silverstone and Haddon 1996); or in this case, for the desire for sameness. Similarly, several Dutch course participants signified that they wanted to follow the course to know what their partner, son, children or grandchildren were so enthusiastic about, to feel involved in the world of significant others around them. Hence, social resources in the form of pressure of peers were decisive in their decision to domesticate a computer (Rogers 1995).

Finally, we found that some participants were eager to gain access to the information offered by the internet. Course participants, for instance, expressed the desire to seek information relating to gardening; nature, 'how things work'; the body; information on public transportation; and about where to travel with a disabled child. Many informants highlighted the feeling of security that knowledge associated with computers and internet provided. This was further enhanced by the majority of the course participants having little, or no, educational prowess.

The motivations we have summarized seem to relate to 'usefulness'. Hardly any of the course participants mentioned motivations associated with having fun or playing with the computer, or using the computer for no other reason but to explore 'what can be done with it'. They seem to feel a pressure to use the computer, with few enjoying the experience. Dutch course participant, Aram, comparing learning to use the computer, which he had to do for his job, with filling out a tax form: not fun, but necessary.

Did the courses satisfy those needs and motivations through the course curriculum and set-up? If the appropriation phase is to be passed successfully, it is vital that the personal meanings attached to the computer are translated into something that fits into their lives and their personal motivations, that is: addressing the cultural capital of its attendants. In these cases, the courses needed to guide course participants in how they could support their children with their computer use, improve the skills needed for further employment chances, and help in learning how and where to find the information for which they were searching. Furthermore, in order to support participants in their desire to 'keep up with the information society', it may have been helpful if they were taught some of the language associated with computers, and to learn about what can and cannot be done with computers, so that they could feel they had a grip on the information society again.[7]

Did the conversion[8] of the symbolic resources that were provided by the course organizers and instructors match the symbolic resources, expectations and desires of the participants? Did such factors lead to their appropriation of the computer? For several Dutch course participants the answer is no, and they became 'informed rejecters' after the course (Wyatt 2004). Early on in the course, they felt pressure from their social environment to keep up with modern society by using computers, whereas after the course they did not feel this pressure and they had some clear arguments relating to rejection of the computer. Participants could not find significance in learning some basic skills such as file management, or searching the internet. As John said after seeing the internet and after finishing the course: 'I feel very disappointed, I really am disappointed. I had imagined something nicer. Now I feel like I wasted my time, it is a real disappointment' (interview: John, Amsterdam). John decided not to buy a computer and not to continue with other courses. This is not to say that a course is 'unsuccessful', the question is whether participants were adequately 'informed', and whether an alternative course design could have conversed a meaning that would have made more sense. In this case, the course did not converse relevant meanings and it did not help movement through the appropriation phase.

The Dutch informants that continued to use the computer after the course had been regular users of the computer and the internet before participating in the course. Interestingly, the functions they used had little relationship to the course content and participants seemed to have found their own more meaningful activities, such as downloading and listening to music, finding information on public transportation, using chat and SMS programs with friends, helping their children with using the internet and photography processing programs. It seems the Dutch course failed to help course participants to find relevant meanings in computers.

The Irish case seems to have been more successful: the informants spoke about how the internet began to 'fit' their lives after the course. It transpired that the course designers successfully found ways of making the technology appealing and discovered instances where the technology could work for the users. The end product resulted in a shift of meaning, where the computer/internet, initially conceptualized as an educational tool for their children, became something increasingly meaningful for the course participant. The quotes below highlight the process of how the computer and internet achieved this transformation:

> I didn't have any previous experience with computers. Oh! I'd say in the beginning I literally didn't know how to turn it on and

now I can do the majority of stuff. There is still stuff I don't know about it but there was things I didn't know how to do like installing stuff, but now I'm installing things.

(Interview: Jenny, Dublin)

In Jenny's view the fact that she can now 'install things' is seen as a measure of her progress or as a positive outcome of the course. The computer has lost its sense of being an impenetrable alien object, and has become a formidable technology, deeply meaningful to her.

This is a common theme among the Irish respondents. Each spoke about their motives for joining the course in objective terms (for example, gaining knowledge for someone else's benefit) only to realize its functions and uses in subjective terms. The informants speak of how the computer/internet achieved a sense of embeddedness and meaning to them through use:

I don't think of it as something special. Maybe I would have beforehand, but seeing it now, I think it is just there ... At the beginning I thought it was great or something special, but I am used to it now. It's just another part of the place.

(Interview: Jenny, Dublin)

It is interesting to note that the computer is still regarded as holding some sort of interest or intrigue for Jenny in the ways she still wants to learn. In a similar fashion Marie confirms this:

I was absolutely terrified of it ... and ... of breaking it or anything else, you know ... but I feel more easy and since I started doing classes and since we got this (computer), I feel easier about the one at work. I feel more relaxed about trying something I wouldn't have tried before.

(Interview: Marie, Dublin)

The Ballymun course was successful in showing how the computer and internet are translated into something useful and meaningful to the participants on the course. It facilitated the domestication of the technology by teaching women the relevant skills and competencies so that the computer/internet could become something they could master and use in a meaningful manner. The Dutch course fell short in this respect as it adopted a 'one size fits all' approach in the course content and in its organization. Instead of designing the course from the participant perspective, addressing the needs and motivations of the participants, the Dutch case used a 'top-down' approach that assumed the skill level and technological competencies of the participants were homogeneous. It offered the participants a course which the participants had to fit themselves around instead of shaping the course to fit the requirements of the participants. In other words, it did not take the cultural capital of the course participants into account.

The appropriation phase is also concerned with issues relating to access and ownership. As stated before, the Ballymun course participants had access to the internet and computers at home while attending the course, whereas in the Westerpark case, not all informants had access at home. Hence, the Irish and Dutch participants differed in how far they had progressed in the phase of appropriation, which also may explain why more Dutch participants reversed the domestication process and decided that computers were not relevant to their lives. In the following section we discuss the relevance of owning a computer and the significance of giving it a place and a time in the home. These factors are crucial during the objectification and incorporation of new technologies.

Objectification and incorporation

During the objectification and incorporation dimensions of the domestication process, the computer is given a physical location and a timetable of use. To support these dimensions, courses need to appeal to course participants in the 'everyday' sense of practicality and usefulness. This is especially pertinent in the case of the Dutch participants who experienced a higher level of use and interaction with the computer during the course period but failed to continue using the computer after the course finished. It seems that the course provided its own rationale for using the computer on a temporary basis for the duration of the course. For example, it was used for completing course homework or practising skills, such as typing. Since many of the course participants did not fully pass the appropriation phase, this use of the computer was not integrated into their everyday pattern of life and they stopped using it all together after the course ended.

In reverse, the Ballymun course concentrated on bridging the gap between course work and everyday uses of the computer, which facilitated the transition from course-focused use to domestic use. This is very evident in the analysis of the time-use diaries which suggest that the computer and the internet have become a greater part of the everyday lives of the course participants. In 5 out of 6 diaries, the media consumption patterns of the course participants clearly show an increased use of the internet and computer following the course. It is interesting to reconcile the changing image/perception of the technology with the evidence produced in the time-use diaries. The following quotes highlight how the informants have witnessed the domestication of the technology.

> To me, it's nearly like the hoover, stereo, but yet it is special. Even, though when you buy something within weeks because you have worked for it and you have bought it and are delighted with it, it loses its novelty like everything does. I found the computer still lost the novelty of being a wonderful thing. But I find it a god send for me the knowledge is still there, I just think there is so much you can do with it.
>
> (Karen, Dublin)

Whether course participants had ownership of their computer influenced the domestication process and this was related to their economic resources and cultural capital. The Irish respondents spoke of how home-use increased the meaning and significance of the technology in their lives. They spoke about the importance of being able to interact with the artefact in a private sphere. In reverse, not all of the Dutch participants had access to computers and the internet at home. Moreover, in the year following the course, each of the course participants with access at home experienced major problems with using the computer for a longer period of time, as their computer broke down and needed to be repaired or replaced.[9]

As an alternative, the Municipality of Amsterdam included access to public terminals consciously as part of the project and several locations were opened to offer increased access to public terminals, in an area considered to be a 'safe' place for women: the public library. However, none of the informants had even considered using public terminals as an alternative, nor did they regard them as attractive. Truus, who had not followed the course, stated that she 'would feel ashamed' if she used it in a public place and it would not go well. It may be the case that the usage of computers in public spaces is less attractive for women than for men. Indeed, Rommes has shown that public terminals users in Amsterdam were mostly young males (Rommes 2002). Using computers in public spaces converses technological competence to the outside world, an image that in our society more readily fits with younger male users.

Some of the Westerpark course participants who did have access to the internet at home did not incorporate it in their everyday-life patterns. For example, Esther and Ine, both women of around 60 from Amsterdam, had bought a computer with their respective partner and spouse. After a while, Esther concluded that her partner should keep the computer in his house, as she never used it. Similarly, Ine, a year after the course, rather than using the computer herself, watched her husband use it. For these women, the phases of domestication do not necessarily follow each other and the process is not completed. It is possible for a user to follow a course, buy a computer and give it a place in the home, but this does not necessarily mean that the user will incorporate the artefact and ascribe it meaning in the home. Hence, the domestication process is not always successful and can stop when the user loses interest in the technology.

Conclusions

In this chapter, we have shown how the potential for domestication of technology is not the same for all users, because some can mobilize resources and capital in a more effective way than others. As a result, some users have to perform more work and adapt their lives more than others, or give up on a new technology altogether. Indeed, as Rogers remarked, new technologies often enlarge pre-existing differences in a society. In the cases presented, pre-existing differences in access to social, economic and symbolic resources impact on the extent to which the domestication process is successful. This notion of resources, both in a material and symbolic sense, is central, and social, economic and cultural resources have been shown to influence peoples' understanding of, and approach to, certain technologies and the ways they may or may not begin to domesticate these technologies. Use of the concept of domestication draws attention to these factors.

In addition, we have extended the current conceptualization of domestication to incorporate the influence of IT courses on the actual process of individual domestication of the computer. We wanted to move away from the idea that only users are active in the domestication process and, instead stress that external factors such as courses are also influential, for example, through the conversion of the meanings of computers via courses or other users. And we demonstrated that domestication is not an activity solely reserved for householders to experience but can also occur outside the home, even though this did seem to be much more problematic, as the lack of use of public terminals demonstrated.

We found that the concept of domestication, with the addition of attention to the different kinds of capital, seems to offer valuable insights for course developers, especially in terms of how to better support disadvantaged users in their domestication process. We have argued that IT courses should not only provide the material resources for users, such as the hardware, the instruction, or access privileges but that they should also support the symbolic resources, such as interest, motivation, the importance and meaning of the artefact to the user. Furthermore, course developers should consider the reasons why users invest time and money into these courses, what they expect to accomplish by completing the course and how the meaning of the computer and internet can change over time in the same way that people's needs and motivations change. We have shown that these expectations and motivations may be very different for 'laggards' than for earlier adopters, and that course designers often make assumptions about participants' individual needs and requirements.

As we have shown, the courses were, to some extent, successful in addressing participants' lack of resources. They addressed the lack of economic capital by participants through offering the courses for free and offering public access to computers. Social capital has proven to be crucial as motivation for using IT. Similarly, Stewart (2002) and Bakardjieva (2002) highlighted the importance of the presence of 'warm experts', knowledgeable friends or family, to help users in their domestication process of ICTs. By employing patient teachers who had some time for personal attention, this social capital was offered to the disadvantaged users we studied. It has, however, also become clear, that the Dutch course designers seem to have overlooked the importance of addressing the cultural capital of the courses participants. The course design did not take into account participants' previous and existing knowledge and meanings associated with computers; let alone that the courses could converse new meanings that fitted the lives of the participants more adequately.

Some Dutch course participants exhibited high levels of computer and internet use during the course and did not continue to use the computer after the course had finished. Hence, the course design needs to improve in conversing relevant meanings relating to the everyday lives of participants. On a theoretical level, this demonstrates that domestication can be momentary, reversed, or non-linear. Hence, we argue that the ideal phases domestication model could be renamed a multi-dimensional model of domestication.

We have shown that both the courses and the involvement and activity of users in all aspects of the domestication process have been crucial. By removing the agency of people or skipping over certain phases the end product (domestication) is disrupted. Courses not only support the domestication process, but conversely can disrupt the process of domestication, especially when the organizers and course material, as in the Dutch case, insist on a fixed or static translation of the computer that fails to complement the cultural capital of the potential user. We feel that courses should provide opportunities for participants to shape or construct their own personal interpretation of the technology through use. We suggest that by focusing the course curriculum on 'everyday' life uses and functions, the meanings associated with the computer become less prescribed and more open to flexible translations.

Notes

1. We are grateful for the financial support of the Information Science and Technology programme of the European Commission for the SIGIS project under which we conducted the case studies reported in this article. We are profoundly indebted to all of those course participants and course organizers who gave generously of their time to help us with the studies. We would also like to acknowledge the input of Katie Ward and of colleagues in the SIGIS network on developing the case studies that this work is based on (Hynes 2004; and Rommes 2003, 2004).

2. As Sørensen *et al.* wrote: 'in social studies of computing, there has been a surprising lack of interest in studying how people learn to use computers' (Sørensen *et al.* 2000, p. 246).

3. We regard the 'incorporation' and the 'objectification' phase of an artefact more as dimensions than as phases, because they do not necessarily follow each other in time.

4. Descriptions of all the course participants can be found at Hynes (2004) and Rommes (2004).

5. In addition, the Dutch courses were sponsored by national government, whereas the computers of the Irish courses were sponsored by the local education authority. The computer hardware was supplied by the 'Tesco: computer for tokens' initiative aimed at furnishing primary and secondary schools around the country with computers.

6. In terms of advertising the courses, potential participants for the Westerpark courses were reached with the help of door-to-door leaflets. The school in Ballymun used a number of methods to attract participants. First, the course was advertised in the local schools via a notice sent home with the schoolchildren or by a notice displayed in the window of the main entrance to the school. Second, the school also employed a home–school liaison officer whose responsibility it was to ensure communication between families and the school. In this role, the officer also invited and encouraged parents to participate in school-run courses.

7. Although for some it may have even been enough to feel connected

to society again to be able to say that they had followed a course, or that they did own a computer (whether or not they used it, as Berg showed: Berg 1999).

8. Whereas in most domestication descriptions, the conversion phase is concerned with symbolic meanings of the computer as they are conversed by its user (in this case, the course participants) as shown in the way the user presents the computer (material and semiotic) to the outside world.

9. This was partly the result of the fact that many of them used second- or third-hand computers. See also Thomas and Wyatt 2000 for the relevance of this for the trickle-down assumption in innovation studies.

References

Aune, M. (1996) 'The computer in everyday life: Patterns of domestication of a new technology', in (eds) M. Lie and K. H. Sørensen, *Making Technology Our Own? Domesticating Technology into Everyday Life.* Scandinavian University Press: Oslo, pp. 91–120.

Bakardjieva, M. (2002) *'Users as Innovators: A Perspective from Everyday Life,'* EASST paper, York.

Berg, A. (1999) 'Minitel, internet and everyday life: Domesticating progress?' in *Workshop on Technology and Modernity: The Empirical Turn.* Enschede: The Netherlands, p. 22.

Berg, A. (1996) *Digital Feminism.* Norwegian University of Science and Technology, Centre for Technology and Society: Trondheim.

Bourdieu, P. (1986) 'The forms of capital,' in (ed.) J. Richardson, *Handbook of Theory and Research for the Sociology of Education.* Greenwood Press: New York.

Cockburn, C. (1992) 'The circuit of technology; gender, identity and power', in (eds) R. Silverstone and E. Hirsch, *Consuming Technologies. Media and Information in Domestic Spaces.* Routledge: London, pp. 32–47.

Frissen, V. (1997) *Gender, ITCs and Everyday Life: Mutual Shaping Process.* COST A4, 6, Brussels, EC.

Gay, P. D., Hall, S., Janes, L., Mackay, H. and Negus, K. (1997) *Doing Cultural Studies; The Story of the Sony Walkman.* Sage Publications: London.

Haddon, L. (1992) 'Explaining ICT consumption, The case of the home computer', in (eds) R. Silverstone and E. Hirsch, *Consuming Technologies. Media and Information in Domestic Spaces.* Routledge: London, pp. 82–96.

Hynes, D. (2004) 'The role of computer courses in the domestication of the computer', in (eds) N. Oudshoorn, E. Rommes and I. v. Slooten, *Strategies of Inclusion: Gender in the Information Society, vol. III: Surveys of Women's User Experience*. NTNU: Trondheim, pp. 167–84.

Lie, M. and Sørensen, K. H. (1996) 'Making technology our own? Domesticating technology into everyday life', in (eds) M. Lie and K. H. Sørensen, *Making Technology Our Own? Domesticating Technology into Everyday Life*. Scandinavian University Press: Oslo.

Mackay, H. (1997) 'Consuming communication technologies at home', in (ed.) H. Mackay, *Consumption and everyday life*. Sage Publications: London, pp. 261–94.

Mansell, R. and Silverstone, R. (eds) (1996) *Communication by Design; The Politics of Information and Communication Technologies*. Oxford University Press: Oxford.

Rogers, E. M. (1995) *Diffusion of innovations*, 4th edn. The Free Press: New York.

Rommes, E. (2004) ' "I don't know how to fit it into my life". The gap between the inclusion initiative "Introduction courses computers and the internet" and the personal stories of the excluded', in (eds) N. Oudshoorn, E. Rommes and I. v. Slooten, *Strategies of Inclusion: Gender in the Information Society, vol. III: Surveys of Women's User Experience*. NTNU: Trondheim, pp. 491–510.

Rommes, E. (2003) ' "I don't know how to fit it into my life". Courses, computers and the internet for "everybody in Amsterdam"', in (eds) M. Lie and K. Sørensen, *Strategies of Inclusion: Gender in the Information Society, vol. 1: Experiences from Public Sector Initiatives*. NTNU: Trondheim, no. 63, 2003, pp. 151–66.

Rommes, E. (2002) *Gender Scripts and the Internet; The Design and Use of Amsterdam's Digital City*. Enschede: Twente University.

Silverstone, R. (2001) *'Under construction: New Media and Information Technologies in the Societies of Europe'*. A Framework Paper for the European Media Technology and Everyday Life Network (EMTEL 2), Trondheim, 20th June 2001.

Silverstone, R. and Haddon, L. (1996) Design and the domestication of information and communication technologies: Technical change and everyday life, in (eds) R. Mansell and R. Silverstone, *Communication by Design, The Politics of Information and Communication Technologies*. Oxford University Press: Oxford, pp. 44–74.

Silverstone, R., Hirsch, E. and Morley, D. (1992) Information and communication technologies and the moral economy of the household, in (eds) R. Silverstone and E. Hirsch, *Consuming Technologies; Media and Information in Domestic Spaces*. Routledge: London, pp. 15–31.

Smith, R. and Bakardjieva, M. (2001) 'The internet in everyday life: computer networking from the standpoint of the domestic user'. *New Media & Society*, vol. 3, no. 1, pp. 91–107.

Sørensen, K. H., Aune, M. and Hatling, M. (2000) 'Against linearity – on the cultural appropriation of science and technology', in (eds) M. Dierkes and C. v. Grote, *Between Understanding and Trust, The Public, Science and Technology*. Harwood Academic Publishers: Amsterdam, pp. 237–57.

Stewart, J. (2002) *Personal and social issues in the appropriation of new media products in everyday life: adoption, non-adoption, and the role of the informal economy and local experts*. PhD thesis, University of Edinburgh.

Thomas, G. and Wyatt, S. (2000) 'Access is not the only problem: using and controlling the Internet', in (eds) S. Wyatt, F. Henwood, N. Miller and P. Senker, *Technology and In/equality, Questioning the Information Society*. Routledge: London, pp. 21–45.

Wyatt, S. (2004) 'Non-users also matter: the construction of users and non-users of the Internet', in (eds) N. Oudshoorn and T. Pinch, *How Users Matter: The Co-construction of Users and Technology*. Cambridge MA: MIT Press.

8 The bald guy just ate an orange. Domestication, work and home[1]

Katie Ward

Boundary management: creating home and managing work

John,[2] a participant running a business from his home study, explained how his work was 'computerized' and how living and working in the same place demanded the management of boundaries separating work from home within the domestic environment. John explained the strategies of boundary management and how clear distinctions were maintained between work and family life. He talked about the rules and patterns surrounding the use and the physical location of the computer and mentioned an anecdote which indicated the fragility of home–work boundaries and the way in which they can easily collapse. A vigilant family member had carefully inspected the contacts of his wastepaper bin, which was kept just outside the study door and announced to other family members, 'the bald guy just ate an orange!' This illustrates both the need for successful, and sometimes the failure of, boundary construction in the home as a means to organize and control or 'domesticate' the internet in the home environment. Access to a computer and the internet facilitates 'home-work' and engenders a situation where work becomes computerized and symbolized by the presence of ICT technology.

Working at home requires not only an ability to complete the day's tasks, but also a degree of skill in the management of physical and symbolic boundaries relating to the public and private spheres and work and family life (Salaff 2002). The importance of 'boundary work' was a reoccurring theme throughout the majority of the 25 home-based interviews[3] that were implemented as part of a larger ethnographic study carried out over two years in a coastal town in North County Dublin, where I lived and worked. The interviews were concerned with the use and 'shaping' of the personal computer and internet media[4] by families in the domestic environment. They ascertained how families thought, felt and discussed the computer and internet media; whether it resolved problems; created arguments, and the extent to which it both transformed and slotted into existing household and family routine.

The purpose of this chapter is to focus on boundary management strategies employed by home-workers[5] to define 'home and family' and 'work space' within the domestic context. Using the data, I demonstrate the dynamic process that emerges from users' attempts to integrate and manage their computer technology within the home. Furthermore, with a focus on the home-workers' domestication[6] of the computer and internet, which facilitates working at home, I suggest that there is a close relationship between the stages of the domestication process, to the extent to which they merge and overlap, highlighting the fluid nature of the process. It will be suggested that the function ascribed to the technology by the user determines the way in which the technology will be displayed. Since one of the main uses of the computer is for work purposes, it is displayed in a study/work room that is distinct from other family space within the household in its spatial and temporal arrangements and rules.

It was clear that computers used for home-work purposes were also used for other activities by other family members. For example, John's wife used the computer to maintain contact with family members. However, when used for home-working, it was apparent that the user working at home spent time thinking about how to shape the technology to meet work-related needs. This involved specific spatial and temporal arrangements, which defined the use and display of the technology. Such arrangements enabled the control of work and provided the means to confine it within a routine. Before moving on to further examine the way in which home workers domesticate their internet technology, which is representative of their computerized work, I explore the notion of 'home' and provide an overview of the domestication concept and its stages.

Where is home? Towards a definition

In exploring the consumption of media technologies, Silverstone (1994) establishes the household as a site for explicating the dynamics, conflicts and values surrounding both the performances of consumption and domesticity and their intrinsic character. Careful attention is given to the understanding of domesticity and it is explicated in three dimensions: home, family and household. In explicating the notion of 'home', Silverstone provides an understanding, which avoids imposing a normative conceptualization onto this complex web of relations. Silverstone (1994) notes that the concept of 'home' has received criticism, suggesting that the idea of household is breaking down, is steeped in patriarchy and an outmoded concept. Yet, despite the problematization of 'home', he claims that notions of it have survived and conceives of it on a symbolic level, where its boundaries are 'under construction':

> Home is a construct. It is a place not a space. It is the object of more or less intense emotion. It is where we belong . . . Home can be anything from a nation to a tent or a neighbourhood. Home, substantial or insubstantial, fixed or shifting, singular or plural, is what we can make of it.
>
> (Silverstone 1994: 26)

Conceptions of home are also informed by the work of other scholars who have defined it with reference to its imagined and symbolic boundaries. Morley (2000) notes, for example, that it is difficult to separate the idea of family from that of home privatization and domesticity. He argues that homes are created not only by networks of connections, but also through consumerism, where the consumption of television is often at the heart of homemaking and the privatization process. Drawing on Douglas' work relating to the idea of the home as a 'gift economy', sustained by a system of exchanges, Morley suggests that viewing television has moved towards replacing social rituals surrounding mealtimes as one of the most significant keys in gift exchange and the ordering or time and space. Significantly, 'homemaking' is frequently depicted on television as a desirable activity and demonstrates the way in which television not only allows the emergence of the private family, but also demonstrates how to perform 'private-ness', domesticity or home; indeed, 'successful' home and family life.

Thus, for Morley, the notion of home is a fluid and imagined construct, which emerges from webs of interaction and communication that identify those included and those excluded. Other scholars have also explored the symbolic value of the home. Berg (1999), in her study of the smart home uses gender as a vehicle to distinguish house and home, she states that 'there is a crucial difference between a house and a home. It is women, in the main, whose work and skills make the former into the latter' (Berg 1999, p. 312).

Following Silverstone (1994) and others I present a version of home which is defined as operating at both a material and symbolic level. 'Home', in this instance, refers to the domestic, private sphere, and is understood as a symbolic space, constructed by the family who live in a particular household. The family is regarded as a web of human relations, whose interactions within a household construct a home: a symbolic entity that articulates the values and habitus of the family, while also finding constitution within those values.

Moral economy of the household: from formal to personal economy

The household is a site which enables the production of a home and within this process, the household has a complex double-edged role, where it is a site for consumption, allowing the creation of a symbolic reality representing 'home'; and the home, in turn, supports the values that allow its constitution and (re)construction. The construct of the home provides grounding for what Silverstone *et al.* (1992) term the 'moral economy of the household'. This refers to the process by which alien and alienating commodities are appropriated from the 'formal' economy and brought into the domestic sphere, where they are inscribed with private meanings and transformed into acceptable symbolic objects, which construct and articulate the values of the home.

Thus, the moral economy of the household is conceived of as both an 'economy of meanings' and a 'meaningful economy' (Silverstone *et al.* 1992, p. 18). The household is identified as a significant unit of consumption; the point at which goods are both consumed and appropriated into the private sphere of domesticity. Households, through their consumption of goods and services, become actively engaged with the formal economy, allowing the appropriation of consumables into the domestic realm; or their appropriation into a 'personal economy of meaning'. Commodities are given meaning according to the values of the home and are redefined, shaped and ascribed a function to adhere to the home's established routines, patterns and social hierarchy of gendered and aged roles. Through their introduction into the household, commodities become enmeshed within an economy of meanings, where they are moulded in accordance with the habitus of the home to produce a 'meaningful economy', which articulates of the values of the home. Thus, the home articulates the values that constitute it, which not only provides a knowledge base enabling 'meaningful' consumption and display of artefacts, but also allows the basis for the creation of a household identity.

For the home-workers in this study, the computer and internet are ascribed status within an *economy of meaning* relating to the organization of work and home; time and space. These arrangements for the technology are implemented through a dynamic process of accommodation and management and articulate a symbolic reality. They also play a role in producing new meanings, domestic arrangements and relationships. Not only do home-workers play an active role in shaping and constructing, domesticating and organizing the computer to contain and organize work, but their domestic arrangements are, to an extent, reconstituted by ICT technology and work. Thus, when explicating the introduction and integration of the computer and internet into the household, attention must not only be given to the users' cultivation of the technology, but the way in which the technology has the capacity to both sustain, reflect and reform domestic arrangements.

This tension is clearly articulated in the work of both Silverstone (1994) and Lie and Sørensen (1996), where it is acknowledged that the domestication process is problematic, not always seamless and sometimes unsuccessful. Indeed, it is argued that in appropriating media technology families not only integrate the technology, but also to a certain extent change their behaviour because of the technology. This theme is implicit through Silverstone's body of work and in particular it is evident when he discusses the way in which television has 'spawned supporting technologies and created new spaces: TV dinners, the TV lounge, the open plan itself (Silverstone 1994, p. 100). The implication is that although families actively engage in the domestication process, the technology plays a role in changing some habits and behaviours. Although he recognizes that media technologies represent a site of struggle and that artefacts can have an impact on human action, he states, 'it is the computer which is, as often as not, transformed by … incorporation, much more than the routines of the household' (*ibid.*, p. 20).

Domestication: a conceptual framework

The 'domestication' concept (Silverstone and Hirsch 1992; Silverstone 1994; Sørensen 1994; Lie and Sørensen 1996, Sørensen *et al.* 2000) informed the analysis of the data as a means to analyse users' struggle to manage the internet and work in the home. This concept has developed from perspectives which emphasize the 'social shaping of technology', where the user is perceived to take a dominant role in defining the nature, scope and functions of the technology. This approach aims to question discourses surrounding technological determinism, where technology is perceived to develop independently of society, having a significant impact on societal change (MacKenzie and Wacjman 1999).

The concept of domestication and subsequent development and criticism (Ling and Thrane 2001), provides a framework for analysing the 'career' of media technologies in the home, and is presented as a struggle between the user and technology, where the user aims to tame, gain control, shape or ascribe meaning to the artefact. When examining the relationship of technology to human action and human shaping socio-technological relations, Sørensen (1994, pp. 3–6) favours an approach that is sensitive to the agency of the user, an approach that 'in principle empowers consumers/users' (*ibid.*, p. 5). 'Tinkering' or the 'production acts of consumers' are seen as key factors in the shaping of the technology. The artefact is given meaning through a 'multi-dimensional process of negotiation, involving humans and non-humans', consisting of conflict as well as collaboration. While users have the capacity to actively shape the technology, the artefact has the potential to influence human action as well. For Sørensen, one of the key questions about the relationship between humans and technology is whether artefacts are used in the prescribed or intended manner or are changed and shaped to meet a specific set of needs.

It is reiterated that 'there is no technology without action', the premise being that users' actions matter, allowing a degree of 'interpretative flexibility' when they attempt to integrate a new technology into the domestic routine. Artefacts then are ascribed with meaning and functionality, which is bound with the reproduction and transformation of relationships. It is emphasized, however, that the domestication process is not necessarily harmonious, linear or complete. Rather, it is perceived as a process borne of, and producing, conflict where the outcomes are heterogeneous and sometimes irresolvable. For example, it is noted that needs and households change, through divorce or children leaving; the implication being that the domestication process must continue, shaping the technology to new relationships and the emergence of new needs in the household.

Similarly, it is suggested, by Silverstone (1994) that technology[7] is consumed within specific and localized contexts, where it becomes inscribed with meaning, while reproducing values and transforming relations. The household is a space where technology is adopted, consumed, argued about and, with varying degrees of success, integrated into domestic culture: the site where technology as an object and as mediator of public culture is shaped to meet the needs and reproduce the values of the home. In exploring the centrality of the media in everyday life and its integration into domestic patterns and routines, Silverstone provides a model through which consumers' relationship with the television can be approached and analysed. It is noted that in bringing media technologies such as television into the home, they must be managed, allowing them to find an appropriate place in the structure of the home. This process is referred to as domestication: 'By domestication I mean something quite akin to the domestication of the wild animal ... a process of taming or bringing under control. Technologies, television and television programmes must be domesticated if they are to find a space or place for themselves in the home' (Silverstone 1994, p. 83).

Domestication, then, refers to the movement of the artefact from the public realm to the private. The consumable, in the process of domestication, is transformed from cold and meaningless product into a desirable part of the home. In appropriating a good, consumers enter a struggle for control and the artefact becomes a site for the negotiation of meanings. For example, when a television is located in the home, rules and routines are applied, to allow the household to sustain routine and rearticulate its values. The domestication of media technology requires active involvement, allowing the good to be integrated into the existing patterns in the household. It is at this level that families produce their media technology, creating them to reflect and articulate the habitus of the home.

The process of integrating media into the household is referred to as the process of 'domestication' where six moments of consumption are identified. This begins with production within the formal market economy and ends at the stage where the family is using the good to make a statement about the values of the home.[8] Following the production stage in the process, and before the consumer reaches the purchasing stage, it is observed that he or she enters the phase of 'imagination', where advertising fuels desire for the artefact. Subsequently, the good is purchased, and this is referred to as the stage of 'appropriation'. This consists of 'objectification' or the active shaping of the object to merge with the physicality of the household and of 'incorporation' or the process of ascribing meaning within household rituals and rules. Thus, throughout the process the object is given meaning so that it not only reaches a 'taken-for-granted' status in the household, but is also used to carry symbolic values about the home to the outside world. This final stage is called 'conversion' (Silverstone 1994; Silverstone and Hirsch 1992).

Silverstone is careful to state that the stages of domestication, 'can be considered as neither discrete, nor necessarily as evenly present, in all acts of consumption (1994, pp. 123–4). Indeed, it is emphasized that this approach to consumption is a model or sketch: an ideal type. In building on this notion, I use examples of data to illustrate the often 'untidy' process of domestication. More specifically, I focus on the 'objectification' and 'incorporation' stages of the domestication process to examine the tensions, changes, organizational processes and value judgements that emerge when a computer and the internet are used in the domestic sphere for work purposes. I provide rich illustrations of the way in which home-workers arrange the household and change temporal routine to accommodate the computer, while also shaping and integrating the computer into the existing habitus of the household. Furthermore, I confirm that the stages of domestication are not necessarily discrete or linear (Silverstone and Hirsch 1992; Silverstone 1994; Sørensen 1994) by suggesting that participants blur the predefined stages of incorporation and objectification, not only rendering them indistinct, but also indicating that the process is far from smooth, frictionless and precise.

Home and work

For those whose work was largely home-based, the computer technology, facilitating homework, presented tensions which manifested as a struggle between the accommodation and management of the technology and its (re)construction as an acceptable and useful artefact and symbol within the household. Although the computer and internet presented challenges and created tensions, it emerged that home-workers did attempt to exercise some control over the technology. When discussing the techniques employed to manage and accommodate the technology and distinguish work from home, participants invariably referred to three factors:

- the careful organization of space, domestic and technological artefacts to distinguish work from leisure/home/family space;
- the division of time into 'work' and 'family/leisure';
- the attachment of specific meaning to all household media to distinguish work and leisure activities.

However, such careful attention to domestic arrangements points not only to a desire to shape the technology and curb the presence of work, but also suggests how the intrusion of the technology can incite certain behaviour patterns, as home-workers begin to accommodate the imposition of the technology in private space. The integration of the computer into the domestic environment is double-edged in the sense that the arrangements made to accommodate the technology also serve as the means to integrate and domesticate it, thus highlighting the close relationship between the management and accommodation of the technology and its reproduction as a meaningful, domesticated artefact. The computer, as a focus for work in the home, while undergoing a 'shaping' process also becomes a catalyst for transformation and I identify the emergence of a complex dynamic between management and accommodation, or organization and acceptance of the internet and its intrusion into the private sphere. For example, although considerable attempts are made to 'tame' the technology in the sense that it is placed in a specific room and ascribed a routine that poses minimal disruption to family life, participants such as John, who had deliberately created a home study, could be perceived as being 'determined' by the technology; the changes to temporal routines and spatial arrangements in the household merely harbouring the encroachment of web-based work into private space.

Those working at home prioritized the negotiation of physical space and spatial and temporal boundaries and in Silverstone's frame of reference, this activity would be understood under the headings of 'objectification' and 'incorporation'. Objectification refers to the display of technology and incorporation refers to the integration of technology 'into the routines of daily life' (Silverstone and Hirsch 1992, p. 24). Although Silverstone recognizes that the boundary between objectification and incorporation is often indistinct, he makes the point that 'there is a difference between use and display [...] which of course has a special relevance to technology' (*ibid.* 1992, pp. 14, 29). For household users working at home in this study, the line between objectification and incorporation is ambiguous. Furthermore, the struggle to manage and accommodate the technology and the active creation of boundaries to distinguish work from home is shown to disrupt the stages of objectification and incorporation, blurring and rendering them indistinct.

When a home computer is introduced into the domestic environment, it becomes integrated into the household's routines and activities (Lally 2002). For participants who worked at home in their own business; as a journalist; freelance; or on a day a week basis, the computer and internet began to represent work, where work activity was facilitated by ICT use. Indeed, the technology symbolized work and this was demonstrated in the way that the computer was seen as a work tool, and in some cases prioritized for work purposes. For example John's children did not use his computer as it was used for work purposes and perceived as 'fragile': 'The children are not into it, but they know that that's work and I can't ... the system is fragile.'

When a computer is introduced into the home and used frequently for work purposes, it becomes difficult to distinguish the technology from work. When asked about how he structured and managed his day, John started to talk about the demands of email, which indicated the way in which the internet technology engenders a situation where work activity is indistinguishable from the features of the technology: 'If you asked those people to break down their working day, how many hours are spent on the mobile or email and a lot of online stuff is the sort of stuff that you would have put off in the past. Email demands a response. I start my day with email.'

Given the close relationship between work and technology it becomes difficult to distinguish where one begins and the other ends. Similarly, work and home overlapped. For example, Michael talked about the close relationship between work and home: 'Work and home overlap. I might be sitting up at my desk upstairs – I might be dealing with domestic matters, but people do that at work.' He noted that such blurred boundaries were not confined to home-workers, but also experienced in traditional workplaces. However, his observation indicates how it becomes important to manage the boundaries separating 'work' from 'family' life and this is achieved through the active implementation and management of strategies to mark the two activities. For example, John talked of the way he separated work from family activities through the use of temporal boundaries: 'I'll occasionally be doing projects that do require me to work at the weekend because you promise a good end product to a tight deadline. When that happens at the weekend, I might say I need one of the days at the weekend. Then the family activities are kept separate.' Conversations with participants included a focus on management strategies and the ways in which the introduction of the technology and computerized work was balanced with its integration into the household routine. The creation of a meaningful 'home and family' space, which was perceived as separate from work was of paramount importance to participants who managed work at home and most participants recognized that conscious attempts are required to manage boundaries.

The internet can disrupt the intricate dynamics and balance of household routine and value system, provoking a need to manage the intrusion; prompting users to reaffirm the family's sense of stability and coherence. The interviews and conversations with users are intriguing, providing insight into, and appreciation of, the manifold processes embarked on by home-workers in attempting to shape and organize the internet. Most users carefully balanced the 'intrusion' of the technology and its ability to disrupt the household's value system, accepting the inevitability of some changes, with active attempts to domesticate the new medium. Indeed, on the one hand, the internet provokes purposeful changes in the household's arrangements, relating to issues such as spatial and temporal arrangements, suggesting that the user is 'shaped' by the technology; yet, on the other hand, the user gives thoughtful attention to the ways the computer can be organized in terms of its function, location, spatial and temporal boundaries and the relationship with other media in the household to maintain and perpetuate the family's value system and sense of stability.

For the remainder of this chapter, the domestication concept and its application to those participants who worked from home are further developed. I demonstrate the way in which participants engage in a struggle with the technology, and the work it brings, in an attempt to achieve a balance between accommodating and managing their intrusion and integration into the home environment. Furthermore, the fluidity of the domestication concept will be highlighted and the way in which the stages merge together, producing a non-linear process of integration.

Domesticating the internet: Objectification and incorporation

As Silverstone (1994) indicates, all the stages in the process of domestication merge together, and for the remainder of the chapter I focus on the stages of objectification and incorporation, illustrating the close relationship between the use and display of the technology and the way in which these stages of domestication merge alongside the struggles and tensions surrounding the integration, management and accommodation of the technology in the home. I show how the two stages are often rendered indistinct in the sense that the organization of routine and rules and the physical arrangement of the household are closely bound with the creation of a physical space to suit a set of specific needs.

Participants made conscientious attempts to create and manage boundaries and all of the participants, when working from home, were keen to separate their 'family' and 'leisure time' from their 'work life' and this involved the creation of symbolic boundaries in the household. They created and attached specific meanings to the computer and internet, confined its use to a particular room and defined times for use, allowing the creation of symbolic boundaries in the home. For example: Jenny and Richard located the computer upstairs so that it would not intrude on the family space in the living room; Siobhan used her laptop for work in an upstairs study. Alex found he had to relocate his computer to an area that was conducive to work as he needed to redefine his leisure and work time: 'It's usually located in the study, it was in the sitting room I would spend far too much time watching TV as well. I would have to be more strict about the TV and the internet.'

John also divided the house so that the study represented work and the remainder of the house symbolized time spent with the family. Indeed, the house had been divided into 'zones', where the front room is used as an office, indicating that a careful decision-making process had been applied to the locating and display of the computer and internet: 'There's a room at the front, which is the office and when I'm in there

I'm at work ... I do shut off from 5.30–8.00, which is when everyone is fed and bathed, busy time for the kids, and then depending on what's going on in the evening I can get back to it.'

John's decision-making process suggests that he has made a set of specific arrangements to control the technology. To some extent John's arrangements have been determined by the imposition of the technology and of computerized work. Yet, on the other hand, John's attempt to contain the technology could also be perceived as an attempt to tame and regain control over it, indicating that domestication is a conflictual and dynamic process. Hence, although John had made special arrangements to accommodate the technology, he successfully imposed a temporal routine on his computer use and work life. Through effective time management, the participant ensured the construction of a domestic 'home life', which involved time spent eating meals with the rest of the family and engaging in routines surrounding children's bath and bed time. To make the distinction more apparent, the participant had established a number of 'rules' surrounding the use of the computer to distinguish it and internet as tools to be used for work purposes. The main use centred on the running of his business; his wife occasionally used the email facility as a means to maintain contact with family and friends abroad, but the four children did not engage with the computer or internet as the participant feared the system was delicate and did not want to risk losing valuable material.

These strategies to manage the technology demonstrate the close relationship between objectification and incorporation, illustrating the ways in which use and display are closely bound when attempting to contain work within the domestic environment. Similarly, Michael was concerned to make the distinction between home and work using temporal routine and the division of space as means for dividing home and work life. He went on to talk about the struggle experienced in maintaining convincing boundaries and the importance of temporal routine in maintaining domestic structure:

> I rarely work downstairs ... I do close the door at 6.00 and relax, because that's work, you do have to close the door at some stage ... It's hard to keep home and work separate – I do try and stop at 6.00 when my wife comes home. If she's coming home late I work late.

Like John, Michael also observed that he managed his internet use via the imposition of temporal routine and the division of the house into zones. The home office was located upstairs and the downstairs was perceived as the area for performing 'home life' as opposed to 'work life'.

Again, a focus on the separation of home and work time and space demonstrates the close relationship between use and display and the way in which participants are often required to make changes to their spatial and temporal arrangements to accommodate and manage the technology and computerized work.

The domestic organization of work and leisure

There is a close relation between use and display of the technology. The dynamic process of domestication, however, can also be identified in relation to the organization of work and leisure. Home-workers pay careful attention to the domestic organization of work and leisure, suggesting that the definition of leisure time and space was paramount in maintaining control over work in the home.

In an attempt to preserve her home life as a space separate from work, Siobhan divided the house into 'work' and 'leisure' zones and devised a strategy relating to financial organization and telephone bill payment. Siobhan accepted that work-related email frequently infiltrated the domestic arena, but in attempt to maintain certain zones in the house as symbols of 'home' installed two phone lines, where the upstairs line in the study room was used for work purposes and the downstairs connection in the living room for leisure and entertainment. Furthermore, the two phone lines allowed the participant to exercise control over the cost of the internet which further differentiated work from home. Having two phone lines ensured that she was in a position to monitor the payment situation; calls from the downstairs line were associated with leisure and therefore perceived as her responsibility: 'When I do that [use the internet for leisure/entertainment/personal research] I pay for my own calls. I have an itemized bill, so any calls for work, I call from the upstairs line. Calls from down here I pay for myself.'

As with John and Michael, Siobhan, in her endeavour to manage work at home was keen to establish boundaries in relation to work and leisure and in doing so gave careful attention to the routines surrounding use of the technology and its display. On the one hand it could be suggested that Siobhan has been shaped by the impact of the technology and computerized work, highlighting the specific spatial and financial arrangements to accommodate the presence of her work. On the other hand, it could be suggested that through the installation and use of two phone lines; the division of the house into zones; financial management; and the creation of specific patterns relating to the consumption of content, Siobhan effectively created 'two versions' of the internet, which had unique patterns and rules relating to use and display, allowing effective domestication and governing of the technology. Nevertheless, it seems that Siobhan has experienced the management and domestication of her technology as conflictual and dynamic in terms of its use for both leisure and work: the manifold nature of the process exemplified by her use patterns. Siobhan discussed, with enthusiasm, her use of the internet for leisure purposes and explained, with amusement, her self-imposed rules of access. Indeed, when the internet was accessed downstairs it was associated with home and leisure and she carried out activities such as personal travel-related research and shopping. By way of contrast, when used upstairs it was strictly as a work tool: 'At home, it is associated with leisure ... I have stopped buying magazines. I go to their website for make-up tips and fashion. I sit down with a cup of coffee and the internet, but that's down here [in the living room] and not up there [in the upstairs study]!'

Siobhan made an interesting point relating to the resonance of specific use and display patterns and their intrinsic value in the maintenance of symbolic boundaries. When using the internet for leisure she sits downstairs ('not up there!') and further defined this activity through sitting down with a cup of coffee and consuming magazine content from the internet. In consuming the internet in a specific manner, Siobhan effectively created her 'own' internet that not only had meaning within her household, but also allowed the management of work in the domestic environment. Furthermore, her use of language is interesting and revealing. Although Siobhan had two phone lines in the home for work and for leisure-related use, she referred to 'home' use in the context of 'leisure' time because she unequivocally associates home with leisure, as opposed to work. This illustrates the importance of boundary creation and management and the ways in which use patterns and display of the technology are closely bound in the management and domestication of the computer in the home. She further defined her work and leisure activities through the use of two email addresses, one for work and one for personal communications. She acknowledged however that imposed boundaries separating work and home sometimes fail.

Similarly, as indicated above, John divided the house into work and leisure zones. These divisions were further reinforced, however, through the meanings that were attached to other media in the household and the way that they were defined in relation to the internet. For example, John strongly associated the television with leisure and relaxation, whereas the internet was used purely for work. Hence, John gave different meanings to the TV and internet as a way of managing work in the domestic environment.

In this household, the television and internet, both in terms of location and use patterns, were set up in opposition to each other as means to protect the boundaries of home from those of work. For John, the symbolism of the television and internet were central in helping to define those boundaries. The internet was perceived as a work tool and not associated with leisure or relaxation, whereas the television was given status as a medium of leisure. In defining the television's function as a tool of entertainment and the internet as a medium of work, the participant has created a situation where the media conserve and separate 'home' from 'work' activity. Again, the attachment of specific meanings to different household media shows that domestication is a dynamic process, in the sense that effort has to be made to give symbolic meaning to all media outlets in the household. Yet, the process of ascribing meaning allows John to gain effective control over his work. Similarly, Alex talks about the way in which he imposes temporal routine on his work and leisure time and the way in which the TV is used to define relaxation, symbolizing an end to work activity: 'I don't use the internet after 8 p.m. I swap over to the TV. I use the internet more for work than entertainment, but I do use it for entertainment.'

Conclusion: a domesticated internet?

Wellman and Haythornwaite (2002) present the internet as a system that is incorporated into the routine of everyday life. They suggest that it has become embedded into community building, family connections, education, complementing individuals' existing networks, attitudes, behaviour and experiences. Similarly, Salaff's (2002) study of home-workers has suggested that the home internet has been constructed as a tool to be integrated into the fabric of everyday life, rather than an entity divorced from mundane domesticity. This chapter has suggested that the integration of computer technology and computerized work into the household and home is a complicated process, where participants must negotiate the intrusion of both the technology and work in their home lives.

The findings from interviews with domestic users have been framed in relation to literature relating to domestic media consumption; specifically, the domestication concept as developed by Sørensen (1994) and Silverstone *et al.* (1992, 1994). I have argued that the integration of technology into the household is most accurately described as non-linear, where the stages of domestication begin to merge together. Certain stages in the domestication process can be recognized in the data, but participants do not impose a linear career onto their technology. Rather than progressing through the stages of domestication, participants often blur and merge specific stages in the domestication process. Many home-workers prioritized a particular stage in the process and organized their computer and internet in a way appropriate to the household.

Using the domestication concept, I have also illustrated ways in which specific rules and routines surrounding spatial and temporal organization are established to govern patterns of use and display of the computer, to accommodate the presence of computerized work. It has become apparent that integration of technology into the household is dynamic, and does not follow a predefined career or process. Working at home is an interesting case to that end. In building a home office, participants not only make decisions about the purchasing and appropriation of technology, but also about specific spatial and temporal arrangements to segregate 'work' from 'family' activity. Home users played an active role in organizing and personalizing 'their' internet, for example, by creating two versions of the internet using different phone lines and different financial arrangements as Siobhan did.

The process is, however, not always without conflicts. It can be ambiguous, implying that the technology has a degree of 'agency'. John for example, a home-worker with young children, made special arrangements when positioning the technology in the household, suggesting a conflictual relationship between user and technology. On the one hand, this can be seen as an active attempt to control and organize the technology to suit the needs of all the individuals in the household, but on the other, it could be suggested that the users are 'determined' to make these arrangements by the very intrusive nature of home-working.

Both Sørensen *et al.* (2000) and Ling and Thrane (2001) refer to the needs of individuals in their theses. Likewise, the requirements of individuals in the household were also significant factors for the participants in this study, when incorporating a computer into the domestic setting. The main aim of home-workers was to create physical and symbolic boundaries between work and home, and participants employed a number of strategies, such as the organization of space, time and media consumption to achieve the management of those boundaries. Home-workers make significant choices about the way in which they organize spatial and temporal routines and individuals' access to the computer as a means of segregating work from home.

Home-workers were concerned with the domestication or organization of the computer and one of the most significant features in this organizational process was the computer's positioning in the relationship with other media in the household. Participants were eager to organize the internet alongside their existing patterns of media consumption and defined their computer and internet use in relation to other media. Engagement with, and meanings attached to other media were also important in terms of participants dividing their homes into zones. For many participants the television symbolized leisure, whereas the computer was associated with work. Thus, like the organization of time and space, the computer and internet's relationship with other media plays a significant role in its domestication. This can be seen in the cases of John and Alex where the television was used to define home and leisure, both in terms of space and time. The challenge offered by other media in the household coupled with the struggle to manage and accommodate the technology may constitute one of the many relevant questions for future domestication research.

Appendix: Participating households

Interview pseudonyms	Household composition (Ads: Adults / Ch: Children)	Occupation (HW: Housewife)
1 Katherine and Brian	2 Ads; 2 Ch (under 5)	Accountant; HW and student
2 Peter, Margaret, Robert	3 Ads; (2 parents and 1 university student)	HW, Management in ICT sector
3 Mandy, Simon, Jessica, Daniel	2 Ads; 2 Ch (9 and 7)	Clerical worker; taxi driver
4 Janet and Gary	2 Ads – children away at university	Lecturer; airport worker, writer
5 Jenny and Richard	2 Ads; 3 Ch (4–11)	Both running own businesses
6 Sam and Joan	2 Ads	Retired
7 Lucy and Alex	2 Ads; 1 baby	Postgraduate students
8 James and Ellen	2 Ads	Journalist; HW
9 Joe, Mary and Sarah	2 Ads; 2 Ch (4 and baby)	Own business (local shop); wife
10 Tim, Maggie, Emer, Rebecca	2 Ads; 2 students (16 and 19)	Teacher; County Council – admin
11 Siobhan and Oliver	2 Ads	Both employed in ICT sector
12 Stephen and Joanne	2 Ads; 3 Ch (under 5)	Artist (own gallery); HW
13 Paul and Karen	2 Ads; 2 Ch (8, 3)	Manager; bank cashier
14 Terry and Liz	2 Ads; 2 Ch (11, 13 + friend)	Teacher; citizen adviser
15 Sam, Helen and Chris	2 Ads; 1 Ch at home and in flat in Dublin	Retired; trainee mgr, marketing

16 Michael and Charlotte	2 Ads; 4 Ch (under 5)	Own business; HW
17 Marie and Patrick	2 Ads; 5 children (11–21)	HW, manual worker
18 David	2 Ads; 2 Ch (13 and 11)	Teacher; HW
19 Vicky and Nick	2 Ads; 1 Ch (baby)	Clerical worker; management
20 Jack and Ruth	2 Ads; (grown 'child')	Teacher; nurse; (artist)

Notes

1. I would like to acknowledge the support of colleagues in the EMTEL II network in the completion of the research. I would like to thank Paschal Preston for his encouragement and mentoring throughout my participation in the EMTEL network and beyond.
2. All names have been changed to protect the identity of the users.
3. See Appendix for details on participating households. See also Chapter 11, by Jo Pierson, on the blurring of boundaries between home and work.
4. Internet media refers to electronic communication in the form of email, bulletin board forums, email listservs and interactive and non-interactive websites. All the participants in the study accessed web-based content through an internet enabled PC. A few participants had, in addition, a set-top box, but preferred to use the PC. The PC was preferred as it allowed navigation using a mouse, whereas the set-top box was perceived as limiting in its capacity for browsing.
5. Home-workers refers to those participants who had chosen to work from home.
6. The domestication concept has been developed in the UK and Norway and has been applied by others in Europe and Canada (see Ling and Thrane 2001; Smith and Bakardjieva 2000, and Introduction of this text).
7. In his body of early work, Silverstone develops the domestication concept largely in relation to television. In later work (1999) Silverstone makes reference to the internet as a medium that is actively shaped and integrated into the everyday domestic environment.
8. The process of domestication has been explored consistently in Silverstone's body of work relating to media consumption. However, there is some variation in the model between the different texts. For example, in earlier work (1992) four stages of domestication are

recognized and in later work (1994) there is elaboration of the initial stages in the consumption process.

References

Berg, A.-J. (1999) 'A gendered socio-technical construction: The smart house', in (eds) D. MacKenzie and J. Wajcman, *The Social Shaping of Technology*, 2nd edn. Open University Press: Buckingham, pp. 301–14.

Lally, E. (2002) *At Home with Computers*. Berg: Oxford.

Lie, M. and Sørensen, K. H. (1996) 'Making technology our own? Domesticating technology into everyday life', in (eds) M. Lie and K. H. Sørensen, *Making Technology our Own? Domesticating Technology into Everyday Life*. Scandinavian University Press: Oslo, pp. 1–30.

Ling, R. and Thrane, K. (2001) 'It actually separates us a bit, but I think that is an advantage: The management of electronic media in Norwegian households,' in *Proceedings of International Conference 'E-Usages'*: Paris, pp. 148–59.

MacKenzie, D. and Wajcman, J. (1999) *The Social Shaping of Technology*, 2nd edn. Open University Press: Buckingham.

Morley, D. (2000) *Home Territories: Media, Mobility and Identity*. Routledge: London.

Salaff, J. W. (2002) 'Where home is the office: New forms of flexible work,' in (eds) B. Wellman and C. Haythornwaite, *The Internet in Everyday Life*. Blackwell: MA, pp. 464–96.

Silverstone, R. (1999) *Why Study The Media*. Sage: London.

Silverstone, R. (1994) *Television And Everyday Life*. Routledge: London.

Silverstone, R. and Haddon, L. (1996) 'Design and the domestication of information and communication technologies: technical change and everyday life', in (eds) R. Mansell and R. Silverstone, *Communication by Design. The Politics of Information and Communication Technologies'*. Oxford University Press: Oxford, pp. 44–74.

Silverstone, R. and Hirsch, E. (eds) (1992) *Consuming Technologies: Media and Information in Domestic Spaces*. Routledge: London.

Silverstone, R., Hirsch, E. and Morley, D. (1992) 'Information and communication technologies and the moral economy of the household,' in (eds) R. Silverstone and E. Hirsch, *Consuming Technologies: Media and Information in Domestic Spaces*. Routledge: London, pp. 15–32.

Smith, R. and Bakardjieva, M. (2001) 'The Internet in everyday life: computer networking from the standpoint of the domestic user'. *New Media & Society*, vol. 3, no. 1, pp. 67–83.

Sørensen, K. (1994) '*Technology in use: Two essays in the domestication of artefacts,*' STS Working Papers 2/94. Senter for teknologi og Samfunn, Trondheim.

Sørensen, K., Aune, M. and Hatling, M. (2000) Against linearity: On the cultural appropriation of science and technology,' in (eds) K. Sørensen, K. Aune and M. Hatling, *Between Understanding and Trust. The Public, Science and Technology.* Harwood Academic Publishers: Amsterdam, pp. 237–57.

Wellman, B. and Haythornwaite, C. (eds) *The Internet in Everyday Life.* Blackwell: MA.

9 Making a 'home'. The domestication of Information and Communication Technologies in single parents' households

Anna Maria Russo Lemor

Introduction

In the most recent US census (Fields and Casper 2001), there were 12 million single-parent households. Population projections estimate that half of the American children born in the 1990s will spend some time in single-parent households (Amato 1999). Despite the growing presence in the USA as well as in Europe (European Commission 2001) of single-parent families, qualitative research on these households is at present fairly limited, especially in relation to mass media. Nevertheless, there is much to suggest the need to explore, more fully, the ways in which this cohort incorporates new and old media use into their everyday lives.

In recognition of the increasing social significance of single-parent families, this chapter, based on the author's dissertation study, stresses the importance of considering family arrangement as an influential factor in individuals' attitudes towards media and their consumption practices within the contexts of everyday life. Indeed, this chapter illustrates how the roles of media and ICTs as symbolic sources and resources in single-parent families are influenced by social, material and emotional factors, which affect their everyday life.

On the one hand, the particular lifeworld of these families strongly supports the complexity of the processes, especially those of appropriation and incorporation of ICTs, involved in the twofold relationship between households and ICTs described in the domestication theory (Silverstone *et al.* 1992, p. 16). On the other hand, these parents' particular family structure and everyday life complicate the concept of the moral economy within the domestication theory, which presupposes only one household as a unit whose boundaries are, although flexible, still traceable. In the case of my informants, the line delimiting their 'home' is rather blurred and confused, since for their families, there are at least two households (the home of each parent and sometimes also the one of a new partner) involved, with their own independent but interconnected moral economies, which have a rather consistent weight on both parents' decision-making processes regarding rules and routines for the children, including, also, their consumption of ICTs. In addition, this 'extended' household is also immersed in what some of the interviewees called 'village', the large social network of friends and non-family members that has a rather influential role in the life of these parents and in relation to the choices of media for their children.

This social network reflects the negotiation and adaptation processes that the interviewees have gone through in order to shape their everyday lives to their changed realities and to adapt and react to the social, cultural, economic constraints that affect their family practices. Therefore, the impact of the values and everyday life practices of the other parent along with the ones of one's own 'village', make ICTs' adoption, incorporation and conversion (Silverstone *et al.* 1992, pp. 20–1) rather complex. Such constantly shifting processes are dependent on a vast array of 'reasons' and happenings that the day brings into the life of these families. Hence, such level of complexity stresses how the processes involved in the twofold relationship between individuals/families and ICTs do not necessarily occur in the consecutive order in which they are presented as part of the domestication process. Rather they are fluid practices, whose meanings and dynamic change according to the particular social, economic and cultural factors involving the household and its members.

Sociological accounts on family diversity and single parenthood

Along with a wide public consensus among academics and lay people, that the best family structure for children is the one produced by marriage among heterosexual couples, in the last decade there has been a growing body of research stressing the necessity of accepting and considering alternative family structures, because there is no effective standard to which family types need to conform (Coontz 1997; Stacey 1999; Demo *et al.* 2000; Dowd 1997).

One of the main issues facing single parents is diminished income as a consequence of divorce or separation. Consistent research relates the problems associated with single parenting to the poor economic conditions that these families experience (Teachman and Paasch 1994). It is poverty rather than single parenthood that is an influential factor in the child development, future career, job placement and self-esteem building (McLanahan and Sandefur 1994). Furthermore, income influences the time the parent spends with the children and, when low it is responsible for the lack of adult mentoring and of educational opportunities.

Other factors affecting the family life of single parents are: the legal allocation of parental responsibilities, the visitation arrangements, the common pressure to ensure that the children maintain a happy relationship with both parents, the forced relocation of one of the parents, and the change of lifestyle due to limited financial resources. In addition, research shows that single parents encounter difficulties in adapting to raising their children without the help of the other adult (Smart 1999). Indeed, both parents experience anger, pain and loss for different reasons and go through a process of self reassessment in order to adapt their role of parenting to the new situation or, in some cases, to create a new identity as a single parent and establish a new relationship with the other parent (Thompson and Amato 1999; Smart and Neale 1999). In post-divorce situations, roles and expectations become fluid and negotiation is essential in order to establish a relationship with a partner who, in some cases, is no longer well regarded. In many of my interviews, this issue emerged in relation to disagreements on children's rules and habits; the parent indicated his or her constant attempt to maintain a 'civil' relationship with the ex-partner for the sake of the children while, at the same time, criticizing the other parent's rules and habits. Indeed, the parenting and relational choices of single parents are continuously negotiated with the ex-partner and current partner (when present), as well as with the children. As a result, these negotiations between ex-partners, current partners, and children played a central role in the articulations of beliefs and practices surrounding ICTs for each of the families interviewed. In particular, most of the parents interviewed expressed their frustrations at having to leave their children in the home of the other parent: an environment they did not find agreeable or have any influence upon.

Audience research on family media consumption and everyday life

Since the introduction of television in the 1950s, many scholars have been interested in understanding the role of media within individuals' private lives. This project is particularly indebted to the strand of critical audience research initiated in the 1980s by James Lull (1980), Dorothy Hobson (1980, 1982), David Morley (1986), Jan-Uwe Rogge and Klaus

Jensen (1988) whose work focused on the household as an important space, in which media play a prominent role as symbolic resources for social and cultural practices within the context of everyday life. In addition, Rogge and Jensen's (1988) study also pointed out that the single-parent families used media to compensate for emotional deficiencies, poverty of experience, lack of closeness between parent and children, and lack of alternative leisure activities owing to the parent's financial and temporal constraints.

Starting in the 1990s, reception studies on families have focused on the introduction of 'old' mass media and 'new' ICTs in the households and their impact on everyday life practices and values. Audience researchers such as David Buckingham (2000), Ellen Seiter (1999), Sonia Livingstone (1997, 1998; Livingstone and Bovill 1999), and Toni Downes (1999) have shown, in their studies of children, differences in media consumption patterns that are related to the cultural and social backgrounds of the parents.

Nevertheless, within household research on ICT use, there is little written on the processes of negotiation that occurs among couples in relation to media consumption practices, especially after divorce or separation. The research on issues of power among married couples within the context of television consumption (Morley 1986; Hobson 1980; Lull 1990) are few and mostly on conflicts and resolutions. However, Walter Gantz (2001) suggests interestingly that as for other matters, television can be either a source of conflict among partners who are already dissatisfied with their relationship or a useful means to bring a troubled couple together. In fact, as my interviews demonstrate, following Gantz, conflicts around media are associated with other aspects of the intimate relationship among the couple. Such conflicts might have been sedated by the overall harmonious and satisfying union and surfaced once the relationship was ended.

Finally, the most influential work for my study lies within the first and most celebrated extensive study on the introduction of ICTs in the household and their impact on meaning-making and everyday life: *The Household Uses of Information and Communication Technologies* project directed by Roger Silverstone between the mid-1980s and 1990s. It is within this research that Silverstone, Hirsch and Morley (1992) developed the domestication concept and where Leslie Haddon and Roger Silverstone (1995) focused, in one of the reports, on the use of communication technologies in lone parents' households. Consistent with my findings, the two British scholars stressed the significance of television and telephones as means of communication and entertainment for the families, due to economic constraints that limit the possibility of alternative recreational activities; and, in the case of the telephone, for social networking and daily arrangements. In addition, in agreement with my analysis, these scholars noted that space and time constraints impacted on the patterns of media consumption, as well as the degree of privacy afforded to individual family members. This chapter, therefore, discusses the constraints that the single parents interviewed face while trying to build a 'home'. Home is utilized in the sense suggested by Haddon and Silverstone (1995): the emotional and conceptual idea of a having a place of residence, a place one belongs to, that, at times, confers security or anxiety, influenced also by public discourses on the family. In particular, the authors stress that obtaining such feeling of 'home' is for single parents an achievement which involves not only having to deal with time and space issues but also it

> '. . . involves, among other things, the appropriation of both objects and machines, meanings and media . . .'
> (Haddon and Silverstone 1995, p. 15)

It is the project of making a home that provides the central framework for understanding my informants' practices relating to ICTs. Hence, it is with this notion in mind, and in the light of literature presented here, that the narratives of my informants, analysed below, contribute to a better understanding of how temporal, spatial, economic and social arrangements influence the uses of, and meanings drawn from, old and new media technologies.

Methodology

This chapter is drawn from the author's qualitative dissertation study (Russo 2003), carried out within the context of an ongoing, multi-year research project, the 'Symbolism, Meaning, and the New Media @ Home'.[1]

The interviewees were selected according to a 'maximum variation sampling' approach, which aims to roughly mirror the demographic characteristics of the American population, and a 'snowball sampling' approach, which refers to the strategy of asking informants to help locate other interviewees (Lindlof 1995). I concentrated on single parents who, at the moment of the interview, had their children living with them at least 40 per cent of the time and were not living with any other adult in the house. I wanted to ensure that they all had considerable experience of daily parenting issues and household responsibilities.

For the purpose of this research, I have analysed the accounts of 6 single fathers and 16 single mothers. They are predominantly Caucasian, although three of them have mixed ethnicity and they were working at the time of the interview in a vast range of professions mostly within the service industry. Three parents had a high-school degree; the others mostly had some years of college, followed by few with a bachelor's, an associate's, or a graduate degree. The families' income ranged from below $15,000 to over $75,000 annually. However, it is important to point out that in divorced or separated households, due to alimony issues, the measure of income is rather different from two-parent families. Indeed, in some families the income was rather unstable due to recurrent changes in child support arrangements as well as in changes in the profession of one of the parents.

For the purpose of this study, almost all of the members of each household have been interviewed twice, once together and once individually. The interviews have been conducted by a team of investigators, including the author,[2] and followed the informants' privacy guidelines issued by the Human Research Committee of the University of Colorado. Thus, names and any other information that could reveal the interviewees' identity have been removed from the transcripts and this study.

Finally, while I acknowledge the bias that the researcher brings to the interviewing process (for more on this topic consult Hoover 2003; Haddon 1998), I still believe that the present study offers an informed and useful analysis of some aspects of single parents' lifeworlds and their everyday life.

Analysis of the experiences of my informants

In the light of literature mentioned above, this section will show how time, space, economic and socio-psychological issues of single parenthood impact on media consumption within the context of everyday life practices, through the voiced experiences of some of my informants.

Temporal and spatial constraints affecting media use

The story of Katy Cabera illustrates clearly how economic and time constraints, as well as the size and shape of the household impact on media consumption. Katy, at the time of the interview, was living in the family housing complex of the university where she worked at as an administrative assistant, while studying for a bachelor's degree in social work. She is 32 years old, Hispanic, and has been divorced for four years. Her ex-husband is in the Navy, as she was previously, and he rarely sees their two children but supports them financially. Their combined income, including child support, is around \$35,000. Katy considers herself lucky because her boss allows her to be flexible with her working hours (32 hours per week). On top of that, Katy is involved in several organizations as a volunteer, many of which include her children. The Caberas live in a two-bedroom apartment. They own one television and a VCR, which are located in the living room, whereas a brand new computer sits in the kitchen. When asked about her media consumption, Katy explained that she adopted a different pattern of use when the children were present from when they were not, while also noting her felt need to adapt her media habits to a very hectic schedule of family activities. In relation to computers, for example, this is what she answered:

Interviewer: How many hours each day do you think you use the computer?

Katy: I don't know that there's an average. I can go a week without it. It just depends, really, on what's going on. ... Ah, when they're (the kids) here, since this is our only television – if they're watching TV, then I'll log on. I'm not necessarily emailing. I may be looking for recipes. Or if something sparks my curiosity, I'll look it up online.

Katy's experience represents one of the many cases where parents' media uses, pressured by time issues, are structured by the need to oversee and entertain the children, run errands, as well as the need to share media technologies. Katy comments on her experience:

Interviewer: I'm curious why you decided to put the computer in the kitchen rather than in here [living room]. Or upstairs.

Katy: I wanted it upstairs eventually. But I haven't bought a desk yet. So it was in the kitchen until I was able to have the funds to buy a desk. And I never have the opportunity [to buy a desk]. I don't want it in here [living room] because I think that there would be too much chaos going on [both Jake and Helena are playing on the floor in front of this as she says this]. At least in the kitchen, it's just off to the side.

Here she explains the computer's somewhat unusual location (in the kitchen) in relation to her need to both oversee the children's internet activities and to engage simultaneously in other household chores. The time pressures of single parenting, combined with the burden of child care, affect both the way that media are utilized and the way rules are negotiated in the home.

Due to time pressures, another common practice for the families interviewed was the negotiation of rules for the children to account for their often hectic and changing daily routines. Indeed, rule negotiations between parents and children are rather common, and dependent, along with weather-related factors, on the daily routines of each family member. Many of the parents interviewed explained that they had different routines for their children in winter and in summer, which in turn would affect their consumption of media as well. Work-related activities also played an important role, especially if the parent has to bring some business home in the evenings or on weekends. As Jeff Stein (41) comments on his daughter's use of media: '... I'd say it varies but ... I guess the more busy I am with things in the house I am doing the more likely she is to be using some form of media ... on the computer and on television.' Jeff has been divorced for seven years and has Rachel 50 per cent of the time. He has his own business, so, like Katy Cabera, considers himself pretty lucky, in terms of the flexibility of his working schedule that allows him to organize his work around his ex-wife's job schedule, so that Rachel would not spend any time in daycare centres. However, at the same time, being self-employed puts a lot of pressure on earning a stable income to make a living, which fluctuates between $20,000 and $35,000, forcing him to work quite a lot.

Economic and temporal issues affecting entertainment choices and attitudes towards media

Along with space, lack of time and money are also responsible for the limitations on recreational activities outside the home and for the scarcity of media within the household. Almost all of the families claimed that they did not have money to invest in computers, cable, stereo systems, or a second or new TV set. Indeed, they tended to stress the desire to fulfil other necessities if they had had the economic opportunity. An example is represented by the case of Anna Lally, a single mother since the age of 16, who never received any financial help from her family nor from the father of her son. Anna has a very old computer handed down by a friend, so slow that it is incapable of being connected to the internet. However, Anna does not have money for a new one and admits that she is not interested in investing in a computer – there are more useful things she could do with her money. As she explains: 'It doesn't seem like a necessity to me. So I'm not motivated to put my money into that. You know, if somebody walked up to me and said, "Here, have a new computer system", and it was internet ready, I'd probably accept it. And I might use it too.'

Anna's case is very similar to the one of another informant, Jill Allen (37). When talking about computers, Jill, the mother of two girls, commented that even if she had money to buy one, she did not have anywhere to put it. In addition, she had never used one, and her parents let her daughters use theirs. However, at the time of the second interview, eight months later, the prospect of owning the parents' computer very soon (since they had ordered a new one) opened a whole new horizon of possibilities for Jill's work enhancement and social networking and, suddenly, 'space' was no longer an issue. Hence, economic constraints can be disguised behind other types of constraint that are felt to be less embarrassing or easier to accept psychologically.

Furthermore, echoing public discourses around the impact of visual media on children, many informants, while acknowledging that watching television is a waste of time or often is just a time filler, could not avoid using the medium for parenting purposes. Therefore, in many cases, they had to compromise their values with their needs. As Roxanne Conner (45, buyer in graphic business, currently unemployed) confesses when discussing the use of media by single parents:

Roxanne: Yeah. Um, well it comes into play because there, it's a big presence, as far as entertainment. The internet and movies and video games and the phone ... I guess that's sort of a media thing ... And ... just, I'm surprised at ... I guess how lenient I am about the whole thing knowing when he was little, or thinking when he was little, 'Oh, I'm certainly not going to park him in front of the TV ... I'm never going to be one of those parents.' And it's just ...

Interviewer: Reality intervened?

Roxanne: Exactly. And very, you know, I don't try and shelter him from it.

Roxanne, at the time of the interview, had recently been laid off from her work as a graphic buyer. She had been working full-time during her two marriages, of which the last ended two years ago, leaving her with the primary physical custody of Jeremy, the son she had from her first marriage. Although Roxanne has never suffered from economic constraints, since her job provided her with financial stability even before both divorces, she had several stories to tell about the stressful life of being a single mother with a full-time job and the role of media in her parenting of Jeremy.

Nevertheless, television is viewed as a waste of time and a negative source of entertainment for children from both two-parent and single-parent families. One difference lies in the fact that, among the single parents interviewed, those who do not have cable often justify this decision firstly, by referencing a moral view of the medium, and secondly, by the fact that it is a financial burden they cannot sustain. Indeed, in the families that do not have cable there is a VCR and often a large number of videotapes that the children watch repeatedly. This practice is justified as being useful because it allows the parents to select the programme for their children and to show it whenever necessary, thus, affording greater control for the parents.

This is the case of the Fallons, who got rid of cable and the big TV set because the mother, Wyonna, thought that her daughters, Jill and Uta, were becoming addicted. In her own words: 'I guess that was my motivation for not having TV – one was cable is expensive – but also we watched way too much TV' (Wyonna, 39, part-time baker, school custodian, student). However, they do own around 200 videos and watch one everyday. In fact, if TV appeared to be negative for the children, videotapes are allowed because they permit the parent to have more control over the content and a more flexible viewing schedule that can better adapt to the hectic and often unstructured life of single-parent households. Besides, the introduction of the VCR, as Wyonna confessed, was also the result of her compromise with the children, who otherwise would have not tolerated living in a house with no TV.

Furthermore, in terms of rules that parents set for their children, there are definitely more detailed and restricted parameters in relation to television than to computers. Indeed, in relation to their children's computer use, my informants do not show the same moral concerns and tend to trust their children's use in terms of sites they visit. As in Downes's (1999) interviews, parents tend to have a different attitude towards the new machines in comparison to television and associate them with educational opportunities. When present, computers are perceived as useful and necessary for children's career development, while for their personal lives they seem to often be seen as useful for social networking, information retrieval and leisure activities, unless they are involved in the parent's profession (Russo 2003).

Custody arrangements, family practices, and media consumption

As mentioned in the sociological literature, divorce and separation require that the parents adapt to the drastic lifestyle changes and build a new parenting role (Demo *et al.* 2000). However, very often with this new identity comes a new life, which is not materially as well equipped as the previous one. In particular, single mothers face the most challenges in trying to run the same household arrangements with a reduced income especially when the separation has not been consensual or when child support is minimal or non-existent. Financial instability post-divorce had, for some of my informants, repercussion on their children's education and leisure activities. Relocation to more affordable neighbourhoods often results in a change of schools, which are not always very strong in their educational structures; college funds are used to pay divorce lawyers; and budgets are tight for entertainment activities and machines.

The experience of relocation and its repercussions on family practices was shared by several of the informants. One case is represented by the Allens, who, since the divorce in 1995, had, up to the time of the interview, changed place already five times and were risking having to move again. Because of financial difficulties, Jill and her daughters had been moving between their own apartment, when they could afford one, and the house of Jill's parents, in which they all had to share one bedroom. Four months before the interview, the Allens moved into a three-bedroom house found through an organization that helps families on a low income to find somewhere to live. However, since Jill had recently kicked out her boyfriend because he was an alcoholic, she was running the risk of being evicted because she was not able to afford the rent on her own. Jill, who never attended college, works on the assembly line in a factory and is planning to pick up a second job in order to afford the rent. Her income at the factory was only $15,000 a year, and she is the sole supporter of her two daughters. The father officially has joint custody but lives far away with his new family and is not involved in the girls' lives. The only help Jill receives is from her parents who have an active role in her life. In terms of leisure activities, Jill complains that they do not participate in many activities as a family because it is too expensive to go out, so their only entertainment resource is the satellite television, a play station, and her parents' computer: 'We talk a lot; it's just that we don't know what to do. It's hard for me to be a single parent, and sometimes it is hard to budget the money.'

Finally, the situation is even more precarious when the divorce has not been settled and child support is not offered. This is the case of Vanessa Miller (35, Wal-Mart cashier) who, after twenty years, left the husband twelve months before the interview and had, since then, moved already three times. She explained how the divorce had been 'tough' on the children, whose grades at school had dropped since she left her husband. Their life had been completely transformed since their household income had dropped dramatically. In relation to media, they no longer had cable or a computer, and that actually turned into a positive situation for Vanessa, as she did not have to worry about what their children were exposed to on the internet or on television. However, their drastic lifestyle change was definitely felt by the entire family. In cases like the Millers, divorce or separation radically changes the mothers' household habits, while the fathers tend to have not only cable television but also computers; and the children, according to their mothers, use them without much parental oversight or restrictions. Indeed, this inclination reflects the economic disparity that is typical in single-parent households between mothers and fathers.

Negotiating media habits with the other parent

An important issue that single parents have to face in their everyday lives relates to their constant need to negotiate children's rules with the other parent, when involved. Both two-parent and single-parent households generally claim to have guidelines regarding the types of material and the amount of media they allow their children to consume. Yet in the interviews there often seemed to be notable differences between the media practices of the parent interviewed and those of the ex-spouse, as if the rules in place before the separation were contingent to the union of the parents, and the parenting practices previously held. Thus, media rules were often a source of conflict and tension with the other parent, which, in turn, affected the children's relationships with them both.

A good example of such conflicting relationships is represented by the story of Rayna Hancock (37). Rayna lives with her 7-year-old son in a mobile home. She is in school trying to attain an associate's degree and presently her income is $13,000 a year. She is divorced and has physical custody of her son; while the father, who sees the child quite regularly, lives with his grandmother, his girlfriend and a new baby. Rayna owns a refurbished computer as well as a television and a VCR donated by members of her church congregation. When Rayna was asked about the type of videos and games that she rented for her son, she explained animatedly that the father's son buys him games and lets him watch films that are too violent. When asked how she dealt with Wes's father on the matter, she replied: 'I don't really have to tell him, he knows, he knows that I don't agree with this and that, but, also I can't expect him to change everything ... he's had to change a lot to meet my expectations.'

Rayna's story is just one among similar narratives of disappointment and incompetence that describe the other parent – mostly the father. Definitely, the reason and modality in which the parents have split up reflect the tone of these conversations.

On the same topic, another interesting pattern emerged within three of the families interviewed, echoing an argument raised by Rogge and Jensen (1988) in their study. Those authors claimed that women tend to recognize computers as pertaining to the male domain and, thus, consciously or unconsciously reject them because they serve as reminders of the conflicts they have with their male partner. One woman, Meredith Ricci, a nurse and mother of three daughters, voiced a similar experience. Her ex-husband works in the computer business and always had many computers in the house. When asked if she discussed media rules with him, she explained that she did not. Computers in particular were not discussed, she said, because they had always been a 'sore spot' in their relationship. Meredith bemoaned the fact that her ex-husband had been constantly on the computer for work and for fun, causing a great deal of tension in their marriage. As a reaction, she said that she had not even wanted to touch one when they had been married, and now barely uses them for the same reason. When asked if her infrequent use of the computer was related to her experience with her computer-user husband, she answered:

> Uhm [yes]. Because I felt like it was taking away from personal time or being able to do anything else you know. It's, it's a scapegoat. It's like the people that read all the time because they can't talk to somebody, you know they sit [miming somebody reading a book].
>
> (Meredith, 41)

Two interviewees, Sarah Taber and Eugene Arrington, similarly blamed excessive television consumption as one of the reasons for their divorces. In both cases, the husband was watching too much television and not devoting enough time to the family in the view of their ex-wives. As a reaction, both of these single parents do not watch television and try to instil in their children the same habit.

Indeed, on the matter of the tension involved in discussing media rules with the ex-husband, Sarah (41, Family Advocate counsellor) explains:

Sarah: That is and it was actually a huge issue when they were young for me. That was another mediating [issue] because he didn't have any boundaries. He would let them watch r-rated movies and ... he doesn't have, that's the part of the parent that he doesn't have. He doesn't pay attention to what they are doing, and what they are watching and ... and he is a TV-holic and that's why I don't, you know, I felt like that I lost my marriage actually to TV.

Interviewer: Because he was watching too much TV?

Sarah: He wakes up in the morning, he turns the TV on and goes off when he goes to bed, you know? And basically our conversations ended and TV was what filled that void so ...

> so I went through years and years without even having a TV at all. ... So I do movies, I like movies but now I am very selective of what, you know, when I watch TV ... so they (her children) have been very exposed to a lot of things that I was very against to, especially when they were younger. As they have gotten older they have gotten, because of me I think, where I come from, I finally realized through single parenting that I couldn't protect them. I can't protect them from their environment, I can't protect them from what's going on over at his house ... in many ways they were still getting what they needed, they needed a father and he was there for them.

This excerpt reflects Sarah's frustrations with her ex-husband's lack of supervision of her three children's television consumption; a frustration that echoes also the reasons for her divorce twelve years ago. Nevertheless, she had to accommodate her ex-husband's different parenting style with her own role as a mother. She learned that she could not control her children's lives when they were with their father, so she decided to instil in them a critical capacity to discern among television programmes, so that they could bring with them her teachings when they were with their dad. In addition, Sarah's recognition that it was important for her daughters to have a father figure in their childhood forced her to compromise her dissatisfaction with the ex-husband television habits.

Conclusions: negotiating media consumption and parenting practices

All the issues examined in this chapter have stressed the importance of understanding media consumption within the social and cultural contexts in which individuals' lives are embedded, along with the particular family arrangements in which their practices are entrenched. Especially when discussing the future of new media technologies in contemporary society, there is the general tendency to assume that media are necessarily desired by all; hence, it is only a question of access and ownership. Conversely, in many cases, as for some of my interviewees, individuals are not interested in pursuing ICTs because they are felt to be unnecessary, or are not viewed as a choice owing to economic or cultural reasons. Although media have become naturalized within the space of family practices, they do not necessarily represent the primary concern of single parents. For my informants, making a 'home' (Haddon and Silverstone 1995), as mentioned earlier, is the most important focus in their lives, while ICTs are not necessarily a priority and, in some cases, they cannot be. Old and new media technologies are, in fact, used and conceived of as useful tools and resources, to the extent they are perceived by parents as relevant to their family and individual practices. Indeed, the single parents interviewed struggle to create a meaningful and stable environment for their children. They try to maintain rules and habits the children had before the split-up, while accommodating the larger demands and responsibilities they are confronted with in their manifold roles as caretakers, breadwinners, nurturers, disciplinarians, parents and playmates.

Further, this chapter has illustrated how social and material factors heavily shape the everyday dynamics of single-parent households, and by extension, the way mass media and ICTs are used as means of entertainment, information and communication in these homes. The narratives of the families interviewed are filled with examples showing how lack of income and/or time impact on the ways that single parents interact with their children and, thus, the modalities in which mass media and ICTs are present and are used within these homes. In these households, social and cultural guidelines are taken as the basis for ICT use but are continuously negotiated in light of the particular conditions in which the family is embedded. Indeed, my informants face the constant need to negotiate between their desires and the necessities that parenting entails when it comes to their family's media consumption.

Moreover, the analysis of the transcripts indicated several ways in which the lack of time impacts on the parents' use of media, especially of computers, for their own consumption and their children's. On the one hand, computers, when present, are recognized as useful, convenient, and affordable tools for maintaining contact with friends and family or for making new acquaintances. On the other hand, time for socializing is rather short as there are demands relating to the supervision of children or running household chores.

Another area in which time and economic factors are evident in affecting the choices that single-parent families make is in the leisure sphere. In terms of entertainment, my interviewees demonstrated the rather limited set of choices that they have for themselves and their children. In many families, the lack of money was responsible for the scarcity and limitations of technologies available in the household. Especially in cases of divorce and separation, some of these parents described the ways in which their lives underwent radical change after their split-up, and, thus, even media consumption habits changed accordingly.

Further, this chapter has stressed the importance of considering single parents' media consumption when investigating issues of power relationships within households and their impact on media uses. Indeed, consumption patterns are recognized to be influenced by the different power afforded by family members according to the (gendered) role that they assume within the sphere of the home (Goodman 1983; Brody and Stoneman 1983). In households with one adult, traditional divisions of role between husband and wife are modified to the need and realities of single parenthood. While the parents interviewed struggle between being the caretaker and the breadwinner, the children tend to acquire a larger role in the management of the household and in the decisions related to family practices (Weiss 1979). Therefore, if the social roles involved in family dynamics are reascribed to contain the particular situation of single parents, then the power relationships within households are also modified. The strong bond that ties single parents to their children creates a different power dynamic from that of two-parent families: a dynamic that is sustained by different structural and emotional positions that affect family practices; the range of cultural resources its members have at disposal for producing meanings; and their media ownership and consumption habits within the home.

As the interviews presented confirm, the parents' negotiation between desires and actual practices in relation to their children's media consumption is also complicated by the relationship with the other parent, when present. Almost all the parents interviewed, regardless of their type of custody arrangement, expressed difficulty in having to accommodate the other parent's ideas and habits in relation to their children's media habits. Not only do material constraints change their family practices but also social and emotional ones. Many informants voiced anger and disapproval of the ex-partner's parenting practices. This situation makes their parenting even harder because they feel that they have to compensate for the other parent's (perceived) ineptitude for the sake of their children, overburdening themselves with stress and responsibilities. In most cases, the ex-partner is depicted as a heavy user of media and ICTs and as being overly thoughtless about the children's media consumption. Finally, parenting post-divorce is transformed and complicated not only by the presence of two households, but also by new family members (for example, a new partner), who often joins the household, and whose presence affect the already fragile power relation established between the two parents.

In conclusion, the uniqueness of the dynamics involving single-parent families stresses the complexity of the articulation of the relationship between individuals and ICTs expressed in the domestication theory. For the single parents interviewed, not only power issues but also an intricate web of economic, social and psychological factors come into play in the daily consumption of, and meaning-making associated with, ICTs. Indeed, the complexity of single-parent families' structure and lives stresses the importance of considering the four stages, in which the practices pertaining to the domestication concept are divided, as flexible phases one can return to, and whose dynamics can always change along with their value within the moral economy of the household.

It is, therefore, only when considering the complexity of parenting practices and the fluidity and variety of family arrangements, for example single-parents' households, that it is possible to understand the role played by mass media within individuals' lifeworlds. Indeed, old and new technologies participate in the intricate web of daily routines adapting and influencing parents' life organization and contexts of interaction. Consequently, as the number of single parents grows, their everyday-life experiences might reshape previously accepted norms of family dynamics and the relationship between family life and information and communication technologies.

Notes

1. For more information on this project please consult its website, http://www.mediameaning.org, or contact Professor Stewart Hoover and Professor Lynn Schofield Clark at the University of Colorado at Boulder, USA.
2. The research team is composed of: Joseph Champ (PhD), Scott Webber (PhD), Michelle Miles (PhD student), Denice Walker (PhD student), Monica Emerich (PhD student), Christof Demont-Heinrich (PhD student), Jin Kyu Park (PhD student), and the author.

References

Amato, P. R. (1999) 'The postdivorce society: How divorce is shaping the family and other forms of social organization,' in (eds) Ross A. Thompson and Paul R. Amato, *The Postdivorce Family: Children, Parenting, and Society*. Sage: Thousand Oaks, pp. 161–90.

Brody, G. H. and Stoneman, Z. (1983) 'The influence of television viewing on family interactions: a contextualist framework'. *Journal of Family Issues*, vol. 4, no. 2, pp. 329–48.

Buckingham, D. (2000) *After the Death of Childhood: Growing Up in the Age of Electronic Media*. Polity Press: Malden, MA.

Coontz, S. (1997) *The Way We Really Are: Coming to Terms with America's Changing Families*. Basic Books: New York.

Demo, D. H., Allen, K. R. and Fine, M. A. (2000) *Handbook of Family Diversity*. Oxford University Press: New York.

Demo, H., Fine, M. A. and Ganong, L. H. (2000) 'Divorce as a family stressor,' in (eds) P. C. McKenry and S. J. Price, *Families and Change: Coping with Stressful Events*. Sage: London, pp. 279–302.

Dowd, N. E. (1997) *In Defense of Single-Parent Families*. New York University Press: New York.

Downes, T. (1999) 'Children's and parent's discourses about computers in the home and school'. *Convergence*, vol. 5, no. 4, pp. 104–11.

European Commission (2001) The social situation in the European Union 2001, *Office for Official Publications of the European Communities*, Luxembourg.

Fields, J. and Casper, L. M. (2001) America's families and living arrangements: March 2000. *Current Population Reports*, P20-537. US Census Bureau: Washington, DC.

Gantz, W. (2001) 'Conflicts and resolution strategies associated with television in marital life', in (eds) J. Bryant and J. A. Bryant, *Television and The American Family*, 2nd edn. Lawrence Erlbaum Associates Publishers: Mahwah, NJ, pp. 289–316.

Goodman, I. F. (1983) 'Television's role in family interactions: A family systems perspective'. *Journal of Family Issues*, vol. 4, no. 2, pp. 405–24.

Haddon, L. (1998) 'Methodological considerations in the UK research on the domestication of ICTs,' in (eds) R. Silverstone and M. Hartmann, Falmer, *Methodologies for Media and Information Research in Everyday Life*, EMTEL Working Paper, no. 5. University of Sussex.

Haddon, L. and Silverstone, R. (1995) *Lone parents and their information and communication technologies, A Report on the ESRC/PICT Study of the Household and Information and Communication Technologies*. SPRU CICT Report Series, no. 12. Brighton, Science Policy Research Unity: University of Sussex.

Hobson, D. (1982) *'Crossroads:' The Drama of a Soap Opera*. Methuen: London.

Hobson, D. (1980) 'Housewives and the mass media', in (eds) D. Hobson, S. Hall, A. Lowe and P. Willis, *Culture, Media, Language: Working Papers in Cultural Studies 1972-79*. Hutchinson: London, pp. 105–15.

Hoover, S. M. (2003) 'Media audiences and their narratives: Field research on meaning and identity in the media age'. Paper delivered at the International Communication Association Conference, San Diego, CA, May.

Lindlof, T. R. (1995) *Qualitative Communication Research Methods*. Sage Publications: Thousand Oaks, CA.

Livingstone, S. (1998) 'Audience research at the crossroads: The "implied audience" in media and cultural theory'. *European Journal of Cultural Studies*, vol. 1, no. 2, pp. 193–217.

Livingstone, S. (1997) 'Changing audiences for changing media: A social psychological perspective', in (eds) by P. Winterhoff-Spurk and T. H. A. van der Voort, *New Horizons in Media Psychology: Research Cooperation and Projects in Europe*. Opladen: Westdeutscher Verlag GmbH.

Livingstone, S. and Bovill, M. (1999) *Young People New Media*. London School of Economics and Political Science: London.

Lull, J. (1990) *Inside Family Viewing*. Routledge: New York and London.

Lull, J. (1980) 'The social uses of television'. *Human Communication Research*, vol. 6, no. 3, Spring: pp. 197–209.

McLanahan, S. and Sandefur, G. (1994) *Growing Up with a Single Parent: What Hurts, What Helps*. Harvard University Press: Cambridge.

Morley, D. (1986) *Family Television: Cultural Power and Domestic Leisure*. Comedia: London.

Rogge, J.-U. and Jensen, K. B. (1988) 'Everyday life and television in West Germany: An empathic-interpretive perspective on the family as a system', in (ed.) J. Lull, *World Families Watching Television*. Sage: London, pp. 80–115.

Russo, A. M. (2003) 'For their families' sake: An interpretive analysis of the role of mass media in single parents' households and their meaning-making practices,' PhD Dissertation, University of Colorado: Boulder, CO.

Seiter, E. (1999) *Television and New Media Audiences*. Oxford University Press: London.

Silverstone, R., Hirsch, E. and Morley, D. (1992) 'Information and communication technologies and the moral economy of the household', in (eds) R. Silverstone and E. Hirsch, *Consuming Technologies: Media and Information in Domestic Spaces*. Routledge: London, pp. 15–31.

Smart, C. (1999) 'The "New" Parenthood: Fathers and Mothers after Divorce', in (eds) E. B. Silva and C. Smart, *The New Family?* Sage: London.

Smart, C. and Neale, B. (1999) *Family Fragments?* Polity Press: Cambridge.

Stacey, J. (1999) 'Virtual social science and the politics of family values', in (ed.) G. E. Marcus, *Critical Anthropology Now: Unexpected Contexts, Shifting Constituencies, Changing Agendas*. School of American Research Press: Santa Fe, NM, pp. 29–54.

Teachman, J. D. and Paasch, K. M. (1994) 'Financial impact of divorce on children and their families', *Future of Children*, no. 4, pp. 63–83.

Thompson, R. A. and Amato, P. R. (1999) 'The postdivorce family: An introduction to the issues', in (eds) R. A. Thompson and P. R. Amato, *The Postdivorce Family: Children, Parenting, and Society*. Sage: Thousand Oaks, CA, pp. xi–xxi.

Weiss, R. S. (1979) *Going It Alone: The Family Life and Social Situation of the Single Parent*. Basic Books: New York.

10 From cultural to information revolution. ICT domestication by middle-class Chinese families

Sun Sun Lim

In this chapter, the domestication framework is applied to ICT adoption by middle-class families in Beijing and Shanghai. It is found that in these households, technology has become an inextricable part of the domestic setting, appropriated and deployed to serve particular functions. However, theirs is not an unbridled embrace of technology but an acceptance underlined by circumspection about its potential downsides. ICTs are therefore concurrently adopted, yet resisted in particular circumstances.

Consumerism in China

The functional and symbolic value of ICTs has made them prime objects of Chinese consumerism, itself a relatively recent phenomenon. The 1990s saw significant growth in personal incomes and ready access to material goods in China's urban cities (Lu 2000). Consumerism has risen and Chinese today express their individuality through consumption, ignoring ideological indoctrination by the state (Wei and Pan 1999). As advertising increases and inspires new wants, there is heightened pressure to keep up with one's peers (Gamble 2003). When the Chinese were less affluent, they aspired to possess four status symbols: bicycles, watches, sewing machines and radios (Yan 1994). With growing wealth, the new status symbols or 'six big items' (*liu da jian*) evolved into: VCRs, televisions, washing machines, cameras, refrigerators and electric fans. Ten years on, this list is likely to include newer ICTs like mobile phones, computers and digital cameras (Euromonitor 2003). In particular, the mobile phone is a potent status symbol owing to its visibility and portability (Goodman 1996). For example, when mobile phones first emerged on the scene in Shanghai, people of higher socio-economic classes were referred to as the 'mobile phone-using stratum' (*dageda jieceng*) (Gamble 2003, p. 157).

The one-child policy, introduced in 1979 (Gu 1990), has also influenced consumption habits, and most urban Chinese families do, indeed, have only one child. These only-children determine a considerable proportion of urban families' household purchases (K. Chan and McNeal 2004), estimated at over US$60 billion annually (McNeal and Zhang 2000). About half of the luxury goods purchased in China are bought for the only child or 'little emperor' (*xiao huangdi*) (Yan 1994). Luxury children's goods markets have shown significant growth (Zhao and Murdock 1996), and the variety of services claiming to enhance the physical and intellectual strength of young children has also expanded (Anagnost 1997). Salient trends can also be noted among young Chinese consumers themselves. Young Chinese who grew up in the 1980s and 1990s were born into an era of affluence and have high consumer demands (Li 1998). They are more responsive to advertising and actively acquire branded (*mingpai*) goods, unlike the older generation who tend to be oblivious to advertising (Chao and Myers 1998; Fan and Xiao 1998). Although materialism is officially discouraged in Chinese schools (K. Chan and McNeal 2004), it has been observed that schoolchildren share their experiences of consuming novelty foods (Guo 2000) and this exchange is likely to extend to other consumer products as well. A good example of Chinese children's consumerism is the craze for the Transformer range of toys (Zhao and Murdock 1996).

Technology adoption in China

Technology adoption in China is keeping pace with the country's economic development. The government places great emphasis on the economy's information sector (Dai 2003; Meng and Li 2002), as evidenced by the establishment of the Ministry of Information Industry in 1998 (Zhang 1999). Chinese people have followed the government's lead by avidly adopting technology and acquiring infotech skills (Leung 1998).

In terms of ICT ownership, affluent urban Chinese households are not dissimilar to those in developed countries. Typically, they own televisions, hi-fi stereos, VCD/DVD players, computers and telephones. They are also trend-conscious and update their electronic equipment regularly. The competitiveness of the workplace has quickened their pace of life and spurred demand for instantaneous communications (Euromonitor 2003). Landlines, mobile phones and the internet are in high demand and the ownership of multiple mobile phones for business and personal purposes is not uncommon in China's big cities. Residents in Beijing and Shanghai own the most mobile phones in the country, at 27.7 per cent and 24.5 per cent, respectively (*Mobile Phones Dominate*

Telecom Sector 2001). Beijing and Shanghai are also the only two cities with over 20 per cent of their residents accessing the internet, at 28 and 26.6 per cent respectively, significantly above the national average of 6.2 per cent (*Shanghai Ranks Second in Internet Penetration* 2004). This is not surprising given that household computer ownership in the two cities is more than twice the national average (National Bureau of Statistics of China 2004).

Chinese people's technology adoption have been linked to their lifestyle orientations. A study of individuals' ICT ownership and media-related activities in Beijing, Shanghai and Guangzhou found that Chinese consumers want to come across as sophisticated and fashionable (Leung 1998). This explained their propensity for visiting video stores and karaoke bars. Computer ownership was associated with the 'life expansionist' lifestyle of wanting to broaden one's horizons through acquiring new skills. VCR and pager ownership and cable television subscription were associated with a more hedonistic lifestyle.

In terms of media use, television viewing remains a popular activity. Media use in China changed radically in the wake of Deng's post-1979 economic reforms, which increased the amount of leisure time. Since the 1990s, leisure time of city residents has doubled to approximately 5 hours per day (S. Wang 1995, cited in Wei and Pan 1999). Television viewing has consequently become a popular activity owing to its convenience and affordability (Chu 1993). With growing internet penetration, reading online news, chatting and playing online games have also become alternative recreational outlets (Zhu and He 2002). On average, the Chinese spend 9.8 hours surfing the internet weekly, predominantly from 8 p.m. to 11 p.m. (*People's Republic of China Yearbook* 2003).

Family values and communication

Despite the political turmoil and social upheavals which modern China has witnessed, the family remains a robust social entity. Family values are to a large extent, still adhered to (Davis and Harrell 1993; Ju 1996) and communication within the family tends to be both rule- and role-bound: 'The hierarchical nature of familial relationships, particularly those between parents and children, dictates the way the family communication is conducted, both verbally and nonverbally' (Ju 1996, p. 139). Traditionally, children are socialized to be obedient (*tinghua*) and to defer to parental authority (Gao *et al.* 1996). While there appears to be growing tolerance towards children's assertiveness, arguably the result of parental indulgence of their only children, young Chinese parents still expect their children to obey their commands (Wu 1996a).

Children in China tend to be closer and more affectionate to their mothers while their fathers play the disciplinarian's role and thus keep a distance from them (Chu 1993). The proverbial 'strict father, kind mother' relationship still appears to hold strong today (Ho 1986, 1987; Zang 2003). Among Chinese families today, the father's influence over the children seems to have declined as Chinese youth adore their mothers and tend to confide in them more (Zang 2003). Mothers also have more control over the children and play the critical role of bonding the family (Jankowiak 1993).

There has been widespread criticism that China's one-child policy has resulted in a society of spoilt 'little emperors' with over-indulgent parents. However, research has shown that conversely, parents of only children are so concerned about the 'spoiled only child' syndrome that they tend to control them rather strictly (Falbo and Poston Jr 1996; Wu 1996a, 1996b). The concept of 'control' (*guan*) has particular currency in the Chinese family (Wu 1996b). In Chinese tradition, parents are duty-bound to control their children and to train them to rein in their impulses (Ho 1986). Parental control is associated not with negative but positive connotations and is regarded as an expression of love and care.

Chinese culture has long emphasized the value of education, believed to be critical for one's social mobility and personal development (Hau and Salili 1996; Stevenson and Lee 1996). Chinese families place great importance on education and are prepared to spend a large proportion on their family income to raise their children's educational level (*New Trends in Chinese Marriage and the Family* 1987). Today, education is still of prime importance to Chinese families, especially urban families, which can afford expensive schooling (Donald 2002). The one-child policy has also exacerbated the amount of pressure placed on only-children to perform academically. It was noted as early as 1987, that parents of only-children in China tend to pin all their hopes for success on them and to have unrealistically high expectations (*New Trends in Chinese Marriage and the Family* 1987). Studies have also shown that Chinese parents' involvement in their children's education is high, manifested in their active supervision of schoolwork and the setting of standards to be met by their children (Chen, Lee and Stevenson 1996). Some parents also arrange additional lessons for their children after school hours, thereby imposing more stress on them (Anagnost 1997). Indeed, cities like Beijing have recently seen an explosion in after-school education ranging from traditional subjects like English and Math to artistic pursuits like painting, dance and piano (Y. Wang and Cui 2004).

Outside of one's immediate family, 'personal relationships' (*guanxi*) is a key societal value that impacts upon individuals' communication with the outside world. *Guanxi* with relatives and friends are integral to social mobility (H. Chan and King 2003; Gamer 2003; Yang 1994). One's relatives, school, residential and business contacts form the core of lifelong *guanxi*, which are meant to endure even after these groups have dissolved and face-to-face interaction has ceased (Chu 1993; Goodwin and Tang 1996). It is widely acknowledged that in China today, one is unlikely to achieve much without knowing the right people and pulling the right strings (H. Chan and King 2003). As the average size of families in China has diminished, the importance of such social networks is likely to increase (Goodwin and Tang 1996). Indeed, the skill of developing *guanxi* is considered so important that it may be encouraged even at a young age (Chee 2000). An important corollary of *guanxi* is 'personal obligations and affections' (*renqing*), a concept of reciprocity which underpins social relationships (Chu 1993; Goodwin and Tang 1996). The '*renqing* rule' dictates that people should maintain contact with their personal *guanxi* network by the occasional exchange of greetings, gifts and visits.

Methodology

This study sought to understand ICT domestication by urban Chinese families through in-depth interviews with families in Beijing and Shanghai – arguably China's two leading cities. Economically, Shanghai is at the forefront, with a local GDP of 600 billion RMB, and Beijing coming in a distant second with 350 billion RMB (*Shanghai Ranks 1st Among Metropolitan Economic Giants* 2004). Their ICT penetration levels are the highest in the country. While a study of ICT adoption in these two cities is, therefore, not representative of the country as a whole, it can be indicative of general trends in technology adoption by affluent, urban Chinese households.

Twenty nuclear families were interviewed in May 2004, 10 in each city. One parent and one child from each family were interviewed, making 40 interviews in total. Given their busy schedules, it was impractical to interview both parents. Instead, families were given the choice of which parent would participate. In all but three interviews, it was the mothers who participated. Chinese families of higher socio-economic status are more likely to possess household durables like personal computers, mobile phones, hi-fi stereos, digital cameras and other electronic devices (Euromonitor 2003). Hence, the main selection criterion was that the primary breadwinner of each family had to be a white-collar employee such as a party or government official, manager, entrepreneur, skilled technician, teacher or administrator. All but one were double-income families with both parents working full-time in various white-collar positions as managers, civil servants, teachers and engineers, and so on. The first wave of families interviewed was identified through the researcher's personal contacts and subsequent waves snowballed from referrals of earlier waves.

For each city, half of the families interviewed had children attending primary school and the remaining half, high school. All but one were one-child families, the exception being a family where the father had remarried and had a son from his first marriage and a daughter from his second. The parents interviewed were aged between early 30s and mid-40s, while the children in primary school were between 7 and 12 years old, and those in high school, between 13 and 17 years old. The parents and children were interviewed separately so that they would not mutually influence each other's responses. Sixteen interviews were conducted in the privacy of the interviewees' homes and photos of household ICTs were taken when permission was granted. At the interviewees' behest, the remaining four interviews were conducted in alternative venues such as cafes or workplaces.

The interview questions were based on the framework of appropriation, objectification, incorporation and conversion (Silverstone *et al.* 1992, p. 21); and necessity, control, functionality and sociality/privacy (Livingstone 1992, p. 117). They focused on the family's daily ICT use, mutual understanding of each other's ICT usage and parental influence on children's media usage. The questions were designed to be open-ended so that interviewees could develop their own ideas and the interviewer had the flexibility to probe deeper when interviewees introduced novel ideas or points of interest. The interviews were conducted in Standard Mandarin (*putonghua*) by a native speaker. Every interview was audio-recorded and each lasted about 45 minutes. Verbatim Chinese transcripts were made and qualitatively analysed, with quotations presented in this chapter subsequently translated into English.

ICTs in the urban Chinese household

All the families interviewed owned televisions, mobile phones, hi-fi stereos and VCD/DVD players. With the exception of a few, most families owned computers, digital cameras and portable music devices. These were, therefore, media-rich households which had incorporated ICT use into their daily routines, in the process reconfiguring the domestic space into communal and/or private zones. ICTs also served as intermediaries in family communication, providing both the channels and the content for meaningful exchange. And while they appreciated the value of ICTs for social advancement, many parents remained vigilant about the possible ills of ICT use and sought to contain them. ICT use in the households studied was thus marked by routinization, reconfiguration, intermediation, social advancement and containment.

Routinization

The importance of ICTs in urban Chinese family life was evident. A wide variety of ICTs was used on a personal or shared basis. Mobile phones and portable music devices were used individually, as opposed to television, stereos, VCD/DVD players and digital cameras which tended to be used jointly. Even families which had multiple television sets claimed that they spent more time on shared rather than on individual television viewing. Computers tended to be used individually although in some households, family members would watch each other surf the net or play online games, while some parents would help their children to search for online information and type assignments. In these households, the computer was a second focal point of family interaction, after the television. Some parents also purchased specific educational ICTs such as English language learning devices (*fuduji*)[1] for their children. As for the location of these media, there was no discernible trend towards children's 'bedroom culture' (Bovill and Livingstone 2001, p. 179). Apart from personally-owned ICTs like mobile phones, portable music devices and *fuduji* being placed in the child's room, all other ICTs were placed in communal areas such as living rooms and studies or in parents' bedrooms. Half of the households had two or more televisions, again placed in either the lounge or the parents' bedrooms. In only one instance was the television placed in the child's bedroom.

The parents used a host of media for work and recreational purposes. Most of them used mobile phones for work-related and social communication. Almost all of them had to use computers at work and were, therefore, reasonably competent in their use. Recreational ICT use included television viewing, playing computer games, SMSing friends and surfing the Net. The children used ICTs for educational, recreational and social activities. Typically, primary schoolchildren would practise English on their *fuduji* or use computers for schoolwork, usually with parental assistance. Television viewing, mainly of cartoons and news programmes, and playing computer games were also popular. Older children surfed the Net for entertainment news or researched assignments, played online games and chatted with friends on 'qq' (instant messaging). Other personalized media use included listening to music on portable devices, checking dictionary definitions on their PDAs, practising English on their *fuduji*, SMSing and playing games on their mobile phones.

All the interviewees expressed extreme need for ICTs, finding them indispensable. When asked to imagine life without these devices, children used words such as 'empty' (*kongxu*), 'boring' (*wuliao*), 'painful' (*tongku*) and 'sad' (*nanguo*) while adults used words like 'inconvenient' (*bu fangbian*) and 'unbearable' (*nanshou*). The ICTs most cited as indispensable were the television, computer and mobile phone.

> Without television, I would feel really bored. Without a computer, I can only refer to books. Without my *fuduji*, reading would be so dull and I wouldn't even know if I were reading well. Without my digital camera, I wouldn't be able to capture all that beautiful scenery and happy memories. Without all of these devices, life would be a complete mess! I can't do without a single one of them. They are all important.
>
> (Xiao Shen, boy, 11)

The perceived indispensability of the ICTs indicated that they had been highly domesticated. In many instances, ICT use was systematically routinized into their daily lives. In particular, half of the families would have the television or hi-fi on from when they arose, so that they could catch up on news or listen to music while they prepared for work or school. Many families also sought to enhance their media consumption experience, such as linking the television to the stereo for better sound quality. Almost all the families incorporated television viewing into their dinner-time routine, after which the children did their homework while some parents would continue to watch television, exercise to music, use computer applications or surf the Net.

Indeed, the entire constellation of domesticated ICTs helped to transform the home into a convivial place for rest and recreation. Given the relative novelty of household ICTs in China, some interviewees were able to compare their lives before and after ICT adoption: 'When we were dating, there just weren't that many media so we'd just play the guitar and sing along or go to the movies. Now we have all these ICTs which we can enjoy together' (Mrs Lu, teacher, 33).

Reconfiguration

As urban Chinese apartments tend to be small, ICTs were often used to delineate private and communal areas so that individuals could enjoy some measure of personal space. The domestic space was reconfigured according to family priorities, which often centred around the child's educational needs. This media-enabled reconfiguration illustrates how the physical setting may influence the technology domestication process. Additionally, the duality of media as both shared and communal, yet private and personal, enhanced their versatility as tools for spatial reconfiguration.

For the Chen family in Beijing, the small size of their apartment necessitated that the child did her homework in the living room where the television was located. As a result, the parents would refrain from television viewing while their daughter was studying, so as not to affect her ability to concentrate. Instead, Mrs Chen would urge her husband to engage in private media use, for example internet surfing. In contrast, the Liang family in Shanghai had the luxury of space. The predominance of individualized, private space in their expansive apartment was balanced by a media-enabled accentuation of common space, which helped to instil a sense of shared existence. Discrete domestic spaces were communalized by linking the stereo player in the lounge to the eight speakers placed in different rooms in the apartment. This shared stereo listening served as a unifying experience that helped to draw the family together:

> From the moment I get home, it's left on until I go to bed so it's on for a few hours. My husband likes it but he has no choice since I like it. He won't volitionally turn it on but since I turn it on, he listens in. My daughter also enjoys the music I listen to ... sometimes she won't like a CD that I play and she'll shout, 'Mum change the CD for me!'
>
> (Mrs Liang, teacher, 32)

In some instances, the domestic space was unwittingly reconfigured when individuated media use resulted in some family members retreating into 'personal spheres' which set them apart from the rest of the family. One child recounted how his father's mobile phone use had disrupted the family dinner.

> my father kept holding onto his mobile phone and walking away from the dinner table. But when he returned to his seat, he continued to look at his mobile phone and continued to SMS. My mother said, 'What's the matter? Hurry up and eat your dinner.' But my father behaved as though he hadn't heard her.
>
> (Xiao Li, boy, 11)

Intermediation

ICTs appear to act as intermediaries, facilitating and fostering communication within the urban Chinese family. Given the success of the one-child policy, nuclear families in urban China today typically comprise only three members, as did all but one of the families interviewed. Daily life in these households seemed largely peaceful and uneventful. There was the notable absence of sibling interaction, either harmonious or discordant, which is common in larger families. With regard to ICT use, sibling competition for scarce resources such as shared ICTs and mutual sibling instruction in the use of ICTs were lacking. Sibling rivalry for parental attention was also non-existent. Instead, the parents interviewed could focus their energies on their one child, and these only-children in turn had no companions in the household other than their parents. In this regard, ICTs play a significant role in fostering this mutual parent–child companionship.

Through the processes of conversion and conversation, ICTs provided a common ground for parents and children to interact meaningfully. Many parents felt that talking to their children about media content was a good way to connect with them: 'Television introduces a common language. Take cartoons, for example. Sometimes my daughter and I will watch cartoons together and she'll teach me how to appreciate them. It's really refreshing' (Mrs Xu, teacher, 44).

Media content was also used to impart values to children:

> I'll ask my daughter to watch particular programmes. If she's unable to catch a programme which I had watched earlier in the day, I'll recount it to her in the evening. Or if I see a report in the newspaper or on television, like a story on how an online relationship had negative consequences, I'll give her a blow-by-blow account, reminding her not to fraternise with just about anyone.
>
> (Mrs Fan, shopkeeper, 44)

Studies set in other geographical contexts have shown how media use can encourage family interaction (Hoover *et al.* 2004; Lie and Sørensen 1996; Livingstone 2002). However, media may be especially important in the Chinese family context, where communication tends to be hierarchical and formal, and characterized by a father–child distance. Some interviewees mentioned how ICT use had helped to lighten the household atmosphere and erode communication barriers:

We always watch television while we eat dinner. Without the television on, I think dinnertime would feel a little awkward.

(Mrs Shen, manager, 41)

When we've just purchased a new appliance and I'm still unfamiliar with their functions, I ask my father for advice. Otherwise, I don't usually speak to him much.

(Xiao Zhang, boy, 12)

Mrs Chen, a 39-year-old manager from Beijing, vividly described how she had used SMS to introduce more levity into communication with her husband, something which she might have been less comfortable doing through voice or face-to-face communication:

Once, I sent my husband an SMS for laughs. I wrote. 'The UN Women's and Children's foundation seeks the pleasure of your company' when really, I just wanted him to come home earlier because we'd prepared a little something for him ... Although the event sounded grand, the venue indicated was really our home, No. 1104! So that was just a bit of fun. If I'd just called him directly, it would have been too dull.

Indeed, most of the parents and children interviewed did not feel that ICTs had impacted their interaction negatively. Instead, they felt that ICTs had helped to enhance family interaction:

These ICTs have brought us closer together. Sometimes when I'm using the computer and there are some functions which my mother is unfamiliar with, I'll teach her and my father will listen in too – it's a really cosy feeling ... We always watch television together also. Without television, one of us would read the newspaper, another would read a book and I'd do my home-work. So television viewing increases the amount of time we spend together ... we'll chat about the stuff we see on television and interesting stuff on our mobile phones.

(Xiao He, girl, 16)

Apart from mediating parent–child companionship, ICTs would them-selves serve as surrogate companions to both parents and children. Among adults and children, ICTs offered a ready and reliable form of companionship. In particular, some parents intimated that they empathized with their children's loneliness, no doubt comparing their children's lot with that of their own childhood where larger families were the norm. In this case, despite their apprehension about excessive television viewing, some parents felt that the television could keep the children company.

> sometimes I feel really sorry for him because he has to have some joy in his childhood and children these days are all only-children so we don't want him to feel too lonesome. But the pace of schoolwork is really fast these days and we can't allow him to deteriorate. So sometimes we let him watch television but not too much.
>
> (Mrs Huang, administrator, 37)

Among adults, ICTs also offered a ready and reliable form of companion-ship: '... I can't do without the television. It would be deathly lonesome. The other products are not that crucial' (Mrs Xie, homemaker, 43).

Interestingly, Mrs Xie was the only parent in the study who was not working full-time. Television viewing thus dominated the time which she spent at home, linking her with the outside world.

Social advancement

Chinese parents seem to regard ICTs as important tools for their children's social advancement. This is not surprising given the country's emphasis on technological advancement, and the marketing strategies commonly adopted for ICTs targeted at children. Advertisers have capitalized on the Chinese belief that education is integral to a child's development, such that even computer games devices have been marketed as 'learning facilitating machines' (*xuexi ji*) (Zhao and Murdock 1996, p. 206). Among parents, there was a general sentiment that ICTs were the inevitable way of the future and that to guarantee upward mobility, their children had to be *au fait* with technology. This observation emerged when some parents shared instances of role reversal where their children had taught them about technology, rather than vice versa. Parents were invariably proud when recounting such instances, seeing role reversal as a positive sign on many dimensions: first, that their children were acquiring skills that would enhance their social advance-ment; second, that their children were learning useful things in school. Third, it demonstrated that the next generation was overtaking the present one, a highly-valued achievement in Chinese culture where children are expected to become 'dragons' (Chu 1993, p. 204).

> I don't have time to figure out how to use these new ICTs whereas my son reads the manuals. So his knowledge is superior

to mine. And because he has computer lessons in school, his knowledge of the internet is also greater. I feel that I should learn a bit more about these new technologies because I can't even answer some of his questions. He feels really proud whenever he teaches me something, like 'You don't even know something so basic?' and my response is 'You're supposed to know more than me.'

(Mrs Zhang, accountant, 44)

Hence, although role reversal runs counter to the hierarchical communication style characteristic of Chinese families, it was largely encouraged by parents and viewed positively: 'We're kind of sneaky. We'll feign ignorance (about these ICTs) so as to 'learn' from our son. And if we're really ignorant about the stuff he teaches us, we'll praise him and he's usually thrilled' (Mrs Huang, administrator, 37).

ICTs were also used to connect with the outside world, facilitating individuals' social advancement within their network of contacts. When tapping into one's *guanxi* network, identifying the exact connection required entails negotiating an often complex web of contacts. ICTs expedite this process as linking from one person to another is greatly accelerated in electronically-mediated communication (Gamble 2003). Many interviewees actively used ICTs to establish or maintain *guanxi*, perhaps in a conscious or subconscious observance of the *'renqing* rule'. Exchanging SMSes, chatting online with friends via 'qq' and emailing digital photos were common ways of keeping in touch. Indeed, the telephone has 'reinvented' traditional Chinese rituals (Gamble 2003, p. 136) where instead of visiting relatives during the Spring festival for example, one can make these ritual 'calls' by phone. Consequently, China's mobile phone network is often overloaded with SMS well-wishes during special holidays (Qian 2003). Several interviewees enthused about the convenience of SMS greetings and one interviewee strove to use the service judiciously so as to preserve its novelty value: 'If it's a birthday, I'll send a salutation. Or if it's a special holiday. But I don't do this frequently. If I did, it would become commonplace!' (Mrs Chen, manager, 39).

Apart from the functionality of ICTs, their strong symbolic value also heightened their utility as tools for social advancement. For some of the children, the possession and use of ICTs helped pave the way towards social inclusion. Peer acceptance is particularly important to Chinese only-children as they lack a sibling network and have to compete with other only-children for companionship (Chee 2000). In such circumstances, the role of peers as friends, playmates and influencers of consumption behaviour become even more important (K. Chan and

McNeal 2004). The possession of trendy ICTs, or the lack thereof, could draw a distinction between the socially-accepted haves and the socially-excluded have-nots. One child's desire for an MP3 player seemed to be motivated by her wish to keep up with her peers and gain acceptance: 'Whenever we go for school excursions and everyone gets on the bus, some kids with MP3 players will fiddle with their players or snooze off and ignore me. So getting an MP3 player would give me something to do' (Xiao Jiang, girl, 12).

Containment

Chinese parents' practice of 'control' (*guan*), so as to train their children to rein in their impulses, was manifested in parental restrictions on children's media usage. These efforts at control were occasionally tempered by the recognition that exposure to ICTs was nonetheless important:

> Our son is just too young to control his computer usage. Once he develops a craze for a game, he just can't restrain himself. But his father thinks it's not a good idea to completely deny him exposure to the computer. So we try to give him some space.
>
> (Mrs Shen, manager, 41)

Such control is borne out of strong parental interest to contain the perceived negative impact of ICT use on their children's education, a key priority of Chinese families. Most of the parents controlled their children's media usage strictly, echoing the findings of Zhao and Murdock (1997) that Chinese children's leisure time was tightly regulated, with priority accorded to schoolwork and educative recreation:

> I only watch a few minutes of television (everyday) ... only after I've completed my homework. But after I've completed my homework, I have to eat dinner, during which I'm not allowed to watch television. Then after dinner I have to practise my piano playing.
>
> (Xiao Wang, girl, 7)

Many parents imposed conditions that ICT use such as television viewing and playing computer games could only commence after the day's homework had been completed. Efforts were also made to incorporate what was perceived as beneficial ICT usage into what little spare time was available. Parental restrictions on children's media usage tended to be bound up with daily routines: 'Our daughter doesn't watch much television. We make sure she eats her dinner at 7 p.m. and that she watches half an hour of news. But sometimes, she can't even afford to watch that half hour because she's just too busy with her studies' (Mrs He, doctor, 48).

In China, the duty to control children falls not only on parents but also on teachers. Since the inception of the one-child policy, Chinese authorities have identified preschool teachers as the solution to parental over-indulgence of only-children (Wu 1996b). It appears that this trend of teachers exerting control over students extends into the students' later years, and to the realm of domestic media use. In particular, some teachers would exhort parents to restrict their children's media usage and even discourage the acquisition of particular ICTs: 'Our son's college teacher prohibited us from buying him a computer for fear that it would affect his studies' (Mrs Xie, homemaker, 43).

Some parents were in turn deferential towards teachers and acted on their recommendations:

> There are so many children's programmes on these days and their teachers don't allow them to watch television. His teachers will ask during parent-teacher meetings, 'Have any students been watching television?' So we try our best not to let him watch too much television.
>
> (Mrs Huang, administrator, 37)

Another common 'containment' strategy was limiting the media content which children were exposed to. With regard to television, there was typically strong parental emphasis on watching news and documentary programmes, while the viewing of adult fare such as soap operas was discouraged. Parental control of internet usage was more varied, ranging from a complete prohibition, to restrictions on accessing particular websites, to occasional supervision: 'In our household, I can't surf the internet. Not that I don't have access, you can see the computer is hooked up to the phone line. Just that I'm not allowed to go online' (Xiao Shen, boy, 11).

In some families, children volitionally restricted their own media exposure. They engaged in predominantly educative media usage, either watching news programmes and documentaries, or surfing the internet for school-related materials. Xiao Feng, a 14-year-old boy, explained how he controlled his own media usage (confirmed separately by his mother who lauded his maturity):

> My parents never restrict me, as long as I don't spend too much time on the computer. Their main concerns are that excessive

usage will affect my eyesight or my studies. Most of the time, I seldom violate the boundaries which I set for myself. I don't go online, or I don't visit unsavoury websites. I use it mainly for research and my studies and I budget a certain amount of time for these activities. The same goes for television.

Conclusion

The rising affluence of urban Chinese households has introduced to China the phenomenon of the media-rich home. In such homes, ICTs are seen not as luxuries but as necessities, integral components of the domestic space. The adoption and deployment of ICTs within the urban Chinese household reflects the 'moral economy' (Silverstone *et al.* 1992, p. 15) of the family vis-à-vis its different members and vis-à-vis the rest of society.

In the routinization of ICT use in the households studied, family values are reaffirmed or challenged, and family priorities, entrenched or reordered. The duality of ICTs as shared and communal, yet individuated and personal, aided the drawing of domestic public–private boundaries in accordance with the families' priorities. The intermediating role which ICTs played in connecting family members and providing surrogate companionship reflected the nature of communication within one-child families and the hierarchical communication style characteristic of Chinese families. The control which parents attempted to exert over their children's ICT use drew into sharp relief the trend towards compartmentalizing children's leisure time and the high regard for educational achievement in Chinese culture. The use of ICTs in social advancement, connecting the family with its *guanxi* network and facilitating social inclusion by one's peers, were symptomatic of the growing importance of ICTs in Chinese society today. The families' ICT domestication was thus set against the unrelenting forces of modernization and the enduring values of tradition.

Media and communications research in China has been predominantly influenced by contemporary communications and cultural studies theory, focusing on *inter alia*, media consumption, media systems and information society, through the application of quantitative research methods such as case studies, audience analysis, surveys and measurement techniques (Hong 2002). In studying media consumption in urban Chinese families using the technology domestication framework and employing qualitative interviews, this chapter has introduced an additional dimension to our understanding of media use in China.

Note

1. Manufactured in China for the local market, these machines enable users to listen to accurate pronunciations of English words and to record and review their own pronunciations. See for example the website of a popular *fuduji* manufacturer, Guangdong Bu Bu Gao Electronic Manufacturing Private Limited at http://www.gdbbk.com/

References

Anagnost, A. (1997) 'Children and national transcendence in China', in (eds) K. G. Lieberthal, S. F. Lim and E. P. Young, *Constructing China: The Interaction of Culture and Economic.* Centre for Chinese Studies, University of Michigan: Ann Arbour, MI, pp. 195–222.

Bovill, M. and Livingstone, S. (2001) 'Bedroom culture and the privatization of media use', in (eds) S. Livingstone and M. Bovill, *Children and Their Changing Environment: A European Comparative Study.* Lawrence Erlbaum Associates: New Jersey, pp. 179–200.

Chan, H. and King, A. Y. C. (2003) 'Religion', in (ed.) R. E. Gamer, *Understanding Contemporary China*, 2nd edn. Lynne Rienner: Boulder, CO, pp. 339–76.

Chan, K. and McNeal, J. U. (2004) *Advertising to Children in China.* The Chinese University Press: Hong Kong.

Chao, L. and Myers, R. H. (1998) 'China's consumer revolution: the 1990s and beyond'. *Journal of Contemporary China*, vol. 7, no. 18, pp. 351–68.

Chee, B. W. L. (2000) 'Eating snacks and biting pressure: Only children in Beijing', in (ed.) J. Jun, *Feeding China's Little Emperors: Food, Children and Social Change.* Stanford University Press: Stanford, CA, pp. 48–70.

Chen, C. S., Lee, S. Y. and Stevenson, H. W. (1996) 'Academic achievement and motivation of Chinese students: A cross-national perspective', in (ed.) S. Lau, *Growing up the Chinese Way.* The Chinese University Press: Hong Kong, pp. 69–92.

Chu, G. C. (1993) *The Great Wall in Ruins: Communication and Cultural Change in China.* State University of New York Press: Albany, NY.

Dai, X. (2003) 'ICTs in China's development strategy', in (eds) C. R. Hughes and G. Wacker, *China and the Internet: Politics of the Digital Leap Forward.* Routledge: London, pp. 8–29.

Davis, D. and Harrell, S. (1993) 'Introduction: The impact of post-Mao reforms on family life', in (eds) D. Davis and S. Harrell, *Chinese Families in the Post-Mao Era.* University of California Press: Berkeley, CA, pp. 1–24.

Donald, S. H. (2002) 'Crazy Rabbits! Children's media culture', in (eds) S. H. Donald, M. Keane and Y. Hong, *Media in China: Consumption, Content and Crisis*. Routledge Curzon: London, pp. 128–38.

Euromonitor (2003) *Consumer Lifestyles in China* (February 2003). Retrieved 14 April 2004, from http://www.euromonitor.com

Falbo, T. and Poston Jr, D. L. (1996) 'The academic, personality and physical outcomes of Chinese only children: A review', in (ed.) S. Lau, *Growing up the Chinese Way*. The Chinese University Press: Hong Kong, pp. 265–86.

Fan, J. and Xiao, J. (1998) 'Consumer decision-making styles of young-adult Chinese'. *The Journal of Consumer Affairs*, vol. 32, no. 2, pp. 275–94.

Gamble, J. (2003) *Shanghai in Transition: Changing Perspectives and Social Contours of a Chinese Metropolis*. Routledge Curzon: London.

Gamer, R. E. (2003) 'Introduction', in (ed.) R. E. Gamer, *Understanding Contemporary China*, 2nd edn. Lynne Rienner: Boulder, CO, pp. 1–10.

Gao, G., Ting-Toomey, S. and Gudykunst, W. B. (1996) 'Chinese communication processes', in (ed.) M. H. Bond, *The Handbook of Chinese Psychology*. Oxford University Press, Hong Kong, pp. 280–93.

Goodman, D. S. (1996) 'The People's Republic of China: The party-state, capitalist revolution and new entrepreneurs', in (eds) R. Robison and D. S. Goodman, *The New Rich in Asia: Mobile Phones, McDonalds and Middle-Class Revolution*. Routledge: London, pp. 225–42.

Goodwin, R. and Tang, C. S.-K. (1996) 'Chinese personal relationships', in (ed.) M. H. Bond, *The Handbook of Chinese Psychology*. Oxford University Press: Hong Kong, pp. 294–308.

Gu, J. (1990) 'Household structure in contemporary China', in (eds) Y. Zeng, C. Zhang and S. Peng, *Changing Family Structure and Population Aging in China*. Peking University Press: Beijing, pp. 92–106.

Guo, Y. (2000) 'Family relations: The generation gap at the table', in (ed.) J. Jun, *Feeding China's Little Emperors: Food, Children and Social Change*. Stanford University Press: Stanford, CA, pp. 94–113.

Hau, K. T. and Salili, F. (1996) 'Achievement goals and causal attributions of Chinese students', in (ed.) S. Lau, *Growing up the Chinese Way*. The Chinese University Press: Hong Kong, pp. 121–46.

Ho, D. Y. F. (1986) 'Chinese patterns of socialisation: A critical review', in (ed.) M. H. Bond, *The Psychology of the Chinese People*. Oxford University Press: Hong Kong, pp. 1–37.

Ho, D. Y. F. (1987) 'Fatherhood in Chinese culture', in (ed.) M. E. Lamb, *The Father's Role: Cross-Cultural Perspectives*. Erlbaum: Hillsdale, NJ, pp. 227–45.

Hong, Y. (2002) 'Preface', in (eds) S. H. Donald, M. Keane and Y. Hong,

Media in China: Consumption, Content and Crisis. Routledge Curzon: London, pp. ix–xi.

Hoover, S. M., Clark, L. S., Alters, D. F., Champ, J. G. and Hood, L. (2004) *Media, Home, and Family*. Routledge: New York.

Jankowiak, W. (1993) *Sex, Death, and Hierarchy in a Chinese City*. Columbia University Press: New York.

Ju, Y. (1996) *Understanding China: Centre Stage of the Fourth Power*. SUNY Press: Albany.

Leung, L. (1998) 'Lifestyles and the use of new media technology in urban China'. *Telecommunications Policy*, vol. 22, no. 9, pp. 781–90.

Li, C. (1998) *China: The Consumer Revolution*. Deloitte & Touche Consulting Group: Singapore.

Lie, M. and Sørensen, K. H. (eds) (1996) *Making Technology our Own? Domesticating Technology into Everyday Life*. Scandinavian University Press: Oslo.

Livingstone, S. (2002) *Young People and New Media*. Sage: London.

Livingstone, S. (1992) 'The meaning of domestic technologies: A personal construct analysis of familial gender relations', in (eds) R. Silverstone and E. Hirsch, *Consuming Technologies: Media and Information in Domestic Spaces*. Routledge: London, pp. 113–30.

Lu, H. (2000) 'To be relatively comfortable in an egalitarian society', in (ed.) D. S. Davis, *The Consumer Revolution in Urban China*. University of California Press: Berkeley, CA, pp. 124–44.

McNeal, J. U. and Zhang, H. (2000) 'Chinese children's consumer behaviour: A review'. *Advertising and Marketing to Children* (March/April), pp. 31–7.

Meng, Q. X. and Li, M. Z. (2002) 'New economy and ICT development in China'. *Information Economics and Policy*, vol. 14, no. 2, pp. 275–95.

Mobile Phones Dominate Telecom Sector (2001) 16 May, retrieved 1 October 2004, from http://english.people.com.cn/english/200105/16/eng20010516_70155.html

National Bureau of Statistics of China (2004) *China Statistical Yearbook 2000*. China Statistics Press: Beijing.

New Trends in Chinese Marriage and the Family (1987) Women of China: Beijing.

People's Republic of China Yearbook (2003) Xinhua Publishing House: Beijing.

Qian, W. (2003) *Spring Festival Greetings Through SMS Break 5 Billion*, retrieved 5 November 2004, from http://www.china.org.cn/english/2003/Feb/55255.htm

Shanghai Ranks 1st Among Metropolitan Economic Giants (2004) retrieved 1 October 2004, from http://www.chinadaily.com.cn/english/doc/2004-03/04/content_311723.htm

Shanghai Ranks Second in Internet Penetration (2004) retrieved 1 October, 2004, from http://news.xinhuanet.com/english/2004-04/08/content_1407796.htm

Silverstone, R., Hirsch, E. and Morley, D. (1992) 'Information and communication technologies and the moral economy of the household', in (eds) R. Silverstone and E. Hirsch, *Consuming Technologies: Media and Information in Domestic Spaces*. Routledge: London, pp. 15–31.

Stevenson, H. W. and Lee, S.-Y. (1996) 'The academic achievement of Chinese students', in (ed.) M. H. Bond, *The Handbook of Chinese Psychology*. Oxford University Press: Hong Kong, pp. 124–42.

Wang, S. (1995) 'Private time and politics: Changes in the leisure activities among city residents'. *Chinese Social Science Quarterly*, Summer, pp. 108–25.

Wang, Y. and Cui, N. (2004) 'Boom of after-school education in China'. *China Daily*, 26 March.

Wei, R. and Pan, Z. D. (1999) 'Mass media and consumerist values in the People's Republic of China'. *International Journal of Public Opinion Research*, vol. 11, no. 1, pp. 75–96.

Wu, D. Y. H. (1996a) 'Chinese childhood socialisation', in (ed.) M. H. Bond, *The Handbook of Chinese Psychology*. Oxford University Press: Hong Kong, pp. 143–54.

Wu, D. Y. H. (1996b) 'Parental control: Psychocultural interpretations of Chinese patterns of socialization', in (ed.) S. Lau, *Growing up the Chinese Way*. The Chinese University Press: Hong Kong, pp. 1–28.

Yan, R. (1994) 'To Reach China Consumers, Adapt to *Guo-Qing*'. *Harvard Business Review*, vol. 72, no. 5, pp. 66–74.

Yang, M. M.-H. (1994) *Gifts, Favours, Banquets: The Art of Social Relationships in China*. Cornell University Press: Ithaca, NY.

Zang, X. (2003) 'Family, kinship, marriage and sexuality', in (ed.) R. E. Gamer, *Understanding Contemporary China*, 2nd edn. Lynne Rienner: Boulder, CO, pp. 281–308.

Zhang, Y. (1999) 'New information technologies and mass communication in Shanghai'. *Media Asia*, vol. 26, no. 1, pp. 3–11.

Zhao, B. (1997) 'Consumerism, confucianism, communism: Making sense of China today'. *New Left Review*, 222, pp. 43–59.

Zhao, B. and Murdock, G. (1996) 'Young pioneers: Children and the making of Chinese consumerism'. *Cultural Studies*, vol. 10, no. 2, pp. 201–17.

Zhu, J. J. H. and He, Z. (2002) 'Perceived characteristics, perceived needs, and perceived popularity – Adoption and use of the Internet in China'. *Communication Research*, vol. 29, no. 4, pp. 466–95.

11 Domestication at work in small businesses

Jo Pierson

I would like to understand the computer, just as I know my car or as I know a tree.

(Florent, fruit farmer, male, 42)

Introduction

Understanding the use of ICT in small businesses via the domestication approach is the core objective of this chapter. Technology use is a central topic in research on organizations, but (very) small organizations have received only limited attention. Little is known on how technology adoption and use take shape in small-scale professional settings. This chapter demonstrates that ICT use in small enterprises is indeed different from large organizations and that the role of the business owner and his social characteristics are crucial for understanding ICT use. This is usually ignored in traditional research on organizational use of ICT, because it often takes a technological determinist view. To account for the role of social actors, it is necessary to take a different theoretical position. The constructivist approaches to technology privilege the mutual shaping of technological and social settings. Neither the technology nor the social is the determinant. Both aspects co-determine each other. The domestication approach applies such a view on ICT use and acceptance but has originally almost exclusively been developed for domestic or household settings. This chapter demonstrates with empirical data that the domestication approach can also be applied to the context of very small businesses. Extending it beyond the domestic setting also contributes to enriching the understanding of domestication.

The findings are based on doctoral research (Pierson 2003). ICTs are defined here as a set of different telephone- and computer-related technologies and services, in particular fax, ISDN, mobile phone, computer and internet. The target user group consists of micro-enterprises, that is the sole proprietors and very small enterprises with fewer than 10 employees (European Commission 1996). Although there are many different delimitations, micro-enterprises belong to the category of Small and Medium-sized Enterprises (SME) but when speaking about SMEs, people usually mean enterprises that are larger. The empirical data consist of a representative survey of 550 micro-enterprises in Flanders (Belgium), together with 200 telephone inter-views and 40 in-depth face-to-face interviews. The latter were selected from two technologically contrasting activities: agriculture, in particular fruit farmers, and white-collar workers, in particular accountants. A major finding that emerges from these data is that an ICT and the owner of a micro-enterprise are certainly not always 'compatible'.

Domestication and small business research

Relevance of small business setting

The small businesses, especially the very small enterprises and the sole proprietors, often have a strong link with the residential context and with domestic motives. Therefore, domestication is a useful concept for understanding both the small business setting and its professional use of ICT.

Technology is one of the central themes of organization studies, with a special interest in the influence of technology on the structure and the performance of an organization. However, when looking at technology use in an organization from the viewpoint of the profes-sional user, mainly management and information studies are relevant. ICT adoption and use in these studies refer to the implementation and use of 'information systems' (IS) or 'management information systems' (MIS). The related subdomains are called 'information systems research' or 'information management studies'. They look at how supply and demand of information in organizations can be mediated by means of technology. This subdiscipline has been subject to the consecutive streams of thought within organization sociology and organization science.[1]

Yet the vast majority of management studies regarding information systems focuses on large to very large companies. The acceptance and implementation of these systems in small companies like SMEs[2] has received less attention (Igbaria *et al.* 1998; Palvia and Palvia 1999; Southern and Tilly 2000). There are various reasons for this. It is clear that small firms did not have information systems in the original meaning of the phrase. The initial concept referred to large-scale internal and/or external networked computer processing systems that are connected with, for example, databases. These kinds of sophisticated systems are of little relevance to SMEs and even less to micro-enterprises. But this is changing with more recent technological developments. The meaning of information systems has been extended to ICTs with a lower threshold (computer, internet, fax, mobile phone, EDI, and so on), yet the statistics show that size still correlates strongly with ownership of these technologies and services. Therefore, it is no surprise that information systems research first looks for settings where these systems are omnipresent. Another reason for the relative neglect of small business is the fact that there is tendency in 'classical' economics to see all companies as equal with regard to ICT adoption and use. Yet it is clear that in their everyday behaviour large enterprises are very different from micro-enterprises. The problem is, as stated by Storey (1994) that 'too often, the large-firm model is taken as given and the small firm is assumed to be a "scaled-down" version of a large firm'. If all businesses are treated similarly, then there is little motivation to look at small businesses separately. They are more difficult to capture given their large number.

Combining factor and actor approach

Given its focus on large businesses, the information systems research alone generates insufficient understanding of ICT use by micro-enterprises. Because of their very small size their ICT-behaviour is to a large extent configured by a single person, i.e. the business owner. Therefore, a sociological view needs to take into account the specificity of the micro-social setting of the owner.

This setting can be examined from an objectivist (factor) and from a subjectivist (actor) approach relating to the epistemological dichotomy in technology studies on how the social can be identified (de Jager and Mok 1989, pp. 305–6). On the one hand, social phenomena, like media behaviour or technology use, are perceived as something that is a consequence of specific *factors* disconnected from persons. People behave in one way or another because of specific structural and/or cultural factors, typically investigated by means of quantitative research like surveys. On the other hand, there is the view that the social reality only exists through the interpreting *actors* that give meaning to this reality. The social reality can, therefore, never be separated from the individual who enacts and experiences it. The latter refers to a descriptive mode that favours an ethnographic viewpoint.

It is possible, however, to study a social phenomenon – for example ICT use in small businesses – by combining both approaches. The idea that the two realms cannot be reconciled is opposed here, following Willmott (1993). It can lead not only to a richer and more diversified analysis of a research question, but also to a more thorough examination. That is needed to understand the situation of the business owner in a micro-enterprise.

Research set-up

This chapter discusses the contribution of the domestication theory, and how this can be associated with the socio-economic reality of the business owner in a micro-enterprise, based on an actor and factor approach. Besides an explanation of the domestication concept, three central aspects in relation to the micro-enterprise setting are elaborated: domestication process, moral economy and blurring of boundaries. Afterwards some dominant trends and findings from the literature on (management) information systems in relation to ICT use are juxtaposed to domestication. Mainstream information systems literature has an objectivist and functionalist angle on the issue of information technology in businesses, with an emphasis on technological and economic explanations. In contrast to this factor approach, the actor approach starting from the interpretation and enactment of the organization members is less developed, although growing. Comparing domestication and IS shows how domestication research complements traditional IS research in relation to small businesses.

The research is based on quantitative and qualitative findings, reflecting a factor and actor approach in domestication. The quantitative analysis refers to a telephone survey conducted at the end of 2000 with a representative sample of 550 randomly selected micro-enterprises in the Flemish district (Belgium), on a total population of 400,000. Yet statistically significant correlations are insufficient for understanding the motives and meaning of business owners concerning their use of ICT. Therefore, the quantitative approach (breadth-wise) was complemented with a qualitative approach (in-depth). This was done by means of in-depth interviews with two a-typical professional activities, fruit farmers (ICT-poor sector) and accountants (ICT-rich sector). Semi-structured interviews with 20 respondents in each profession were executed based on a topic list inspired by domestication research. These 40 interviews are further framed by an additional quantitative sketch of both sectors, based on two surveys of 100 respondents each.[3]

Domestication concept

Domestication refers to the activity of 'domesticating' or taming and cultivating a wild animal in order to make it a pet (Silverstone and Haddon 1996). It is a metaphor for 'absorbing' a strange technology into the context of the everyday life. This refers to the reciprocity of 'fitting in' and 'fitting to' between the ICT and the user context (Punie 2000). The domestication perspective is not only about how (potential) users behave in relation to the technology and vice versa. The way people deal with ICT can also be an articulation of existing practices, conflicts and meanings within the user community.

The domestication perspective originates from views within the cultural studies, especially since the 1980s, from those authors that focus on media as technology, instead of media content and genres.[4] Bausinger (1984) talks about consuming and absorbing technological tools or instruments. Content and technology cannot, of course, be separated, but there can be difference in focus.[5] One of the first empirical analyses where both aspects were elaborated is in *Family Television* by David Morley (1986). Besides the programme preferences, the study also discusses the meaning of the remote control. However it is only late in the 1980s that the technology-as-text approach gets substantial attention (Haddon 1991).

> Like the sounds and images which constitute the 'software' of mass communication, its 'hardware' might equally be seen as a collector of signs that have multi-accentual social meanings – capable of being decoded and appropriated in a plurality of ways within the context of household cultures.
>
> (Moores 1993, p. 9)

This meant a shift from text and genre orientation within the cultural studies to patterns and routines of action in using media technology (Frissen and Wester 1997). The technological objects, like television (and later expanded to other ICTs), are to be situated within the context of reception, linked to social relations, structure and power dynamics. The aim is 'to frame the analyses ... within a broader framework of the role of various media in articulating the private and public spheres, which (hopefully) allows us to articulate these micro-analyses to broader perspectives on macro-social issues of politics, power and culture' (Morley 1992, p. 40).

Domestication in micro-enterprises

Containing the idea of 'domesticity', it is no surprise that the notion of domestication is mainly linked to the home and the household. Some authors have extended the notion to the mobile user (Haddon 2004, pp. 99–115). Only a few scholars have used the concept for explaining ICT use in a work environment (Frissen 1999; Lie and Sørensen 1996; Sørensen *et al.* 2000). Yet there is the implicit assumption that this rich and multi-layered concept can indeed be applied in other contexts as well.

> Both the structures and the processes which we will be describing have a wider relevance, and the process of domestication, especially, should not therefore be seen as something which only takes place in the home. It should inform discussions of technological change in a wide range of institutional settings.
> (Silverstone and Haddon 1996, p. 46)

It is argued in this chapter that the concept is not only useful for explaining the adoption and use of technology in micro-enterprises but also indispensable for a better understanding of ICT use. The basic elements of the domestication approach will be checked against the empirical findings to show this. These basics are the domestication process, the moral economy and the blurring of boundaries.

Domestication process

A distinction is made between different phases that occur in the domestication process or – in the words of Lie and Sørensen (1996) – in making the technology one's own: commodification, appropriation and conversion (Silverstone and Haddon 1996, pp. 61–5). This phasing of the domestication process has been criticized because it contains a notion of linearity that has similarities with a diffusionist approach to innovations (Punie 2000). However, the different elements used in the description of the domestication process do have a value of their own in explaining central aspects of the introduction and acceptance of ICT in a residential context. Therefore, it is examined if and how these elements are applicable in the context of a small-scale professional context.

First there is the link with the development, production and marketing by means of 'commodification'. This refers to the industrial and commercial processes by which services or technologies, like ICT, are marked with a specific function and identity within the consumer society. In this way they enter the public forum of the formal market economy as a commodity. This underscores the idea that ICTs not only have material or functional features, but also a powerful symbolic connotation, as is being externalized in advertising and in public discourse. However, this connotation is dependent on the imaginative work that the potential or actual user undertakes as they participate in the consumption process.

The next phase of domestication is called 'appropriation'. This is the moment when an object is acquired and thus gets a new owner. It is defined as the passage from the formal economy to the moral economy: commodity becomes object (Silverstone *et al.* 1992, p. 22). Once the object or the technology is owned it has to be accepted into, and made to fit in, the existing domestic culture of place and time use.

The phase of 'conversion' concerns the display of the acquired artefact, which makes again the link with the outside world. The meaning of objects is used as 'currency' in the interplay with the public environment. In the early days of the mobile phone, for example, this object was foremost seen as a status symbol. The same goes for young people boasting to each other about their gaming skills. This kind of display enables designers and developers to pick up information that can be brought into the innovation and marketing of new products and services.

The phases in the process of domestication also occur with business owners of micro-enterprises. This is illustrated with findings from the survey and the interviews. In the commodification phase the technological artefact or ICT gets a specific public meaning. In the case of micro-enterprises the phase mainly takes place within or by the sector itself. The sector-related stakeholders and media play a very prominent role in this regard. It appears that most fruit farmers and accountants get information and images on professional ICT (like the online connection with the fruit auction for fruit farmers or the professional literature for accountants) from their professional organizations, from specialist journals and from contacts with colleagues in their sector. This also applies to more generic ICT technologies and services (like internet), although general media (for example, television and radio) also have a prominent role. Commodification means here that sector-specific channels – like specialist journals – shape the public meanings of ICTs.

Appropriation signals the transition from public to private meaning. The micro-enterprises try to accept the ICT in their own everyday work and life. This is not self-evident. The appropriation of internet applications, for example, takes place mainly via the computer. Yet it is the latter that forms the main obstacle for most fruit farmers. The survey showed that three out of five farmers did not have a computer. Even when a PC was available in the company, one third of the business owners did not use it. When the business owner did use the computer, it was generally (54 per cent) not on a daily basis. This means that professional appropriation (defined as using the computer daily for at least half of the time for professional motives), only occurred with 12 per cent of the fruit farmers. As a consequence, the professional domestication of the computer and of the applications that run on a computer is a rather laborious process. This has also to do with the negative perception of office work and everything that relates to that (like computers). For many fruit farmers office computers are at odds with the specificity and practices of their job: 'The purpose of a fruit farmer is to be and to work in his orchard, and not sitting behind that stupid computer, isn't it?' (Florent, fruit farmer, male, 42).[6]

Some farmers see it as a 'necessary evil', while only a few perceive the computer as really helpful for the job. Only when the computer is seen as a kind of elongation of fruit farming technology (for example cold store, sorting machine), will the appropriation take place in a more natural and evident way, because of the professional need, recognizability and therefore reconcilability. In this way a fruit farmer states that a(n) (office) computer does not belong in a fruit-farming business: 'because you cannot do much with it, can you? It is an expensive investment, which does not yield anything directly' (Ronny, fruit farmer, male, 47). Yet in the same interview, Ronny argues: 'You could say that informatics and the computer are indispensable in the control of modern greenhouses.'

The situation is totally different in the case of accountancy, which is mainly an office job. Having no computer is exceptional among accountants. Computer ownership amounted to 86 per cent of the business owners, at the end of the year 2000. One could say with a witticism that the literal distance to a computer in the work environment equals the mental distance to the computer.

In the conversion phase the private technological object re-enters the public domain and is used for communicating meaning to the outside world. A good example is the accountants' use of the internet. The interviews took place during the autumn of 1998, when the internet began to break through in Flanders. Consequently, at that time there were only few professional internet applications available that were really useful for an accountant. Nevertheless, many respondents in the accountancy group felt more or less obliged to have internet, often based on 'client push'.

> Clients get younger ... So once these people become clients, they probably will all communicate via e-mail. At that moment you cannot afford to not follow this trend. So, it is almost a necessary evil. For the moment I do not have internet, but at a certain moment I will have to give in.
>
> (Marc, accountant, male, 43)

The main reason for their adoption and use is that (potential) clients see them as all-round advisers with regard to company administration. Clients expect their accountants to be informed about matters such as internet. So it was important for these accountants to show the outside world that they have and understand new media. Conversion becomes a part of the business process, legitimating ownership and use of ICTs, such as the internet. This results in a greater than average internet penetration – 80 per cent of the accountants against 44 per cent of all micro-enterprises at that time. Despite its low direct usefulness, 48 per cent of all accountants with a computer claim to be online daily at least half of the time for professional reasons. This also shows how the concept of 'perceived usefulness' in the information systems literature (see below) can be complemented by the domestication perspective.

Moral economy

One of the key concepts in the domestication perspective is 'moral economy' (Silverstone *et al.* 1992). The notion of the household as a moral economy, as a kind of opposite to formal economy, is based on anthropological and historical research. It appeared that the meaning of an object (for example money) is subject to transformation as it is appropriated, that is when it crosses the boundaries between the public world of individual and commodity-based transactions and the private world of domestic reproduction. In the latter, other agreements and values dominate, in particular, those that are associated with longer-term interests of the social order. Given that the meanings of objects are negotiable, Silverstone *et al.* state that they are 'vulnerable to the active or reactive work of individuals and households as they transform and translate the public and alienating offerings of the formal economy into accessible and acceptable terms' (Silverstone *et al.* 1992, p. 17).

The notion of 'moral economy' can be explained in different ways. 'Economy' refers to the fact that households are economic entities in that their contribution to the production and consumption are part of the general public economy. At the same time, the household is also an economic entity that acts on its own. 'Moral' refers to the way that the meaning of public activities like work, relaxation or shopping is being negotiated through the knowledge, values, norms, assessment and the aesthetics within the household. The latter aspects are the result of the background and the biography of the household, its separate members and of the in-house politics. Silverstone *et al.* summarize this as follows:

> The moral economy of the household is therefore both an economy of meanings and a meaningful economy; and in both of its two dimensions it stands in a potentially or actually transformative relationship to the public, objective economy of the exchange of goods and meanings.
>
> (Silverstone *et al.* 1992, p. 18)

ICT behaviour in small companies is a typical illustration of the moral economy idea. The presupposition is that business owners in any company act according to the formal economy logic. This relates to the idea that all enterprises, large or small, have the same relationship with technology. However a small business should not be perceived as a large business at a small scale. 'The analysis here strives not to see small business as large business in microcosm. It recognizes small business as an "uneasy stratum" with characteristics of labour as well as capital – an institution that can only be fully understood when seen in its social and economic context' (Mariussen *et al.* 1997, pp. 65–6).

This presupposes that the situation in a micro-enterprise with regard to adoption and use of ICT can be identified as a moral economy. In the household, the main question is: how does the public environment affect the private context of the family? When looking at micro-enterprises the question is: how does the private (social) context of the business owner affect the public (economic) world of business use of ICT in small companies, and vice versa? Findings from the survey and the interviews illustrate this. First, this refers to how personal characteristics from the private context (co-)determine the adoption and use of ICT in the business. Second, the point of attention is the relation between the technological capabilities of the micro-enterprise and the private setting.

The notion of moral economy is used here to indicate how the private sphere (personal traits, private interests, social contacts, household norms and values) permeates the professional sphere and how this shapes ICT acceptance in micro-enterprises. Significant characteristics are: education, age, gender, hobby and relational setting – especially the educational level, whether or not having a higher education degree, significantly explains ICT adoption (fax, ISDN, mobile phone and computer). Yet internet is an exception, because education does not seem to play a role with regard to adopting and using the internet in the business. So once the computer is acquired it is not the educational level that influences online access and use.

The situation of a business manager of a micro-enterprise is very different from that of a business manager of a large company. In the latter, ICT acquisition and use is more dependent on formal decision processes. This is especially the case where technological experts are involved, who (can) approach the technology from a more rational professional-economic logic. Yet the self-employed business owners mostly do not have access to this kind of expert and often they themselves do not have the full technological capabilities. The survey confirms that most business owners claim to know only a little, or very little, about the internet, computer and even mobile phone: respectively, 76 per cent, 61 per cent and 54 per cent.

The question is then, to whom can they turn for support in decisions regarding computer and internet? The survey shows that most business owners do not at first look for outside support when taking decisions with regard to computers and the internet in their business (for example, buying a PC, installing new software). Despite (sometimes) limited knowledge, most business owners, by far, trust their own judgement and knowledge (69 per cent). However, if additional help is needed they first turn to people nearby, mostly family (17.5 per cent).[7] In only very few cases (5 per cent of the micro-enterprises with personnel) is a specialist consulted.

The surveys among fruit farmers and accountants show similar patterns. Fruit farmers mainly trust their own judgement (61 per cent), when making decisions about computers and the internet. Family members hold a strong second place (22 per cent). Accountants have, on average, more computer skills. It is, therefore, no surprise that 80 per cent claim to deal with computer issues themselves. For additional help they look to specialist support outside the firm (like the computer store) (26 per cent) or they ask somebody in the company (16 per cent). Having a partner who knows as much, or more, about computers occurs in 38 per cent of the cases, compared to 70 per cent of the fruit farmers. The interviews indeed showed that the (female) partner is often more informed about ICT. When asking if a fruit farmer and a computer go together, the answer is:

> No. Except when your partner also works in the business, then a computer is possible. The wife does more the personnel registration and the bookkeeping and stuff ... My wife doesn't have to be outside in the rain and the wind.
>
> (Kristof, fruit farmer, male, 25)

In many cases the technological capabilities are related to the division of roles, where one person is responsible for the 'outside work' (fruit farming), while the other takes care of the 'inside work' (administration, calculations, and so on).

Blurring of boundaries

In order to understand the domestication of ICT in relation to the moral economy of the micro-enterprise, other aspects also need to be taken into account. Haddon and Silverstone (1993, p. 4) state:

> Central to an understanding of the moral economy of a household, and central therefore to an understanding of the

place of ICTs in the home, were issues of the organization of space and time, gender and age difference, and *the relationship between public and private dimensions of everyday life*. (Own emphases)

Public and private dimensions can refer to different aspects of social life, like political discourse (cf. Habermas's public sphere), solidarity, but also to work (in contrast to private or free time). It is the latter meaning that is especially relevant in the context of a micro-enterprise. Both concepts – public and private – are however 'inter-relational'. This means that one can only be delimited in relation to the other (Silverstone 1996).

Business owners of micro-enterprises often experience an overlap in place and time between public and private world. This idea is often indicated by the notion of 'blurring of boundaries'.[8] The survey shows that for two-thirds of all Flemish business owners (66 per cent) the place for work coincides with home. More than three-quarters of the respondents (76 per cent) have no clearly delimited working hours. The situation of most business owners in a micro-enterprise, therefore, corresponds with the situation of teleworkers, that is, people working (part of their time) from home.

The workplace of teleworkers is (partly) situated at home. Experiences of teleworkers and small-business owners, therefore, are similar. Technologies often migrate from appliances for work to appliances for home use by other members of the family. The reverse phenomenon also occurs, when household communication technologies like the telephone, are used for professional motives. This demands specific requirements (for example, who answers the phone, not occupying the phone during work hours) (Haddon and Silverstone 1994). A similar public–private interaction can be found in micro-enterprises.

ICTs that have entered the household environment of the teleworker interact with the moral economy. This can have an indirect impact on the existing arrangements, expectations and routines within the household. The 'culture' and organization of the household will have to conform to some extent to the work prerequisites. This adaptation is not always easy or without conflict (Haddon and Silverstone 1993, p. 94). It could mean that the moral economy will take on more specific characteristics of the formal economy. De Gournay and Mercier (1997, p. 151) observe that when telephone-related ICTs in the home are also being used for work, this often leads to professional 'imperialism' and to 'disinvestments' in private communication. There is a tendency for professional communication to gradually absorb and diminish the private sphere. This means that an environment formerly characterized by spontaneity, improvisation, leisure and non-rational behaviour, becomes increasingly subject to control and management. The children, for instance, need to be quiet during a telephone conversation for work.

This kind of self-imposed rationalization is a sign of the gradual loss of private autonomy. De Gournay and Mercier (1997, p. 381) describe three tactical attitudes as symptoms of this development: the import of professional rationality, the tendency for postponed and unidirectional communication and the need for individualistic communication. The latter stimulates the use of mobile phones, because they enable direct personal contact. The possibility of targeted personal reachability is for many people more important than the mobility aspect of a cell phone. Apparently the professional sphere has a dominant influence on the ICT use, when it merges with the private sphere.

ICT use in micro-enterprises is indeed subject to the blurring of boundaries between public and private sphere. This is, for example, visible in the mixed use of different ICTs. The internet and the mobile phone, especially, are professional tools that are also used privately.

Almost half of the business owners (48 per cent) use their cell phone from work at least half of the time for private matters. This mixed use differs according to gender. Micro-enterprises with female business owners use their cell phone significantly more for private affairs (37 per cent women, more than half of the time) than business with male entrepreneurs (17 per cent men, more than half of the time). This indicates that ICT use is more than only a matter of the formal economy. The blurring of boundaries in terms of place and time also increases the mixed internet use at work. The internet is used by 37 per cent of the respondents at least half of the time for private matters. One of the reasons for private computer and internet use is that they are perceived as a kind of hobby (12 per cent of the business owners). It is no longer just a tool – the use becomes a goal in itself.

The business owners whose working hours are not strictly separated from their private (or free) time benefit more from a cell phone, because they want to be reachable for work purposes. Some fruit farmers have acquired a mobile phone so that business contacts do not have to call at home first: 'It was for those situations that my wife needed me. So if somebody came to our house who needed me, like a salesman of some company, while we were picking fruit or were in the fruit auction' (Jos, fruit farmer, male, 45).

This is especially perceived as a problem when the partner (mostly the wife) dislikes acting as a secretary. This also relates to the growing need for individualistic communication (see above), where the mobile phone enables targeted personal reachability (de Gournay and Mercier 1997).

The business owners without fixed working hours can be reached during work for urgent family-related calls. In this way ICT is used to bring the private sphere in the work sphere. The degree to which this blurring is allowed depends on the attitude of the business owner in question (de Gournay and Mercier 1997). Work and home need to be placed on a continuum, where the possibilities range from 'integration' to 'segmentation'. The work of the business owner of a micro-enterprise is typically characterized by integration, as is illustrated when asking if it is possible to make the distinction between work and private life:

> Not easy. I try to keep them separated somewhat but it is not easy, especially with those greenhouses. These are a concern that preoccupies you day and night ... Particularly periods in the autumn when we are harvesting and so ... At night at 10 p.m., after watching TV, you always feel the urge to go and check the computer, to see if everything is all right. You cannot say at 5 p.m., now I close the door behind me.
>
> (Jos, fruit farmer, male, 45)

Some people are able to make that distinction, however: 'Yet, if I close the door, I am a happy person. Do you really think that I am thinking about this apple or that stupid pear for a whole day? Never' (Piet, fruit farmer, male, 41). Nippert-Eng (1996, pp. 1–7) talks about 'boundary work' of work and home, when she describes the process through which people concretize the mental territories of work and home into physical ones and learn to transcend as well as preserve these realms. Each individual takes a position, which has to be negotiated within a number of constraints, using a number of 'tools', like ICTs.

However, it is not only the ICT that enables access to the private sphere. It also occurs that the private sphere enables access to ICT. Often the children of the business owner start using a computer. Afterwards they convince their parents that they can also use the computer for work. Another possibility is that the partner already uses a computer for her or his own job (outside the micro-enterprise). She or he is then more capable of doing the office work on the computer, which is a strong impetus for having an office computer in the micro-enterprise.

Trends in studies on information systems

In IS research, ICT adoption and use is discussed within the context of identifying successful information systems. The main goal is to find the most optimal technological system for a specific organization and a way to implement this system successfully. 'Success' has been defined in different ways, depending on the author (Windrum and de Berranger

2002): the number of available ICTs, pre-defined organizational objectives reached, assessment of the management team, and so on. Yet the criteria for measuring success that are used most frequently are 'user satisfaction' and 'the adoption and use of information technology' (DeLone and McLean 1992). User satisfaction here means the so-called 'user information satisfaction', that is 'the extent to which users believe the information system available to them meets their information requirements' (Ives *et al*. 1983).

Another criterion often used for measuring IS success is the adoption and the use of IT. In their meta-analysis of empirical literature Mahmood *et al*. (2001) give an overview of the most significant factors that explain ICT use in organizations. They conclude that the degree of use is heavily dependent on the degree that one sees the IT system as useful and on the perceived user-friendliness. This relates to the Technology Acceptance Model (TAM), focusing on perceived innovation attributes (Davis 1989). In TAM the belief-constructs 'perceived usefulness'[9] and 'ease of use'[10] are related to the attitude towards and the (intentional) use of media technology. Later on, the perceived usefulness has been supplemented with variables like experience, subjective norm, image, job relevance, output quality and result demonstrableness. Also the degree of organizational support for information technology is a significant factor.

These functionalist IS approaches are aimed at investigating conditions and factors for successful ICT implementation. When an information system is not successful, there is a tendency to qualify the user as 'incapable', or even to 'blame' the user of being unwilling to use the information system. So the problem is not the technology, but the user. Even when concentrating on user satisfaction and adoption and use of information technology, the concept of 'success' is still rather vague. On the one hand, user satisfaction focuses on the aspect of information and the degree to which the concerned user is satisfied about the information he gets via the system. Yet the notion of information is not always made very clear. In this way also the aspect of communication is neglected. On the other hand, when IS research looks at adoption and use of information technology they refer to organizations in general – mostly large companies. As a result, extrapolations to the small-business setting can only be made with extreme caution.

Conclusion: professional domestication in micro-enterprises

It is demonstrated that the notion of domestication holds a central position in explaining ICT use in small enterprises. As a result, traditional views based on management and information systems research need to be complemented with a social constructivist view. Researching businesses that domesticate technology should ideally integrate both a factor approach and an actor approach. The factor approach puts forward how formal business and social characteristics, like turnover and education, are linked with adoption and use of ICT. The actor approach highlights that business owners themselves perceive communication technologies in relation to both work and home. Looking at domestication in micro-enterprises from those two angles enables a more complete view to be obtained.

In addition to confirming that the domestication concept can be used beyond the household setting, the analysis of micro-enterprises also enriches the understanding of domestication. The argument is that a distinction should be made between adoption (or non-adoption) and actual use of ICT in the professional context.[11] Non adoption of specific ICT is mainly related to the lack of professional added value. In the survey more than half of the respondents (56 per cent) indicated 'no need' as the reason for not having internet in the business. This shows how internet is often perceived as irrelevant to one's job. The prominence of 'no need' also is highlighted elsewhere (European Commission 2000; Punie 2000).

With regard to adoption, the domestication of ICT runs smoothly within the work environment when the technological object is connected to familiar means of production. The mobile phone makes sense for fruit farmers, for example, it can be used to automatically alert the farmer when there is a possible breakdown of the heating in the greenhouse. The same goes for a computer attached to the sorting machine. In the case of accountants this refers to the bookkeeping software. In all these examples, the technology or application is experienced as a natural part of the job. When the business owner is convinced of the usefulness of a certain technological tool for work, the adoption runs smoothly. Barriers to adoption largely disappear when the tool is seen as being indispensable to the job. Professional usefulness is a powerful motive for ICT adoption.

Once adopted, and once the ICT gets a useful function within the work context, the reciprocity of 'fitting in' and 'fitting to' between the ICT and the entrepreneur takes place. One of the chief outcomes is the importance of professional users recognizing the familiar in a new technology. This refers to the notion of 'banalisation' (Mallein and Toussaint 1994a, 1994b). Professional domestication will occur more easily when an ICT is not perceived as something too innovative or extraordinary, but as something that fits into everyday work routines and practices. The ICT is just one of the many professional tools. One rather prefers an ICT that accommodates the own work praxis. Frissen (1999) comes to the same conclusion when investigating the relation between ICT and work in everyday life. This relates to the basic idea in domestication that:

> *domestication is fundamentally a conservative process,* as consumers look to incorporate new technologies into the patterns of their everyday life in such a way as to maintain both the structure of their lives and their control of that structure. (Own emphases)
> (Silverstone and Haddon 1996, p. 60)

It seems that this also occurs in the professional setting of the micro-enterprise. This means that the acceptance occurs via the recognizability with existing ICTs. A recently adopted ICT will, therefore, be used in a similar way as comparable technologies or applications. Just as households initially perceived the television as radio with images, many fruit farmers perceive the mobile phone as a plain old telephone without wire, which one can take outside in the orchard. The greater the recognizability with an existing technology, the lower is the resistance for the average business owner to use it. This also is the case for the internet, though in a reverse way, Internet is seen as a computer application and because computers are perceived by many people as 'difficult', internet is also regarded as difficult to use.

Domestication incorporates the paradox of inertia and progress with regard to the innovation process in very small businesses. When technological innovation gets appropriated and integrated gradually, it becomes an everyday working tool to be used efficiently and possibly in innovative ways. Yet at the same time, domestication also fosters inertia, by putting up barriers against new (and perhaps better) ICTs with a similar function. These innovations have to compete with the existing technological culture, use patterns and routines in the business. In the interviews the accountants were very enthusiastic about their own text-based (MS-DOS) accountancy software that – according to them – was the best in the world; and all other programmes were less ideal. A graphical user interface is not even considered:

> But as to bookkeeping programs, I don't think I would change easily. I have been looking at other programs in the past. But I find that every time mine comes out best. So I stick with it. This is really my decision. It is not really worth it to look any further. It's just good!
> (Jeanine, accountant, female, 57)

The domestication process enables as well as constrains technological innovation in small businesses. This is of crucial importance for a better understanding of ICT adoption and use in a professional context.

Notes

1. This refers to three different approaches of organization research. The first approach is the 'scientific management' approach (Taylor 1947), with the machine as the metaphor for the organization. In reaction to this, the 'human relations' approach was developed (Mayo 1933). Here we find a strong link with social psychology, where the organization is seen as a 'living organism'. The 'process approach' (or 'systems approach') is sometimes identified as a third wave of IS research (Harrington 1991; Leeuwis 1993, pp. 34–6). Here organizations are compared with processes. This starts from the theory of 'open systems', where systems of human activities are in constant interchange with their environment.
2. SMEs in the information systems literature are often defined according to American standards, that is, companies with fewer than 500 employees. This is, however, quite large for European standards and certainly for Belgian or Flemish standards.
3. For the analysis of the statistical results a significance level (alpha) of 0.05 is maintained.
4. In Hall's encoding/decoding scheme the 'technical infrastructure' is already mentioned as one of the components (Hall 1973).
5. See also Maren Hartmann's contribution, Chapter 5.
6. In order to guarantee anonymity, only the first name is indicated. In addition, some of the respondent's basic characteristics are given: profession, gender and age.
7. These figures refer to the whole population of micro-enterprises.
8. See also Chapter 8 (Katie Ward) in this book.
9. 'The degree to which a person believes that using a particular system would enhance his or her job performance' (Davis 1989, p. 320).
10. 'The degree to which a person believes that using a particular system would be free of effort' (Davis 1989, p. 320).
11. A similar approach of differentiating adoption and use with regard to domestication in the residential context was introduced by Punie (2000). See also Punie (2004).

References

Bausinger, H. (1984) 'Media, technology and daily life'. *Media, Culture & Society*, vol. 6, no. 4, pp. 343–51.

Davis, F. D. (1989) 'Perceived usefulness, perceived ease of use, and user acceptance of information technology'. *MIS Quarterly*, vol. 13, no. 3, pp. 319–41.

de Gournay, C. and Mercier, P.-A. (1997) 'Entre la vie privée et le travail: décloisonnement et nouveaux partages'. *Proceedings of International Conference 'Penser les usages – Imagining uses'*, Bordeaux, pp. 379–87.

de Jager, H. and Mok, A. L. (1989) *Grondbeginselen der sociologie: gezichtspunten en begrippen*. Stenfert Kroese: Leiden.

DeLone, W. H. and McLean, E. R. (1992) 'Information systems success: the quest for the dependent variable'. *Information Systems Research*, vol. 3, no. 1, pp. 60–95.

European Commission (1996) 'Recommendation of the Commission'. *Official Journal of the European Communities*, no. L 107/6, European Commission: Luxembourg.

European Commission (2000) *The European Observatory for SMEs: Sixth Report*. Luxembourg, ENSR – KPMG Consulting – EIM Small Business Research and Consultancy, European Commission: Luxembourg.

Frissen, V. (1999) *ICT en arbeid in het dagelijks leven*, Werkdocument 71. Rathenau Institute: Den Haag.

Frissen, V. and Wester, F. (1997) 'De interpretatieve onderzoeksbenadering in de communicatiewetenschap', in (eds) J. Servaes and V. Frissen, *De interpretatieve benadering in de communicatiewetenschap theorie, methodologie en case-studies*. Acco: Leuven, pp. 13–37.

Haddon, L. (2004) *Information and Communication Technologies in Everyday Life: A Concise Introduction and Research Guide*. Berg: Oxford.

Haddon, L. (1991) 'The cultural production and consumption of IT', in (eds) H. MacKay, M. Young and J. Beynon, *Understanding technology in education*. Falmer: London, pp. 157–75.

Haddon, L. and Silverstone, R. (1994) 'Telework and the changing relationship of home and work', in (ed.) R. Mansell, *Management of information and communication technologies: emerging patterns of control*. Aslib: London, pp. 234–47.

Haddon, L. and Silverstone, R. (1993) *Teleworking in the 1990s: A View From the Home*, SPRU/CICT Report Series no. 10, SPRU. University of Sussex: Brighton.

Hall, S. (1973) *Encoding and Decoding in the Television Discourse*. Stencilled Occasional Papers, University of Birmingham: Birmingham.

Harrington, J. (1991) *Organizational Structure and Information Technology*. Prentice-Hall: New York.

Igbaria, M., Zinatelli, N. and Cavaye, A. L. M. (1998) 'Analysis of information technology success in small firms in New Zealand'. *International Journal of Information Management*, vol. 18, no. 2, pp. 103–19.

Ives, B., Olson, M. and Baroudi, J. (1983) 'The measurement of user information satisfaction', *Communications of the ACM*, vol. 26, no. 10, pp. 785–93.

Leeuwis, C. (1993) *Of computers, myths and modelling: the social construction of diversity, knowledge, information and communication technology in Dutch horticulture and agricultural extension.* Unpublished PhD, Landbouwuniversiteit: Wageningen.

Lie, M. and Sørensen, K. H. (1996) 'Making technology our own? Domesticating technology into everyday life', in (eds) M. Lie and K. H. Sørensen, *Making Technology our Own? Domesticating Technology into Everyday Life.* Scandinavian University Press: Oslo, pp. 1–30.

Mahmood, M. A., Hall, L. and Swanberg, D. L. (2001) 'Factors affecting information technology usage: a meta-analysis of the empirical literature'. *Journal of Organizational Computing and Electronic Commerce*, vol. 11, no. 2, pp. 107–30.

Mallein, P. and Toussaint, Y. (1994a) 'L'intégration sociale des technologies d'information et de communication: une sociologie des usages'. *Technologies de l'information et société*, vol. 6, no. 4, pp. 315–35.

Mallein, P. and Toussaint, Y. (1994b) 'Technologies de l'information et de la communication: une approche sociologique pour la conception assistée par l'usage'. *Communications & Strategies*, no. 5, pp. 77–99.

Mariussen, A., Wheelock, J. and Baines, S. (1997) 'The family business tradition in Britain and Norway: modernization and reinvention?' *International Studies of Management and Organization*, vol. 27, no. 3, pp. 64–85.

Mayo, E. (1933) *The Human Problems of an Industrial Civilization.* Macmillan: New York.

Moores, S. (1993) *Interpreting Audiences: The Ethnography of Media Consumption.* Sage: London.

Morley, D. (1992) *Television, Audiences and Cultural Studies.* Routledge: London.

Morley, D. (1986) *Family Television: Cultural Power and Domestic Leisure.* Comedia: London.

Nippert-Eng, C. E. (1996) *Home and Work: Negotiating Boundaries through Everyday Life.* University of Chicago Press: Chicago and London.

Palvia, P. C. and Palvia, S. C. (1999) 'An examination of the IT satisfaction of small-business users'. *Information and Management*, vol. 35, no. 3, pp. 127–137.

Pierson, J. (2003) *De (on)verenigbaarheid van informatie- en communicatie-technologie en zelfstandige ondernemers: Een gebruikersgericht en innovatiestrategisch onderzoek naar adoptie, gebruik en betekenis van ICT voor zaakvoerders van micro-ondernemingen*. Unpublished PhD, Vrije Universiteit Brussel: Brussels.

Punie, Y. (2004) 'Een theoretische en empirische benadering van adoptie, gebruik en betekenis van informatie- en communicatie-technologie in het dagelijkse leven', in (eds) N. Carpentier, C. Pauwels and O. Van Oost, *Het on(be)grijpbare publiek: een communicatiewetenschappelijke exploratie van publiekonderzoek*. VUBPress: Brussel, pp. 175–200.

Punie, Y. (2000) *Domesticatie van Informatie- en Communicatietechnologie. Adoptie, gebruik en betekenis van media in het dagelijkse leven: Continue beperking of discontinue bevrijding?* Unpublished PhD, Vrije Universiteit Brussel: Brussels.

Silverstone, R. (1996) 'Introduction: information and communication technologies and the articulation of the public and the private', in (eds) R. Silverstone and M. Hartmann, *Media and Information Technologies and the Changing Relationship to Public and Private Space: EMTEL Working Paper No. 2*. University of Sussex: Brighton, pp. 3–6.

Silverstone, R. and Haddon, L. (1996) 'Design and domestication of information and communication technologies: technical change and everyday life', in (eds) R. Mansell and R. Silverstone, *Communication by design: the politics of information and communication technologies*. Oxford University Press: Oxford, pp. 44–74.

Silverstone, R., Hirsch, E. and Morley, D. (1992) 'Information and communication technologies and the moral economy of the household', in (eds) R. Silverstone and E. Hirsch, *Consuming Technologies: Media and Information in Domestic Spaces*. Routledge: London, pp. 15–31.

Sørensen, K. H., Aune, M. and Hatling, M. (2000) 'Against linearity: on the cultural appropriation of science and technology', in (eds) M. Dierkes and C. von Grote, *Between Understanding and Trust: The Public, Science and Technology*. OPA: Amsterdam, pp. 237–57.

Southern, A. and Tilly, F. (2000) 'Small firms and information and communication technologies (ICTs): toward a typology of ICTs usage'. *New Technology, Work and Employment*, vol. 15, no. 2, pp. 138–54.

Storey, D. J. (1994) *Understanding the Small Business Sector*. Routledge: London.

Taylor, F. W. (1947) *Scientific Management*. Harper: New York.

Willmott, H. (1993) 'Breaking the paradigm mentality'. *Organization Studies*, vol. 14, no. 5, pp. 681–719.

Windrum, P. and de Berranger, P. (2002) *The Adoption of e-Business Technology by SMEs*. Unpublished manuscript, MERIT-Infonomics Research Memorandum series, Maastricht.

PART III
Outlook

12 Domesticating domestication. Reflections on the life of a concept

Roger Silverstone

All concepts, once having gained the light of day, take on a life of their own. Domestication is no exception. And readers of the preceding pages will have gained a sense of the threads, some elegantly twisted, some uncomfortably knotted, that have emerged over the last twenty years, as researchers have tried to use its spongy texture to define a way of thinking about the incorporation of technology into everyday life – a way of thinking which seeks to be true to experience and practice.

All concepts are metaphors. They stand in place of the world. And in so doing they mask as well as reveal it. They offer an invitation to compare, to seek illumination from somewhere else, to confront an opaque reality with perhaps another one, and to divine some meaning from their mutuality. Concepts that survive are, most often, simple ones. Domestication is once again no exception. Perhaps this is surprising, since the world they reach towards and attempt to frame is far from simple, and far from stable. They survive, perhaps, through their eloquence, and they disintegrate when the distance established between the world and its thinking becomes too close or too far.

All concepts attempt to address an empirical reality, to offer the basis for description, illumination and, with luck, explanation about the world: to contextualize it and project it beyond the moment. The invitation, if not the injunction, is to think one way, and not another. It is to claim a preferred reading of the world, more accurate to its dynamics and its power. But there is also a tinge of normativity: an expectation of how things should be, ideally.

These are the bases on which a concept's usefulness can be, and will be judged. Domestication is no exception here. In this concluding chapter, I want to review, inevitably with the benefit of hindsight, what was originally being claimed in framing the study of media, technology and everyday life through such a metaphor, and what has become, and might yet become of it, as it and the world which it addresses, inexorably change.

Origins

In the beginning there was technological determinism. Part of this, of course, was common sense. As the twentieth century took hold, science and technology were seen as laws unto themselves. It was part of everyday culture to marvel at, but also to demand, the next great invention, the next great machine (I remember the first sellotape. No more sealing wax and hessian string on brown paper parcels). Science and technology were changing the world, enabling communication when none had been possible before, storing and retrieving information in increasingly paperless spaces, improving the quality of life, re-skilling, transforming the exercise of power in both public and private settings, shrinking distances. Machines were becoming faster, smaller, more efficient, more robust, more sensitive to human needs. Their capacity to define how human beings would live with them, their transparent and irresistible claims on the future, the obviousness of their direct and immediate benefits: for health, wealth, and humankind were unchallenged. Engineers believed in this, politicians believed in it, capitalists believed in it and so did we, the humble consumers, even when we bewailed the risks and dangers of too rapid innovation, and too confusing and destabilizing a transition to the next stage of modernity.

In history and sociology there is an equally long – indeed arguably much longer – version of the technologically determinant. Not unreasonable, one might think, when it comes to spurs, clocks, gunpowder and the compass, or even to writing, printing and the telescope, but arguably more challenging and contentious when it comes to the fine tuning of information and communication technologies in the increasingly complex and fluid global society of late modernity. Yet in all these cases, what was being done was a singular reading, more or less: from technological to social change, from the emergence of the machine and its systems to the conduct of everyday life, without the interruption of the wayward and the human, without the disturbance of the emotional, the non-rational, the perverse. And without these factorings of human need and desire on the one hand, and of institutional interests and power on the other, the story was never going to be completely convincing. Though it could never be entirely wrong either.

By the 1980s, in the fields of science and technology studies, and perhaps less radically, in the fields of media and communication studies, this otherwise singular narrative of socio-technological change was beginning to be challenged. From Latour (Latour 1987) to Williams (Williams 2003), an arc of scepticism and humanism – some might say of a more radical materialism – began to redefine the boundaries between

REFLECTIONS ON THE LIFE OF A CONCEPT

humans and machine. These theoretical approaches would continue to pose a challenge, offering their own version of magical realism, particularly in the case of Actor Network Theory (ANT), in which technologies and bodies were offered as equivalent, where machines spoke to the human and the human to machine, and where technological consequences were social and social consequences technological. In ANT power was diffused, rhizomatic, sub-Foucauldian, intangible. In Williams, it was in your face: post-Marxian, shouting vested interests and global needs. In both, by and large, the focus was on the creation of technology, its invention, mobilization and distribution: in other words its appearance, but not its consequence. While this might be less completely the case for Williams, he too embraced new media technologies, cable, video, the early signs of interactivity, as providing, potentially and, in his case, hopefully, the drivers of (revolutionary) social change.

Media studies had by this time begun its own journey away from determinism, in the guise of media effects, and towards constructivism, in the guise of audience freedom and creativity. The talk was of semiotic democracy, choice, agency, as if somehow the encompassing world of both material and symbolic resources were only there for the taking: as if their limiting constraints, their resistances, their preferences, their demands, were avoidable, infinitely negotiable in the transactions of everyday life, through which individuals and groups made sense of their worlds. This sense was increasingly dependent on their relationships to information and communication technologies and mediated content; the emergent and contested meanings, that flowed eternally through their social and symbolic spaces.

The notion of domestication was a product of this moment. It was an attempt to grasp the nettle of socio-technical change where it could be seen to be both mattering most and where it was almost entirely taken for granted: in the intimate spaces of the home and household. It was an attempt too, naive perhaps, to link the way that we thought about our contemporary relationships to the objects and forces beyond immediate control to those consistencies in human history and culture which indeed, precisely through those relationships, defined our humanity, our capacity to be in the world. Domestication was something human beings did to enhance and secure their everyday lives.

Wild animals then, wild technologies now: what's the difference? In both cases, unconstrained, they pose threats and challenges. In both cases, brought within the fold, they become sources of power and sustenance. Domestication is practice. It involves human agency. It requires effort and culture, and it leaves nothing as it is. Perhaps therein lay an early error in its formulation: the impression that somehow only the technology was transformed in its appropriation into the household, the impression too that such a process was uncomplicated, linear and without its own contradictions. This is not just about failure: the dying PlayStations on the roof of the wardrobe or the advanced functionality of the telephone lying dormant, or the video recorder becalmed in a sea of blank tapes: nor is it, as it would later become, the hyper-intensity of instant messaging or file sharing, examples of a kind of 'über'-domestication, now believed to be two of the great triumphs of spontaneous media consumption.

The domestication of information and communication technologies, on the contrary, notwithstanding its often apparent ease, a process smoothed by marketing eloquence and fine design, nevertheless, confronted established social arrangements and cultural values, at individual and collective levels, as indeed many of the empirical studies in the preceding chapters have amply demonstrated. Both parties to the interaction, the human and the technological, and in both material and symbolic ways, were, and are, in a constant dialectic of change. A dialectic of change that is unending, that takes place across different temporalities and different territories, and that is indeed the very stuff of what everyday life now consists: the stuff of electronic communication, information gathering, media gossip and media literacies; the stuff, indeed, of mediation, the stuff of private and of public life.

Domestication was a seen as a process – a process of consumption – in which consumption was linked to invention and design, and to the public framing of technologies as symbolic objects of value and desire. Domestication described a process of consumption that drew its inspiration from the work of Jean Baudrillard (Baudrillard 1988), Michel de Certeau (de Certeau 1984) and Daniel Miller (Miller 1987), that described consumption not as passive, but as active. The truism, then and now, was that consumption was also production, a form of engagement in material culture that was increasingly seen to be the case particularly in the media, where any and every kind of textual engagement drew on personal, social and cultural resources in such a way as to leave the original, if such a thing could be identified, as significantly affected in use. No stone unturned. No text untouched. No technology untransformed.

The attempt to fix this otherwise amorphous process into the fabric of the everyday, the hooks that still try to link its continuities and contradictions to the conduct of the everyday, lay in the specification of the dimensions of appropriation (commodification, objectification, incorporation, conversion). Again one needs to be careful about their reification, and to try and understand what it is that they are pointing towards. They address the components of a process in which information and communication technologies are located in time and space, in the intimate times and spaces of the household and at the interface between those spaces and the public worlds of discourse and definition, and of the functionalities and potentialities that such technologies in their systemic manifestations afford, and to which they lay claim. Domestication as a process of bringing things home – machines and ideas, values and information – which always involves the crossing of boundaries: above all those between the public and the private, and between proximity and distance, is a process which also involves their constant renegotiation. How could it, in an age of telephone and radio, of computer networking and mobile telephony, be otherwise? And likewise, domestication can only be understood as relational. While it can be empirically observed in the private spaces of the front room or the bedroom, and while it can be analysed in the negotiations of ownership and control of both new old machines and the consumption of content, within the micro-pores of the domestic setting and in the family or household relationship, the concept is, in its essence, dependent on the juxtaposition of inside and outside, and on its continuous negotiation.

Domestication bridges, a priori, the macro social and the micro social: the continuous affordances of the wild and the environmentally abundant out there, with the mobilization of material resources, skills, cultural values and social competences and capabilities in here. This is so, notwithstanding the sense that the boundaries around the home (of which more shortly) are no longer what they were, that homes, hearths, households in an age of mobility and fracture no longer have the defensible borders that were once presumed to be their defining feature; and that individuals, as they break free from the sedentariness and nuclearity of family life and bedroom culture, shatter the bounds of established domesticity. The sociological changes are unarguable, but the phenomenological conditions remain. Information and communication technologies have become a significant component of the carapace of such personality and domesticity, both in their location and their dislocation; and, precisely, in their capacity to help the individual and the collectivity to define and sustain their own ontological security wherever they happen to be.

Commodification, a more accurate framing of the otherwise too general appropriation, and conversion, both link what goes on inside to what goes on outside the home, or indeed within any other organization in which technologies and their content are introduced into the complexities of an enclosed social organization. Commodification refers to that component of the process of domestication, which in design, marketing, market research, the knowledge of pre-existing consumer behaviour and the formation of public policy, prepares the ground for the initial appropriation of a new technology. Machines and services do not come into the household naked. They are packaged, certainly, but they are also 'packaged' by the erstwhile purchaser and user, with dreams and fantasies, hopes and anxieties: the imaginaries of modern consumer society. This aspect of domestication: its inevitable and necessary initiation, operates for the individual (my mobile), the household (our broadband) and, as Jo Pierson has eloquently shown (Chapter 11), the organization (our network).

Conversion involves reconnection; the perpetuation of the helix of the design-domestication interface. Consumption is never a private matter, neither phenomenologically nor materially. It involves display, the development of skills, competences, literacies. It involves discourse and discussion, the sharing of the pride of ownership, as well as its frustration. It involves resistance and refusal and transformation at the point where cultural expectations and social resources meet the challenges of technology, system and content. Of course such an interaction is fraught. There is an essential tension between the technological and the social which has to be worked out at every level, from the political and the personal. Neither party is stable in this, though both, as it were, seek that stability. So designers and manufacturers, as well as policy-makers, construct their objects and functionalities with ideal users and optimum conditions of use in mind: in their own ideal world of laboratory life, they have worked out the benefits and adjusted to the risks; the technologies are designed to be robust, functionally effective and socially consequential. Users want the perfect fit: an enhancement of the quality of their everyday lives without its destabilization; an extension of personality and power without a disruption of identity; a freeing from the constraints of community, without a complete dislocation from the moral order of society. This is the constitutive dialectic of projection and preservation that users bring to any innovation: preservation of the present, projection into the future, and one that constantly challenges the linear logic of diffusion (see Introduction), as well as the hoped-for maintenance of individuals' power to control their own private space, their own media ecology.

Objectification and incorporation are the strategies, or maybe, if one is to be true to de Certeau, the tactics, of domestication. Objectification and incorporation involve placing and timing. The complexities and instabilities of domestic life, both well established and essentially fragile, move to meet the new arrival. Information and communication technologies by definition offer a restructuring of the position of the household and its members, both internally in the interrelationships they have with each other, in the micro-politics of gender, generational and sibling rivalries, and externally as the threads of connection and disconnection, proximity and distance, extend into public spaces or into the networks of the diasporic or the displaced.

Objectification (the location of information and communications technologies in the material, social and cultural spaces of the home) and incorporation (the injection of media technological practices into the temporal patterns of domestic life), together are the infrastructural components of the dynamics of everyday life, both, it should be said, within and outside the formal boundaries of the household. Neither leave the existing patterns of social life untouched; new machines claim new spaces and new patterns of participation; new content challenges existing rules of behaviour or codes of familial practice. But just as equally such technologies enable the management of fracturing social orders, connecting broken homes, or enabling family life to extend beyond the physical and the face to face. This is not a matter of either technological or social determination so much as, at this modest domestic level, the mutuality of transformation that requires human participation and a modicum of human responsibility. And the question for us, as researchers, is that of understanding the nature of that interrelationship and its significance both for those who are engaged, on a daily basis within it, and for an understanding of the wider ramifications of this dialectic at the heart of socio-technical change.

The latter issue is material. Technologies are political. Their innovation is motivated by political and economic interests and agendas. This is hardly new and hardly original. But power, and policy, is never simply exercised, in this sphere, just as in any other. And an account of its complexities and failings (even if in order to improve, ultimately, its efficacy) depends on the disentangling of social process from the otherwise singular rationality of unreflective governance. There are unequal powers, of course, but no determinations, in the innovation of information and communication. The concept of domestication, with its all metaphoric strengths and weaknesses, is designed above all to intervene in the otherwise singular account of technological change and to instate the human at its centre, not in any dewy-eyed romantic way, but to force all of those concerned with its nature to confront the responsibility that all actors must take, both producers and consumers, for the decisions they make, the choices they pursue, and the practices they develop in the creation of the increasingly sophisticated and increasingly salient strategies of communication and information seeking in this late modern, global, world of ours.

Such an observation, one to which I will return in the final section of this chapter, leads neatly enough to the next of the key terms associated with the concept of domestication: the moral economy of the household.

The moral economy of the household

My colleagues and I were struck, in the very earliest phases of our empirical research, by the efforts made by parents of dependent children (and of course by the children too) to manage, monitor and contain the influx of technologically-mediated content into their home, to establish patterns, codes and expectations of behaviour coherent with their own values and those that they wished to preserve. Nuclear or not (and of course many of them, particularly in single-parent or aging households, were not at all nuclear), these primary social groups, consciously or unconsciously, depended for the security of their daily existence on the emergence of a sustainable but particular common sense: a kind of signature set of values that held them together in the face of the traumas of the public and the mediated world, in the face of the challenges of peer groups and networks, and of the arrival of unacceptable messaging services and websites and personal videos. The relationships that formed around such innovations had to be grounded somehow, just as in the latest manifestation of moral ordering, the individual and mobile young, as both Maren Hartmann (2005) and Knut Sørensen (Chapter 3) suggest, are constructing their personal (but shareable) morality in similar ways. These moral positions are also grounded in a sense of self, and in ideals of appropriate values and behaviour that are equivalently (and by definition) sustaining of identity and culture.

Our early research also revealed, perhaps less surprisingly, how different families and households organized their own affairs, managed their finances, exchanged and used money and other material and valued objects as a way of maintaining peace, order and economic viability within their four walls (and of course within their extended relationships). It was interesting to note where and how these informal and often taken-for-granted arrangements broke down, with whom and under what circumstances and, of course, how they affected, and were effected by, transactions that involved the purchase of information and communication technologies, or subscription to their services. In the obverse it was also clear that in many families and households the abstract values associated with money in the formal economy would not need to be, and were not, upheld: the private economy of help, reciprocity and nominal payments for services rendered, did not depend on any models of rational value and fixed rates of exchange. It seemed to us, empirically, that such economic arrangements were grounded in a family or household's sense of its self, a sense of self that could be justified, more or less, with respect to traditions and the articulation of value, and that such values and consequential practices constituted, both in their manifest consistency and in the struggles to maintain them, quite literally, a moral *economy*.

What makes an economy moral? What makes morality economic? In what sense is domestication a moral force?

In the 1980s there was a certain sheepishness around discourses of morality. I suspect there still is. The moral economy emerged from the historical analyses of E. P. Thompson (1971) whose work on the transition from traditional forms of economic life to that of capitalism contrasted a set of arrangements and practices on the one hand grounded in tradition and respect for the individual within a definable and viable community, and the shattering of those often less than rational or less than efficient procedures for distribution and exchange, which advancing capitalism imposed, irrespective of local conditions, beliefs and values. Such a perception of dichotomization was reinforced in the anthropological work of Parry and Bloch (1989) on the meaning of money, and of course in a whole slew of research exploring exchange and reciprocity as a component of economic life.

Economies (all economies, even, strictly, capitalism) are built on moral precepts, in so far as it is presumed that the relationships they prescribe as both desired and optimum between participants have inbuilt judgements of value – above all (though implicitly), the values ascribed to the participants themselves, to the human participants, in the exchange. The public, formal, *zweckrational* (Jo Pierson's calling on Max Weber in this context in Chapter 11, is extremely suggestive) economy of the Protestant ethic and of modernity placed participants within it, in their anonymity and distance. The predominant values were those of abstract calculation, efficiency and the pursuit of profit. The private, informal, *wertrational* economies of traditional societies and personal spaces, brought participants together in the full plenitude of their identities and social roles, where transactions were not necessarily governed by immediate expectations of reciprocity, equivalence or profit.

Notwithstanding the obvious empirical objection that, at the end of the twentieth century, and perhaps even more now, any boundary between these could no longer be seen as viable. This was notwithstanding the fracturing of family life on the one hand, and the intrusiveness of public claims and demands on the other. Notwithstanding the obvious contradictions and instabilities at the heart of any family life or household culture, such that perhaps what might be seen as its defining characteristic lies in the absence of domestic coherence rather than its consistency. Notwithstanding the increasing mobilities of individuals and groups and the breaking down of tradition and ritual at both personal and national levels, and therefore the argument that such a notion – a notion of a moral economy – is no longer sustainable, I want to sustain it.

In one sense the notion of the moral economy is naively empirical. It asks the questions in what ways, if at all, households or families create for themselves private and personal cultures, which have consequences for the way in which the anonymous, homogenizing technologies and services of public and commercial life, are used and valued. And, from a lateral perspective, the question arises too of how we can relate an understanding of patterns of information and communication technology use, resistance, participation and the rest to what we can understand as the culture of the unit whose activities with which we are concerned. In this sense, and without apology, the moral economy is a simple sociological notion, bringing into a single frame the convergence and contradictions of values and practices, and drawing comparatively not so much (though this may have been unclear originally) on a distinction between the moral and the immoral, but on the ontological differences between constitutive forms of socio-economic order and behaviour.

How can we be so sure, empirical evidence apparently to the contrary, that such distinctiveness in economic and social life, that a distinctiveness which underpins what we want to call the private still survives – that it still survives even when we hear so little of it in the speech of those who talk about their media practice; or that it still survives when we can no longer see tangible boundaries around families and households?

There is a whole range of categories and referential practices which we use, and which have been used throughout this book, to locate these framing specificities in the use of information and communication technologies, both old and new, and which – in locating them – become impossible to understand without a grounding reality in reproducible social practice. Ownership, belonging, performance, ritual. There are common senses, etiquettes, narratives, memories, dreams. The consumption of technology is suffused by hopes and fears, threaded with exhilaration and anxiety. The struggles over literacy and control, over their mastery in the personal and the communal manifestations of the home and household, as well as in their extension via the media into a global realm, are specific (if not at some point generalizable) and they are specific to the specific: I do media and technology differently from you. Sometimes, and most superficially, and for the most part, those differences are not significant. But significance itself is a slippery thing. From the point of view of the machine and its systems, my difference and the moral economy in which it is grounded and legitimated, barely disturbs the surface of the commercial and political water; but from the point of view of me and mine, and those like me, that difference is material. It grounds my identity and, in its wider salience, could very well intrude into the generalities of the formal economy in ways that would become both unexpected and disruptive. That is why we study it. A search for salience, and its accounting.

Articulations

A perception about the household (I will come to the relationship between household and home in the next section) as a moral entity opens up another aspect of this conceptual matrix: the issue of articulation. I do not think that this was ever terribly clear or worked through, yet it seemed to have a resonance, as a way of defining the dynamics of the distinctive appropriation of information and communication technologies and media technologies, as both material and symbolic objects and as content, into domestic space.

There are a number of unresolved issues here and, as Maren Hartmann points out (Chapter 5), most of them revolve around mediated content. In an early, but actually quite distinct use of the term articulation (Silverstone 1981), the reference was to structural linguistics and the levels of significance arguably present in natural language. The question that this initial discussion raised was the extent to which television, in its textuality, and as a semiotic system, could be considered such a language. The judgement inevitably was that it could not, at least in the terms in which the problematic was posed at the time.

When it came to domestication, the notion of articulation emerged as an attempt to answer quite a specific, and a rather different, question. It was the question of the distinct nature and function of information and communication technologies in the social and cultural environments of the household. All technologies once appropriated, found, in one way or another, their time and place in that space, and in their placing were articulated as material and symbolic objects into the fabric of everyday life. Information and communication added an extra dimension. This was their second articulation, for they brought, through the communications they enabled, a range of content-based claims, the hooks and eyes of mediation, which established but also disturbed the relationship between the private and the public spaces of communication and meaning. The doubling itself was perceived as double: on the one hand the mediated communications, perhaps above all of broadcasting (in news, soap opera, advertising and the rest), were seen to provide the effective communications to reinforce claims of public technologically-mediated culture in domestic settings. It was as though the technologies were not inert (as a washing machine might be considered inert) but brought with them, as if in a fifth column, the means for their further integration and sophistication into everyday life (actually, of course, the process of innovation and diffusion requires all technologies to some degree to do this, above all in the creation of dependency).

Information and communication technologies, however, must also be seen to enable the substantive articulation of meaning, mediating distance and proximity, personality and community, and the relations between public and private spaces, activities and values. But they do so only through the mediation that the social processes of reception, in brains as well as in homes, generate in the dynamics of consumption. If there is to be a third articulation (and I am nervous about such a proliferation) it lies in the activities of the household itself as the microcosmic location of the social and cultural work that is a constituent part of the way in which public and private meaning and communications are constructed and sustained at the interface with technology.

This is, in general, not a terribly challenging idea. But it is difficult to pin down empirically. It requires, again as Hartmann points out, a thorough-going epistemological and methodological commitment to ethnographic approaches to research. And it requires something that was consistently underrepresented in the early research: both an interrogation of texts and meanings, of their production and consumption in the home, as well as of the ways in which the processes of articulation, particularly now with mobile and personal technologies, have exploded beyond the boundaries of domestic space, and have led to various kinds of private appropriations of, and within, the public domain.

Such an observation allows the argument to move on one further step. For it brings us face to face with the problem of the household and the problem of home.

Household and home

Households, we are told, are no longer what they were. They have become virtual, traumatized by the fracturing of cross-generational cultures, peer-group pressures, the vulnerability of marriages and the ephemerality of social relationships. They have become virtual, too, through the radical attack on their integrity that information and communication technologies have generated: the old ones, like television and video, as they have swarmed through the various private spaces of suburban (and other) dwellings, enabling local and personal bedroom cultures to develop, disconnected from the whole; and the new ones, the Walkman, mobile phone and the internet, breaching the walls of otherwise sedentary media consumption, and driving connectivity, sociability and personality into the wild prairies of public space. Households are having a hard time of it: no longer recognized objectively as containers of social and economic life, no longer stable in value or consistent in practice, no longer secure on the tossing seas of mediated globalization and personal networking, no longer morally or ethically self-regulating. Above all, the boundaries around the household are breaking down. Thresholds are crumbling. The distinctions between public and private spaces and frames of reference, always particular to society and culture, are losing their force and their significance. Public, private: who notices any more, who cares?

There is something familiar in these arguments, and, if I may be forgiven for saying so, something both familiar and wrong. They reproduce the arguments, still *au current*, surrounding the present and future of the nation-state in the face of rampant globalization. There is no need to rehearse all of these arguments, merely to say that their flaw consists in their exaggeration of the new global challenges to the power of the state, to its own power within its own borders and to its capacity as a political unit to command its own destiny on the trans-national stage; and, finally, in its consequential suggestion that such challenges are terminal. Yet the nation-state, albeit transformed and less secure in a number of different ways, is still paramount in the regulation of its own domestic affairs, both economic and social, and it still holds (depending on the resources it can command), considerable sway globally, in political, economic and even environmental agendas. The nation-state is still a pillar of global society, even though pock-marked by the steady erosion of the acid of trans-nationality, and by the bullets of neo-imperial adventures.

The parallel with the household, while not exact, is close enough to be plausible. Households, within the domestication enterprise, were defined as social, economic and political units, within which a certain stability of transactional culture in each of these domains enabled the days to pass without trauma, and enabled values, however provisional and fragile, to be created, sustained and transmitted. Households have an objective reality within the macro-institutional frameworks of the state: the source of taxes and the recipients of social benefits, the primary political and socializing unit. People move in and out of them, of course. They are fractured by divorce and personal independence. They are, however, consistently present, not to say ineradicable, in the social investigation of technology and mobility, and as the necessary starting point of any investigation, even of their vulnerability to self-conscious denial (so, as individuals in their own self-reflective discourses, seem to value 'the household' not at all, they nevertheless ground their dismissal on its absolute presence and the implicit recognition that without the structure it provides their lives would be impossible). In these investigations (there are many examples in this book), the household is still there as the starting point and as the ground base for an understanding of the social dynamics of media change.

And then there is a further parallel: between the national and home. Maria Bakardjieva (Chapter 4) prefers home to household, and, in many respects, for good reasons. The shift from the material to the phenomenological is a necessary one, for a sense of place and placement, a sense of belonging, a sense of location, is in each case and in their over-determination, just that: a sense, a perception – something inside, intangible, fluid, mobile, transferable as well as ontological. The notion of home is as a projection of self, and as something that can be carried with you; a notion of home that extends from a place of origin to a dream of redemption; a notion of home that attaches to the keypad of a mobile phone or Blackberry, a technological extension of the self, and one which means that you are never out of reach, never disconnected. It is a notion of home that is performed on a daily basis through interaction rituals both with other individuals and with the technologies that enable those interactions.

There has, however, to be a dialectic between the phenomenology of home and the political economy (roughly speaking) of the household. Indeed, it is within this dialectic that so many of the tensions and contradictions surrounding the take-up, use and consequences of use, of information and communication technologies are to be found. The dialectics of proximity and distance, of the personal and the political and, as I will discuss shortly, the public and the private, are in each case to be found at the interface between where I actually am and where I think I am (or remember being, or wish to be); and at the interface between me and my machine and my interlocutors and my sources of information, power and identity. The sense of place, which sometimes we wish to call – more or less benevolently – home, is a sense that geographers and sociologists have for some time understood well. I discussed these ideas and their importance, in this context, in *Television and Everyday Life* (Silverstone 1994). And it, therefore, follows that place, location, meaningful space, is something that increasingly now depends both on our capacity to domesticate the technologically new, but also on our, technologically-enhanced, capacity to extend the domestic beyond the confines of the household.

Home, then, is no longer singular, no longer static, no longer, in an increasingly mobile and disrupted world, capable of being taken for granted. But if the human condition requires a modicum of ontological security for its continuing possibility and its development, home –

technologically enhanced as well as technologically disrupted – is a sine qua non. We cannot do without it, within or without the household. To be homeless is to be beyond reach, and to be without identity.

Domestication today

The empirical chapters preceding this one have taken the concept of domestication into the brave new world of digital technologies, those that have extended the range and speed of global reach, and those which have taken the personalization and the mobilization both of the machine and of everyday life to new levels. All sorts of things are changing and it is hardly surprising that it is the breaking down of all that is solid in the domestic realm that catches the eye. The household has become a relational category in which its borders and boundaries can no longer be taken for granted and which shift, if not with the winds, at least with the variations of technologically facilitated movement, both symbolic and material, as individuals engage electronically with the public world: in the invigoration of otherwise traditional social networks distinctive to their own society (Lim, Chapter 10); in managing the challenges of single parenthood (Russo Lemor, Chapter 9) and fractured or migrant lives (Berker 2005); in the attempts to integrate the socially marginal into the mainstream (Hynes and Rommes, Chapter 7); and in the negotiations within the household, and between those within it and those outside it, for a proper and sustainable place for a personal node in the network society (Ward, Chapter 8).

Perhaps the primary articulation in this new miasma of communication, one that was insufficiently in evidence in its early formulation, is that between the public and the private. It is increasingly a commonplace to observe that the electronic media have taken this interface by the scruff of its neck. And in some senses, the distinctiveness of what might constitute the new in new information and communication technologies, will find its definition in the consequences that their innovation has for our positioning in the world, and in the redefinition of the boundaries between the personal and the communal, the intimate and the shared, the self and other.

There is a distinction to be made, I think, and quite a profound one, between the primarily *centripetal* mediated cultures of the twentieth century and the increasingly *centrifugal* mediated cultures of the twenty-first. In the first, *mediated centripetal culture*, the cultures of press and broadcasting, whose orientation is towards the bounded community, be it the nation, the region or the neighbourhood, and to the ingathering of a shareable cultural and social space, what was (and of course still is) involved is public talk and private performance: the circulation of images and stories in public provide the resources in private for reading, viewing, talking, identification and the sharing of values. In the second, in the realm of *mediated centrifugal culture*, it is much more a matter of private talk and public performance (Katz and Aakhus 2002), where, in the public spaces of villages and cities, and in the equivalently public spaces of the internet, it is the sharing of differences which provides the connectivity.

Now it is the turn of private conversations to occupy public spaces, and in their public performance (in blogs and in the public voices of the mobile telephone, as well as in the display of the otherwise private lives of public figures on front pages and television screens) creating new kinds of public cultures. These changes are, arguably, so significant that the familiar boundary between the public and the private is no longer clear. And the performative, in so many different guises, comes to be a defining characteristic of this digital culture of ours. Digital technologies allow the breaking down of the conventional walls around the person; and the *make-over*, literal, symbolic, digital, increasingly comes to dominate the heartland of mass, popular, mediated, culture.

Katie Ward's account (Chapter 8) of the domestic struggles in the village on the Irish coast to manage the competing demands of home and work, and of the organization of everyday life around the new possibilities of interaction and networking, provide an exemplary case study of how these large-scale technologically re-released changes are being confronted in the still viable and vital domestic spaces of her informants. And Sun Sun Lim's account (Chapter 10) of *guanxi* in China provides another version of this mediated restructuring, or in this case the mediated reinforcing, of a culturally distinct version of what constitutes an extended private space and network. Here a traditional form of social organization, one that represents a distinctive manifestation of domesticity, rather than being undermined by technological change, is being both enhanced and changed as information and communication technologies become increasingly adopted and domesticated. We should not forget the enormous importance of cultural difference in the processes of domestication and innovation. Western models, contentious though they already are, do not necessarily travel that well despite what we think of as an increasingly homogenous globalized world.

Domestication and morality

Earlier I asked the question, in what ways domestication could be considered a moral force? It is a question that has begun to be asked at various points in this book so far, and I guess it is about time that the nettle was more firmly grasped, hard though it will be to do so, and inconclusive too.

To put it crudely, morality refers to the ways in which human beings relate to each other and orient themselves to the world. All communication has then some claims to morality; for all communication requires that primary engagement. Domestication involves the appropriation of the new into the familiar, or as we now would wish to see it, perhaps more accurately, as a process in which that appropriation is attempted. The challenges that new media pose to the settled and the familiar, evident in the ways in which new forms of broadcasting, and new networking and mobile technologies, have made their impression on everyday life, are in many, if not all respects, also fundamental challenges precisely to those more or less established and taken-for-granted ways in which individuals and groups position themselves in the world and in relation to each other.

To take, and to distort, a distinction which the political philosopher, Michael Walzer (Walzer 1994), uses in a much more sophisticated way, one can nevertheless in this, our context, speak of morality, as being either thick or thin. Thin morality is the morality of custom and convention. It is the morality, by and large, of which Bakardjieva, Hartmann and Sørensen speak. It is the morality of behaviour and practice, a morality of etiquette and convention, of formal and informal rules – those developed within the confines of domestic spaces, those developed to articulate a boundary around the personal and the private in public spaces, and indeed those embodied and systematized in regulatory frameworks, as constraints on public behaviour, too.

These are the forms of behaviour, modes of expectation, the mores, that provide for a modicum of sensibility and personal integrity (and security) as new technologies and technologically inspired practices disturb the customs and expectations of established forms of communication and the comfort of familiar networks. Perhaps this is the morality of the double articulation, the articulation of technology, a morality which depends on, and incorporates, the changing affordances of new media as they present themselves in the daily round, a morality of practice, a morality of contact, a morality of management, a morality of the day to day. Thin morality is a morality inscribed into the minutiae of the taken for granted, in the following of daily rituals and in the repairing of those rituals when confronted by threats from outside; and as such this is the dimension of morality which underpins our quotidian frameworks for conduct and propriety.

Thick morality, as I intend it here, is the morality of disinterested responsibility, responsibility that comes with agency, that comes with choice, that comes with communication. Responsibility that comes with recognition of, and care for the other. Media, all media, old and new, are also fundamentally implicated in this dimension of the moral order, for in the connections they enable or disable, in the mediation of proximity and distance, in the possibilities they create for defining the boundaries around the self and in the capacity to position the self in the world of strangers, they provide an infrastructure for practical and ultimately non-reciprocal ethics in local, national and global settings. Thick morality involves an ethics that extends beyond the immediate demands of the face-to-face, one that engages, or invites engagement, with otherwise distant humanity. Thick morality is implicated in the articulation of content and consistencies of communication, for it depends on judgements of meaning and significance, of value, of positioning. In so far as the media provide that framework (and many would argue of course, that they either do not, or indeed undermine such a possibility) then the processes of domestication have material significance for the human condition.

But in this context, domestication, as many have pointed out, is double edged. On the one hand, and in its original under-reflexive formulation, domestication as a conservative response to the challenge of technological change, can be seen as a way of absorbing such threats and denying such opportunities for new kinds of reflexivity into the cosy familiarity of a private moral space, the family, the household: comfortable in its own sense of its self, clear about what it values and what it does not; determined to protect those values from the disturbances of otherness. In some senses domestication is, by definition, a process of moral defensiveness, and in so far as technologies are moulded to (or rejected by) private values in private cultures, then what is at stake is the preservation of the core of a personal world against all-comers.

We know, of course, that this is not how it is, but that it is *partly* how it is: this defensiveness is one aspect, one driver of the dialectic of socio-technological change. The contrary and the critical position, the moral counter, as it were, comes precisely in the supposed success of this aspect of domestication, in its neutralization of the potential for real change and new engagements which new media promise and of course from time to time succeed in creating.

Both Lorenzo Simpson (Simpson 1995) and Mike Michael (Michael 2000) have pointed to this politically retrogressive dimension of domestication: that its force is precisely to reject the novel and the possibility of change. Accepting those challenges inevitably involves challenging what one already accepts. And this is hard to do, even for the young who embrace, in every other respect, the liberation of mobile telephony. From this perspective it would be the failure of complete domestication, the persistence of a kind of moral itch or irritation, which changes in communication practice ought consistently to provide, which would be the key to unlocking the value potentially present in new information and communication technologies. It is the irresistibility of this moral itch that underpins Raymond Williams's hopes, and those of others before and since, for technologically facilitated social change.

So the question we could, and should be asking, one which this review of the concept of domestication perhaps surprisingly has led to is, how does such innovation enable a better world, and a more responsible and more sustainable relationship with the world which it now brings more and more radically into focus? In so far as domestication fully succeeds, it could also be said to be failing: for in its attempts at cultural anaesthesia, in its resistance to the radical possibilities and expectations at the heart of communication change, it blunts the force of the moral claims intrinsic to innovation in technology, as in other spheres, and refuses the claims for a wider sense of responsibility for the world, and for those who share it with us: a world which those technologies increasingly construct and command, in their global reach.

References

Baudrillard, J. (1988) *Selected Writings: Jean Baudrillard*, (ed.) Mark Poster. Polity Press: Cambridge.

Berker, T. (2005) 'The everyday of extreme flexibility – the case of migrant researchers' use of new information and communication technologies', in (ed.) R. Silverstone, *Media, Technology and Everyday Life in Europe: From Information to Communication*. Ashgate: Aldershot, pp. 127–42.

de Certeau, M. (1984) *The Practice of Everyday Life*. California University Press: Berkeley, CA.

Hartmann, M. (2005) 'The discourse of the perfect future – young people and new technologies', in (ed.) R. Silverstone, *Media, Technology and Everyday Life in Europe: From Information to Communication*. Ashgate: Aldershot, pp. 143–60.

Katz, J. E. and Aakhus, M. (eds) (2002) *Perpetual Contact: Mobile Communication, Private Talk, Public Performance*. Cambridge University Press: Cambridge.

Latour, B. (1987) *Science in Action: How to Follow Scientists and Engineers Through Society*. Harvard University Press: Cambridge, Mass.

Michael, M. (2000) *Reconnecting Culture, Technology and Nature: From Society to Heterogeneity*. Routledge: London.

Miller, D. (1987) *Material Culture and Mass Consumption*. Blackwell: Oxford.

Parry, J. and Bloch, M. (1989) *Money and the Morality of Exchange*. Cambridge University Press: Cambridge.

Silverstone, R. (1994) *Television and Everyday Life*. Routledge: London.

Silverstone, R. (1981) *The Message of Television: Myth and Narrative in Contemporary Culture*. Heinemann Educational Books: London.

Simpson, L. C. (1995) *Technology, Time and the Conversations of Modernity*. Routledge: London.

Thompson, E. P. (1971) 'The moral economy of the English crowd in the eighteenth century'. *Past and Present*, vol. 50, pp. 76 136.

Walzer, M. (1994) *Thick and Thin: Moral Argument at Home and Abroad*. University of Notre Dame Press: Notre Dame, IN.

Williams, R. (2003) *Television: Technology and Cultural Form*. Routledge: London.

Index